200 best
canned fish
& seafood
recipes

For tuna, salmon, shrimp, crab, clams, oysters, lobster & more

Susan Sampson

Robert
ROSE

For complete cataloguing information, see page 279.

Disclaimer

The recipes in this book have been carefully tested by our kitchen and our tasters. To the best of our knowledge, they are safe and nutritious for ordinary use and users. For those people with food or other allergies, or who have special food requirements or health issues, please read the suggested contents of each recipe carefully and determine whether or not they may create a problem for you. All recipes are used at the risk of the consumer.

We cannot be responsible for any hazards, loss or damage that may occur as a result of any recipe use.

For those with special needs, allergies, requirements or health problems, in the event of any doubt, please contact your medical adviser prior to the use of any recipe.

Design and production: Daniella Zanchetta/PageWave Graphics Inc.
Editor: Judith Finlayson
Copy Editor: Gillian Watts
Indexer: Gillian Watts
Food Photographer: Colin Erricson
Associate Food Photographer: Matt Johannsson
Food Stylist: Kathryn Robertson
Prop Stylist: Charlene Erricson

Cover image: Tagliatelle with Tarragon Lobster and Asparagus (page 206)

We acknowledge the financial support of the Government of Canada through the Book Publishing Industry Development Program (BPIDP) for our publishing activities.

Published by Robert Rose Inc.
120 Eglinton Avenue East, Suite 800, Toronto, Ontario, Canada M4P 1E2
Tel: (416) 322-6552 Fax: (416) 322-6936
www.robertrose.ca

Printed and bound in Canada

1 2 3 4 5 6 7 8 9 FP 20 19 18 17 16 15 14 13 12

Contents

Acknowledgments

This book is dedicated to my husband Robert. For 34 years, he has appreciatively consumed whatever I brought to the table. From the weird to the wonderful, from failed experiments to five-star meals, he ate it all. Somehow, he also remained slim, which peeves me to no end.

I compiled this book in overdrive. I owe thanks to my mother Margaret Horvath and mother-in-law Christel Sampson, who pitched in with the endless scullery duties without ever being asked. Many thanks also to editor Judith Finlayson and designer Daniella Zanchetta for their patience, hard work and diligence.

Introduction

When I told people I was writing a cookbook starring canned seafood, I heard a lot of jokes about slaving over a hot can opener and stocking up for civil emergencies. There is a certain snobbery surrounding tinned fish, but it also has fans in the millions. Trouble is, even devotees don't always know what to do with a can of fish or seafood, beyond mashing it up with mayo or tossing it into a casserole with condensed soup.

A decade ago, as food editor at the *Toronto Star*, I opened a story file and scribbled "Start with a Can of Tuna" on the label. I never did write that story, as daily newspaper deadlines and a steady stream of urgent food news got in the way. However, I remained convinced that a home cook could get creative with canned tuna and its cousins.

In the kitchen, my repertoire ranges from haute to folksy. Fortunately, canned seafood is there to respond to my whims. It's easy to downscale or upscale recipes depending on the type of seafood I select. Tuna, for instance, runs the gamut from inexpensive water-packed fish to pricy belly fillets in extra virgin olive oil. When I crave a taste of crab, I can snack on a dip whipped up with a little can of flaky crab or wow guests with a refined salad starring white crabmeat chunks. I do love to get fancy, so on the weekend I might make a pot pie using canned lobster meat. But as a working mother I also realize that the world is spinning too fast. It's tough to get weekday family meals on the table or stuff lunches into those brown bags late at night. That's when humble canned salmon comes to the rescue. When you're pressed for time or money, it's nice to know you can raid the pantry.

Fresh seafood is dandy, but canned seafood is ready when you are. It's a speedy alternative to fast food. It's generally nutritious, economical and convenient. And a lot of varieties of seafood are interchangeable in recipes, so you can swap what you have on hand (Where appropriate, my recipes suggest such substitutions. You can view a complete list in the substitutions chart on pages 272 to 278). So yes, enjoy fresh fish when you have it, along with the time to fuss with it and the money to pay for it. But feel free to use canned fish in situations that are less ideal — when you are in a hurry, when you are penny-pinching or when you have to customize dinner for those picky kids.

This book includes both traditional and updated recipes, new creations and twists on classic fish dishes. All the recipes start with plain or smoked canned seafood, in water or oil or sometimes with a bit of embellishment. No pickled, pâtéed, spiced, sauced or ready-to-eat concoctions — they speak for themselves.

The key to cooking with canned seafood is this: treat it as a different species from fresh fish. The flavors and textures are different. Consider, for example, the canned cocktail shrimp, the smoked oyster, the salted anchovy — different beasts entirely from their fresh counterparts. Don't treat canned seafood as a sad second-class substitute. Don't try to turn it into something it's not. Instead, work with the differences. Handle it gently and remember that it has already been cooked during the canning process. The techniques and recipes in this book will help you make the most of canned seafood. Have fun experimenting.

Happy cooking,
Susan Sampson

A World of Canned Seafood

Choices, choices. From tuna to crab, many varieties of seafood are available in cans, at a wide range of prices depending upon the species (lobster is always an upscale choice) and quality (sockeye trumps pink salmon). The seafood may be wild or farmed. It may be packed in water, oil, broth or a combination thereof, or simply in its own juices. It may be salted, smoked, spiced or swimming in sauce. It may be flaked or in fillets or skinless and boneless. It may have been canned in North America or imported from faraway places such as Thailand.

Supermarkets and specialty grocers stock the usual suspects, including tuna and salmon, as well as some surprises. In multicultural Toronto, where I live, the products on the shelves reflect the neighborhood. In Little Portugal I found canned cod and squid in its own ink. In Greektown I picked up cod liver, tarama and octopus. In Chinatown I found pike conger in a strangely sweet tomato sauce. In areas that Italian people frequent, shopkeepers sell plenty of anchovies, and the Brits enjoy their kippers.

Consumers do indeed have a wide world of canned seafood to choose from. As popular, plentiful and familiar as canned seafood may be, however, consumers still look at the labels and get confused. This guide to choosing and using canned fish and seafood should help.

The Shopping Basket

Fish

Tuna

Tuna is the second most popular seafood in North America, after shrimp, and has a strong following in Europe. Although tuna is an everyday pantry item, shoppers faced with the array on supermarket shelves can get dizzy trying to figure out what kind to buy. Some labels are full of information while others are vague and puzzling. This guide will help you make a selection.

Types of Canned Tuna

First of all, which species do you want? Chances are the tuna is albacore, yellowfin or skipjack, and the label will say the meat is white or light. Here's how to decode that information:

- Albacore is choice, meaning good-quality or preferable. The proverbial chicken of the sea, it is prized for its firm, pale flesh and mild flavor. Albacore (also known as tombo or longfin tuna) is labeled "white tuna."

- Yellowfin and skipjack are classified as "light tuna" and cost less than albacore. Depending on your bias, they taste more flavorful or fishier than albacore. Skipjack is the smallest type of tuna but boasts the biggest market share.

The majority of tuna eaten around the world is skipjack. Scientifically speaking, it is a close relative of tuna rather than a true tuna species. Yellowfin (also known as yellowtail or ahi) is the largest of the commonly canned tunas. It has a better reputation than skipjack, thanks to its slightly milder flavor and lighter flesh.

- Two other light tunas that are sometimes canned are tongol and bigeye. Never say never, but you are unlikely to find bluefin tuna in a can. Sushi-makers fight over this expensive and endangered fish; it has the darkest, fattiest flesh.

- The bonito is a cousin of tuna; scientifically speaking it belongs to the same family. If bonito is in the can, it must be labeled as such. Bonito has a strong flavor and high fat content. You can use it as you would tuna. Do not confuse bonito with *bonito del norte*, a term the Spanish may use to describe high-quality albacore tuna.

Size Matters

Canned tuna is also classified by the size of the chunks. You can get a loin, pieces of loin or the flakes that fall off when tuna is processed. The larger the chunk(s), the more expensive the tuna, because intact tuna is more attractive and has a better texture.

- Solid tuna is a single piece of loin. It is usually albacore but sometimes yellowfin.

- Chunk tuna consists of large pieces of fish. Chunks are usually yellowfin or skipjack but sometimes albacore.

- Flakes are just that. They range from albacore to bonito. The best are simply pieces that have flaked off albacore loins. The worst look dark, taste tinny, feel mushy and smell fishy.

- Grated or shredded tuna comes in uniform particles but must not be a paste. Decades ago it was used in cooking as you would use flakes, but today it is not commonly stocked in supermarkets. It may be used commercially or in prepared sauces or dips.

- Specialty items include tuna fillets packed in olive oil and, at high-end shops, belly tuna.

Other Tuna Choices

Tuna comes in shelf-stable tins, pouches and bottles. It can be packed in water, olive or other oils or broth, or a combination thereof. Some premium tuna is smoked. All containers are shelf-stable.

The bestselling tuna is versatile middle-of-the-road chunk light tuna packed in water. Most consumers buy water-packed tuna to save money and calories. However, tuna packed in oil is richer and smoother, with a more concentrated flavor. If you are going to spend the calories, buy tuna in olive oil. It is a healthier fat than refined vegetable or soybean oil.

Using Canned Tuna

All types of canned tuna can be used in recipes in this book, including salads, sandwiches, casseroles, pastas and more. However, some are better choices for certain recipes, and I've specified which. Generally speaking, use solid or larger-chunk tuna for salads, casseroles or curries. Buy chunk tuna or even flaked white tuna if you are going to mash it up in dips and the like. For cooked dishes, many people favor light tuna such as yellowfin or skipjack over albacore (not only is light tuna less expensive, it has a fuller flavor). Because it costs more, save tuna in olive oil for green salads, sandwiches and pastas where it takes a starring role. Save the most luscious, high-end fillet and belly tunas packed in olive oil for salads, sandwiches or sushi. Don't cook with them — no sense gilding the lily.

Can Sizes

Tuna usually comes in 6-ounce (170 g) cans. Nowadays you may find 5-ounce (150 g) cans because some manufacturers have reduced the size in the interests of improving profitability. A 6-ounce (170 g) can of chunk light tuna, drained but not pressed, yields ¾ cup (175 mL). A 3-ounce (85 g) can of solid light tuna in olive oil, drained and broken into large chunks, yields a scant ½ cup (125 mL) and about 1 tbsp (15 mL) oil mixed with juices from the fish.

Salmon

Salmon is next on the list of popular canned fish. Wild Pacific sockeye and pink are the two most common kinds of canned salmon.

Types of Canned Salmon

- Pink salmon (also known as humpback) is the lightest, mildest and leanest species of salmon. Its flesh is soft and mild (or bland, depending on your taste). Pink salmon costs less than red sockeye.

- Sockeye's firm red flesh and rich taste make it the king of canned salmon. Sockeye has the second highest fat content of the popular salmon species. Premium sockeye may be labeled blueback, a moniker that refers to the color of its scales in salt water during the period when it is fattest and tastiest.

Three other species of Pacific salmon are usually sold fresh or smoked. However, they may also be canned. These are not available in all regions. If you want a specific type of salmon, you may have to shop for it online.

- Chinook is the largest and fattiest of the Pacific salmons, with velvety dark orange flesh rich in healthy omega-3 fats. It is also called king, blackmouth or spring salmon.

- The small coho (also known as silver salmon) is milder tasting and leaner than sockeye or chinook.

- The least expensive salmon is chum, also called keta, dog or calico salmon. It has lean, mild orange-pink flesh that tends to flake.

What's in the Can?

Salmon is canned in its own juices or in water. The skin and soft bones are edible; the amounts vary from can to can, depending on the original size of the fish. Alternatively, you can buy boneless, skinless salmon in cans. The pieces are usually solid or chunks, but I have seen flaked salmon. Canned smoked salmon is a premium product sold in specialty food shops or upscale supermarkets.

Using Canned Salmon

Any type of canned salmon can be used in the wide spectrum of recipes in this book. For certain recipes the more expensive sockeye is a better choice than pink salmon, which I've noted when necessary. I generally prefer sockeye because it is redder and richer-tasting. But in most cases you can successfully substitute less expensive pink salmon. Generally speaking, you won't need boneless, skinless salmon, but you can use it if desired.

Farmed Salmon

Some of the salmon found in cans is Atlantic salmon. Since the collapse of the wild fishery, Atlantic salmon is almost always farmed. (Salmon farms are located on both the east and west coasts of North America. Some salmon is also farmed organically in Europe.) In contrast, three-quarters of canned Pacific salmon is wild. To choose, check the label. It will usually specify Atlantic salmon or say "wild" — the latter being a marketing plus.

Can Sizes

Two common can sizes are 7½ ounces (213 g) for regular salmon and 6 ounces (170 g) for boneless, skinless salmon. A 7½-ounce (213 g) can yields about 1 cup (250 mL) salmon with the backbone removed. A 6-ounce (170 g) can of boneless, skinless salmon yields about ¾ cup (175 mL). Both were broken into chunks and drained but not pressed before measuring.

Mackerel

Mackerel may be popular in countries as far-flung as Britain and Japan, but it gets no respect in North America. Some people complain it is too "fishy," but I find it surprisingly tasty. And the price is right — sometimes 25 percent less than tuna or salmon.

Canned mackerel is readily available in supermarkets. The oily, flaky, dark, soft flesh is packed in water, brine or olive or other kinds of oil. Large segments are stuffed into full-sized cans, while small tins hold fillets or sardine-like pieces.

Mackerel makes a tasty addition to anything from salads to casseroles. In recipes it can often be used in place of tuna or salmon.

Can Sizes

A common can size is 4 ounces (125 g), which yields about ½ cup (125 mL) flesh, drained but not pressed, and 3 tbsp (45 mL) oil and juices.

Cod

Cod has been pricy since the collapse of the massive fishery off the Grand Banks of Newfoundland. However, cod from the North Pacific and the northeast Atlantic near Iceland is still abundant. Cod is best appreciated fresh, but you may come across canned cod in specialty stores. The label may say "bacalao" or "bacalhau," the Spanish and Portuguese names for cod, particularly when it is salted.

Cod comes canned in olive oil, sometimes with slivers of garlic. The flesh is white, firm and mild. Since it is hard to find and comes in small amounts, I save canned cod for Brandade (page 58) or The Grand Aïoli (page 56), two dishes that typically call for cod. But there is no reason why you can't use it in a variety of canned fish dishes.

If you come across a tin of cod liver, forget the jokes and grab it. Cod liver is the foie gras of the sea. Smoked and packed in its own oil, it is silky, luscious and rich in healthy omega-3 fats. Cod liver is delicious simply spread on toasted baguette or plain crackers, maybe with some tiny cornichons or other pickles alongside.

Can Sizes

Canned cod is too rare a commodity for me to declare a common can size. However, one Portuguese import comes in a 4-ounce (120 g) can.

Sardines and Sprats

What is a sardine? It is not a species but rather a marketing term. The name comes from the Mediterranean island of Sardinia, one of the first places sardines were canned. Today's sardines are immature soft-boned, oily saltwater fish that travel in schools by the millions. A canned sardine may be a juvenile pilchard, herring or sprat. Fish become sardines once they are crammed into a tin (like sardines, so to speak) with their peers.

Half a century ago, sardine canneries were bustling on both coasts of North America. Today sardines are a harder sell. Consumers' tastes have changed; many seem to object to the bold flavor, strong scent and humble reputation of sardines. That's too bad. Sardines are one of the healthiest canned fish choices for you and the environment — abundant, sustainable, low in mercury and full of calcium and heart-healthy oils. This is a good time to revive their reputation.

Size Matters

When buying sardines, the smaller the fish and the more in the can, the higher the quality. All sardines are juvenile fish, but the youngest and smallest are more tender and mild. Hence the comical vintage motto from one manufacturer, "Fish she is very small."

Types of Canned Sardines

Sardines are packed headless but whole, usually in vegetable or olive oil but sometimes in spring water to suit modern tastes. They may also be "slightly smoked," as one label describes it. Some sardines are labeled "silds," which are juvenile herrings. Small sardines may also be labeled "Jutlands." Also available are boneless, skinless sardines; they are firmer and less likely to fall apart in cooking. Besides the proverbial sardines on toast, these little fish are good in salads, sandwiches and pastas.

Can Sizes

A standard can size is 3.75 ounces (106 g). It contains about six sardines, or about ¾ cup (175 L) broken and drained but not pressed sardines and about 1 tbsp (15 L) oil with sardine juices. The same sized can of brislings contains about 20 sardines, or about ½ cup (125 mL) whole sardines, drained but not pressed, and about 1 tbsp (15 mL) oil with juices.

A standard 4-ounce (120 g) can of boneless, skinless sardines contains six fish, or about ½ cup (125 mL) broken and drained but not pressed sardines and 2 tbsp (30 mL) oil with fish juices.

For sprats, the most familiar brand comes in a 5.6-ounce (160 g) round tin. It contains about 30 sprats, or 1 cup (250 mL) sprats, drained but not pressed, and about 2 tbsp (30 mL) oil.

Beware of those oversized tins of salted sardines. The tins are very big and round and are labeled "salted sardines." Sardines and salt are the only two ingredients, and the can weighs 21 ounces (600 g). These are not your grandma's easy-to-eat sardines on toast. Beheaded, smelly and packed in lots of coarse salt, they must be washed, gutted, deboned, filleted and cooked before you can use them.

Keep a special lookout for petite brislings in extra virgin olive oil. These sardines are the finest, tastiest and highest in omega-3 fats. Brisling sardines are usually the young of a specific species, called sprats, from icy northern waters. When smoked and preserved in oil, sprats go by their own name rather than being lumped under the sardine marketing banner. These petite, fatty, herring-like fish look pretty and taste deliciously smoky. They are tinier and more delicate-looking than standard sardines, with finer, bronzed skins and an appealing milder flavor yet firmer flesh. Sprats are a treat on their own with a spritz of lemon, but you can also use them to upscale any of the sardine recipes in this book or as substitutes for other smoked fish. Beware, though: they can be quite salty.

Also going by its own name on labels is the stickleback. Rarely seen in mass markets, this little specialty canned fish looks and tastes similar to sardines. It can be used like sardines in recipes.

Kippers

Kippers belong to the busy herring family. *Kipper*, however, is not the name of a fish. A soft, fat grown-up herring becomes a kipper when it is kippered: lightly salted, split (butterflied) and cold-smoked. Whole kippers look strangely like Siamese twins.

The kipper is best known as a U.K. breakfast staple. On the North American side of the pond, many shoppers are mystified by kippers. You can substitute kippers in dishes that call for smoked fish, add them to omelets or simply eat them straight with a squeeze of lemon juice. The convoluted way to warm kippers is to immerse the can in boiling water for five minutes, then run cold water over the can for 10 seconds, until it is safe to handle. But

instead of messing about, open the can, transfer the kippers to a microwave-safe dish and zap them for a few seconds. Before cooking with kippers, break them into flakes with your fingers.

Types of Canned Kippers

Canned kippers are soft and ready to eat. They are fillets, not whole fish, with a light smokiness and a texture similar to that of canned mackerel. Some are skinned. The label may say "seafood snacks."

> ### Can Sizes
> One typical can is 3.5 ounces (100 g). The yield is about ½ cup (125 mL) kipper fillets broken into chunks and drained but not pressed.

Anchovies

Anchovies are the little fish that could. The true anchovy is a fatty little Mediterranean fish related to the herring. But there are more than a hundred varieties of anchovy swimming in the world's oceans. Their salty, lip-smacking flavor has made them a vital kitchen ingredient since the ancient Romans used them to prepare a fermented sauce/condiment called *garum*. Today the anchovy is a secret ingredient that sneaks into all kinds of food to deliver pizzazz. Anchovies may be hidden in plain sight, in pasta or Caesar salad, or discreetly added to Worcestershire sauce or Vietnamese fish sauce. Anchovies fare worse with the public when they take on starring roles. The anchovies-on-pizza debate, for example, has undoubtedly been raging as long as there has been pizza.

> ### Read the Label
> Check labels carefully: there's a difference between naturally smoked herring and herring with a smoked flavor added. Herrings may also be labeled "golden smoked" instead of "kippered"; these have a more intensely smoky flavor than kippers. Golden smoked herrings are boneless herring fillets smoked over natural fires until they turn golden.

Types of Canned Anchovies

These tasty little fish come in tins or jars, usually flat but sometimes rolled. Unlike most canned fish, anchovies are not sterilized using heat (they'd turn to mush) and contain no artificial preservatives. Instead, anchovies are "semi-preserved" or "partially preserved" — cured using salt and oil. They are filleted, salted, packed in tins or bottles and then immersed in oil. Thus they are considered an "artisan" canned fish.

Check labels and spring for the anchovies in extra virgin olive oil. The irresistible salty oil is a bonus in itself and can be used to enhance your anchovy dishes. Anchovies in extra virgin olive oil are available in supermarkets, in refrigerated cases near the seafood or deli offerings.

"Semi-preserved" equals semi-perishable, so keep unopened cans in a cool location; at home it's safest and simplest to store them in the fridge and keep track of the best-before date. Ideally, anchovies should be kept in a refrigerator at 41°F (5°C); under those conditions they should be good for six months. Once the can is opened, the anchovies must be refrigerated; they will keep for about two months. Transfer them to a little storage tub and make sure they are submerged in oil. Don't be afraid to freeze stray anchovies if you must. Just wrap them individually in foil or plastic.

Cooking with Anchovies

Before using anchovies, rinse and pat them dry to remove excess salt. Some cooks soak anchovies in water, milk or wine to soften them. Anchovies can be pounded into a paste, mashed with a fork or dissolved in hot olive oil on the stove.

Can Sizes

A 2-ounce (50 g) tin is standard. It contains about 15 anchovies and 1 tbsp (15 mL) oil.

Anchovy Paste

You may find anchovy paste, which comes in tubes, more convenient to use and milder-tasting than fillets. Note, however, that the paste contains more than anchovies. Additions may include oil, vinegar, water and spices. About ½ tsp (2 mL) anchovy paste is the equivalent of one anchovy fillet. Keep anchovy paste in the fridge for up to a month after it has been opened.

Roe

Roe is better known as caviar. The female fish's eggs and their pouches are called roe or hard roe, while the male fish's sperm and testes are called milt or soft roe. Roe may also be referred to as "berries."

There's something about those little berries popping on the palate that has captivated cultures around the world. Roe is extracted from all kinds of creatures, from herring to sea urchins. It is served every which way, from the exotic (pulled from fish roasted on a bed of pine needles) to the everyday (on buttered toast). It comes raw, pickled, dried or fried. It is sold by upscale restaurants and by street vendors. It ranges from haute cuisine's beluga caviar to that jar of lumpfish roe you pick up in the supermarket.

Types of Canned Roe

Canned caviar comes in little jars or tins. It may be brined or pasteurized, meaning that it has been heated to hold microorganisms at bay but not fully sterilized. Thus it requires refrigeration. Store it in the coldest part of the fridge, at the back. If desired, you can surround the jar with crushed ice. However, do not freeze caviar; this breaks the cell walls.

- Nothing beats the prestige of sturgeon roe. Purists say it is the only genuine caviar. The best in the world is extracted from wild sturgeon in the Black and Caspian Seas: beluga (top grade), sevruga, ossetra and the rarest, sterlet. However, these wild sturgeon stocks have been fished almost to extinction. While the fishery recovers, so-called "guilt-free" caviar is supplied by North American farmed sturgeon, as well as by other sea, lake and river sturgeon. Sturgeon caviar is served with specific etiquette and special spoons — you don't just nosh on it. Interestingly, as is the case with many gourmet seafoods, caviar didn't start out as a luxury item. It was so abundant in the early 19th century in the U.S. that saloons served caviar to make their customers thirstier.

- Salmon eggs are a small step down from sturgeon roe. They are big, pink and easily crushed or broken. Salmon roe is called "red caviar" to distinguish it from sturgeon eggs. It is also popular with sushi makers, who use it in maki rolls and as garnishes.

- Lumpfish caviar is at the opposite end of the scale from the premium varieties. Called "mock caviar," this workaday roe is naturally an unappetizing gray, so it is dyed shiny black or neon red.

- Tobiko (also known as flying fish roe) is a sushi mainstay. It is orange-red, but it may be dyed. Tobiko prices vary quite a bit but some are on par with lumpfish. However, I prefer tobiko's delightful crunchiness.

- Tarama is a specialty item used to make the pink Greek dip called taramosalata (see page 49). It is inexpensive salted, cured carp (or sometimes cod) caviar, processed with oil and densely packed in jars. Producers are likely to dye it varying shades of pink because pink taramosalata is so familiar to food lovers.

Using Canned Roe

Dyed caviars should be rinsed to get rid of excess dye and preservatives. To rinse caviar, place it in a fine-mesh sieve, run cold water gently over it, then turn it out onto a paper towel to absorb moisture.

Can Sizes
Lumpfish roe is commonly sold in a 2-ounce (50 g) jar. It contains about 3 tbsp (45 mL) roe.

Crustaceans

Shrimp

Shrimp are sold in shelf-stable cans. Because of the heat applied during processing, canned shrimp are firm and dry and crumble easily, even during rinsing. They are best incorporated into dips and sauces rather than being used on their own. They also make cute garnishes on canapés and the like. If you want to add whole canned shrimp to a dish, mix them in gently at the end of the cooking time.

Types of Canned Shrimp

Shrimp are packed in water and priced by size — the larger, the costlier. Size descriptions vary from brand to brand. Miniatures may be labeled "salad," "cocktail" or "tiny" shrimp, followed by small, medium and large. Some are deveined; the label will say so. Deveining (removing the intestinal vein) is preferable but not vital. In the smallest shrimp, deveining is merely cosmetic. In larger ones, however, the vein may contain grit.

Can Sizes
The standard can size is 4 ounces (106 g). This yields about ¾ cup (175 mL) drained small shrimp.

Crab

There are more than 4,000 varieties of sea and freshwater crabs. The most commonly consumed are North America's blue crabs and Asia's blue swimmer crabs. It takes 10 to 15 crabs to extract 1½ pounds (750 g) of meat. No wonder crabmeat is expensive!

Types of Canned Crab

Crab may be shelf-stable or pasteurized, packed in cans or tubs. Pasteurized crab must be refrigerated. It has a shelf life of about 18 months. Once opened, handle it like fresh seafood: keep it in the fridge, securely packaged, and consume it within two days. Although generally more expensive, pasteurized crab is preferable. Shelf-stable crab is heated to a higher temperature for a longer time than pasteurized crab, and this can take a toll on the delicate meat. However, shelf-stable crab is fine in dips and some salads, sandwiches, soups and pastas when you want to enjoy crab more economically.

Grades of Crabmeat

Crabmeat is graded by the size of the pieces. There is also a differentiation between meat from the body and from the claws. Designations vary by brand.

In crabspeak, the chunks are called lumps. White meat is from the body, or carapace. Claw meat is pink-brown and comes from the pincers, swimming fins and legs. Which tastes best is up to the taster. Some people prefer the milder white lump crabmeat, others the "crabbier" claw meat. Pricewise, white and lump trump brown and flaked.

The largest lump white meat comes from the muscles that power the swimming fins. There are only two per crab, and the bigger the crab, the bigger the lumps. This top grade is given appetizing names such as "colossal," "imperial" and "jumbo." A step down are varieties such as "super lump" (broken jumbo lumps and large pieces of body meat), "special" (small pieces from the body) and "backfin" (large and small pieces).

Large lump crabmeat is best for salads, or for when the boss is coming for dinner. Versatile special and backfin grades work in dishes ranging from soup to casseroles. Flaked crabmeat is okay in some dips and sandwich spreads, but be careful with it — enthusiastic mixing can turn it into a paste. Use claw meat for recipes in which you want the most crab flavor. It's also good for finer-textured, easier-to-work-with crab cakes.

The designations on shelf-stable cans include lump, chunk, white meat, flake (white), claw, leg and pink (claw and white meat). Cans labeled "15% leg meat" include mainly fine shreds with small whole leg chunks (do not confuse this with the heartier "claw meat"). Flake or "salad" crab is least expensive; some is so fine it appears minced. In spite of its name, salad crab is too fine for green salads, but it can be mixed with mayonnaise in spreads and dips.

Crabmeat should be moist and springy and smell of briny seawater, not ammonia — a sign of spoilage. Lump crabmeat should be creamy white (no grays, blues or greens, please). Check labels for best-before dates. Don't keep leftovers sitting around while you wait for culinary inspiration. Freezing is possible but not recommended. If you must freeze crabmeat, it's best to first add the crab to a prepared dish.

Can Sizes

Two standard sizes include the 4.25-ounce (120 g) shelf-stable can and the 15-ounce (440 g) container. Can sizes vary, and as recipes often don't require a full container, I've given volume amounts in most of the recipes. About 4 ounces (125 g) of small lump or claw crabmeat, drained but not pressed, equals ¾ cup (175 mL).

Lobster

Lobster canning was big business a century ago, when little lobsters were dubbed "canners." Not so today, now that fresh lobsters are easier to transport. Canned lobster meat will save you time and effort because it's been removed from the shell, but it won't necessarily save you money.

Types of Canned Lobster

Lobster may be frozen, pasteurized or shelf-stable. Cold-canned lobster is cooked, then packed in brine and frozen. Keep it frozen until you are almost ready to use it, then thaw it in the fridge and use it within two days. Pasteurized lobster comes in cans or plastic tubs with metal lids; it is heat-treated for longevity but must be refrigerated. Like cold-canned lobster, it is sold in some supermarkets and at most fishmongers. If you're looking on supermarket shelves you may find lobster in shelf-stable cans, but don't count on it.

Canned lobster tends to be waterlogged or chewy, so it is best chopped and incorporated into cooked dishes or sauces.

Can Sizes

There isn't a lot of choice when it comes to canned lobster. The sizes I have most often come across are an 11.3-ounce (320 g) can of lobster frozen in brine and a 6-ounce (170 g) tub of pasteurized lobster. However, availability may be different in your area. In the recipes I give volume amounts. About 4 ounces (125 g) canned lobster in small chunks, drained but not pressed, equals ¾ cup (175 mL). You can use leftovers to make any of the delicious lobster recipes in this book (see chart, pages 272 to 278).

Mollusks

Clams

Clams are the most popular of the canned bivalves, for good reason. They cut down the work and expense involved in cooking iconic dishes that range from clam chowder to clam pie to spaghetti with clams.

There are more than 2,000 varieties of clams, from hard-shell to soft-shell and from saltwater to freshwater. These days clams are mostly farmed, but you can find wild clams in a can too. East Coast hard-shells are called quahogs and are categorized according to size: button, littleneck, topneck, cherrystone and chowder. They live in deeper water. West Coast hard-shells include Pacific littlenecks, pismos and butter clams. Soft-shell clams live in tidal areas. Their shells are not actually soft but rather thin and brittle. They don't close fully because their siphons protrude. Soft-shell clams include steamers, razor clams and the comical-looking geoduck, with its huge siphon.

Types of Canned Clams

Clams that are commonly sold canned range from those ubiquitous baby clams to their meatier cousins. The baby clams, including yellow clams and tiny manilas, are so delicate they can get lost in casseroles or hearty noodle dishes. However, they are fine in some dips, soups and pastas. Baby clams are commonly packed in water in cans or jars. You may also find them smoked and packed in oil.

For most dishes I prefer the larger, meatier canned clams, particularly surf clams. Depending on one's point of view, they are either pleasantly chewy or tough. Personally, I appreciate that they give you something to sink your teeth into. They look better and taste substantial in chowders and on pizza. Some are canned whole, some chopped. Availability and types vary from area to area. Big surf clams (also known as sea, hen or bar clams or skimmers) and pink clams (also known as machas) are mild and sweet. Ocean clams (also known as quahogs) are darker and more pungent.

Clam Juice

Another handy pantry item is shelf-stable bottled clam juice, which is sold in most supermarkets. If you don't have fish stock you can substitute equal portions of clam juice and water or stock. Do not use the liquid from a can of clams, because it is likely to contain additives such as preservatives.

Can Sizes

Can sizes vary quite a bit. The 5-ounce (142 g) can is a standard size in my area for both baby and surf clams, but your experience may differ. The yield in drained whole clams is 1 cup (250 mL) baby clams or 1½ cups (375 mL) surf clams.

Oysters

Canned oysters have little in common with fresh oysters in terms of taste and texture, but they are delicious in their own right. Oysters may be wild or farmed.

Types of Canned Oysters

Oysters are elegant and luscious when smoked and canned in oil (usually vegetable or seed oil). They may be petite, medium or large. In North America, smoked oysters caught on only after the Second World War. They were popularized by smart 1960s hostesses, no doubt sporting beehives and stilettos as they passed them around as hors d'oeuvres.

Canned boiled oysters are available in some supermarkets but are sold mainly to the food service industry. Packed in water and/or their own liquor, these soft oysters can be difficult to work with. Try them chopped or mashed in dips, for instance, or prepare an impromptu oyster stew with cream and fresh herbs.

Oysters are usually brown but sometimes you will see a green tinge, which is perfectly fine. The color comes from large amounts of chlorophyll from green seaweed, which the oysters feed on when rough seas tear up their beds.

Can Sizes

Smoked oysters are commonly packed in a 3-ounce (85 g) tin. There are about 21 small oysters and 1 tbsp (15 mL) oil in a tin.

Mussels

Canned mussels have a lower profile than canned oysters but are well worth a try. Mussels are usually cultured, or farmed.

Types of Canned Mussels

Mussels come smoked or plain. In both cases they are smaller and milder-tasting than canned oysters. The plain canned mussels, with their creamy texture, are more pleasant than the plain oysters. Smoked mussels are less popular than smoked oysters but are just as good. Use them as you would smoked oysters. In recipes you can switch one for the other.

Can Sizes

Smoked mussels are commonly packed in a 3-ounce (85 g) tin. There are about 25 mussels and 1 tbsp (15 mL) oil in the tin.

Squid

Squid surely tastes better when labeled "calamari," its Italian name. It's from the Latin *calamarium*, meaning inkpot.

Canned squid is most kindly described as an acquired taste. The heat of canning is hard on squid, which must normally be cooked quickly or for a long time but gently. No recipes in this book call directly for canned squid, but it may be substituted for other canned seafood. If you like canned squid, check the chart on pages 272 to 278 for ideas on how to use it.

Types of Canned Squid

Squid is packed in its own ink and oil or simply in inky brine. Pieces from the body have a bitter edge; tentacles are milder. Canned chunks are preferable to whole baby squid. The latter has the texture of disintegrating rubber bands, and the innards have to be pulled out.

Can Sizes

Canned squid is not widely available. One standard can size is 4 ounces (120 g).

Octopus

Octopus, unlike squid, is surprisingly tasty from the can — if you like octopus to begin with. It is normally chewy and meaty, so it seems to stand up fine to canning. The flavor is almost smoky or nutty. Chunks are packed in oil, often olive oil. I have used canned octopus on pizza and it can be substituted for other canned seafood in some salads and pastas. For ideas on how to use it, check the chart on pages 272 to 278.

Can Sizes

Canned octopus is not widely available. One standard can size is 4 ounces (120 g).

A Brief History of Canned Seafood

Napoleon famously noted that an army marches on its stomach. The production and popularity of canned food was driven by soldiers, from the Napoleonic Wars to the American Civil War. On the battlefield, where refrigeration and cooking equipment were scarce to nonexistent, they consumed vast quantities of canned meat, fish and vegetables.

In North America the first canned seafood appeared almost as soon as canning was invented. It started with oysters and lobsters, which in those days were abundant, not the luxury items they have become. Sardines and salmon followed in the mid-1800s. By the 1880s, mackerel, clams and crab had been added to the roster. Canned tuna did not appear until the early years of the 20th century, and then only as a replacement for sardines during a shortage. But tuna quickly caught on with the public. Five years after the first commercial offering of albacore, the number of cases produced had grown a hundredfold.

In the mid-19th century, canned food was a novelty and a status symbol. Today it is usually perceived as a symbol of humble nourishment. It's probably not surprising that sales of canned goods increase during recessions, when unemployment rises, salaries drop and our desire to hunker down at home increases. As for canned seafood in particular, it has evolved into a super convenience food in the kitchens of busy people. It comes in a wide range of interchangeable varieties, letting you easily move from downtown to uptown to suit the occasion. If you're in a rush to feed hungry children, there are plenty of beloved basics, such as tuna salad, to keep them happy. If you want to upgrade, it's easy to switch to, say, crab salad on a bed of baby greens.

The father of canning was Nicolas Appert, a French confectioner, chef and brewer. He began to experiment with canning in 1795 after Napoleon offered a prize to anyone who could invent a way to preserve food for his soldiers and sailors. It took Appert 15 years to meet the challenge. He canned food in glass, in the forerunner of what we now call the Mason jar.

Not long afterwards, Englishmen developed new methods using iron cans, which were unbreakable and coated in tin to prevent rusting. Unfortunately the cans were sealed with toxic lead solder. Modern cans are made of steel coated with tin or laminates or aluminum, which are fine. However, it's wise to look for labels that indicate the plastic linings are free of the controversial chemical bisphenol A (BPA).

Is that a tin or a can or a tin can?

Cans were originally called tins because the metal was tin-plated. Nowadays "tin" is a Britishism. I call the puck-shaped containers cans and the oval containers tins, but you can call them whatever you wish. Manufacturers play with sizes and variations in containers, although they all serve the same function: to preserve food. Some "canned" seafood, such as imported tuna, comes in a jar. Some, such as crabmeat, comes in a plastic tub with a metal lid. The latest thing is the metal-and-plastic pouch.

What Is Canning?

All food contains bacteria, which, over time, will cause it to spoil. One way to prevent spoilage is to seal food in a sterile, airtight container and subject it to enough heat to destroy microorganisms. This canning process cooks the food and changes the taste and texture.

Canned seafood may be shelf-stable or pasteurized. Shelf-stable seafood is sterilized using high heat. It can be stored at room temperature. Pasteurized seafood is heated to lower temperatures for shorter periods of time. This reduces the number of harmful microorganisms but doesn't inactivate them all. The food lasts way longer than it would *au naturel*, but it must be refrigerated to increase its shelf life (the same as with pasteurized milk). Pasteurization is usually reserved for higher-end products such as crabmeat.

Heat sterilization can mar the taste and texture of delicate seafood. Two other, less popular methods used to preserve canned seafood are curing (for example, salted anchovies) and freezing (for example, lobster in brine).

From the Sea to the Cannery

Here are some snapshots of a complicated process: seafood's trip from boat to cannery to market.

On the Ship

Seafood can spoil even before a ship docks. Crustaceans such as shrimp are most notorious for going off quickly. Fattier fish, such as mackerel, spoil quite rapidly too. So a lot of techniques are used to maintain freshness once a catch is pulled from the sea. The seafood may be refrigerated, iced or frozen, kept in cold or frozen brine, or partially processed on the boat or in mini-plants close to shore before being shipped to the cannery. For example, if destined to be canned as skinless and boneless, fresh-caught salmon is gutted and the head and eggs are removed; then it may be frozen. Herrings, which are caught in vast numbers, are frozen in blocks of ice in shallow layers, as they are too delicate to pile up. Shrimp may be peeled and frozen before leaving the boat. Clams may be cooked and frozen or shucked and refrigerated.

Another option is keeping the catch alive. To eliminate waste, sardines are kept in the sea for three days after being caught, a process called thronging. Crabs are either delivered live to the cannery or sent to a mini-plant for steaming, "picking" (extracting meat by hand), grading and freezing.

At the Cannery

Once seafood reaches the cannery, it is either refrigerated, frozen or immediately processed. It is sorted by species and/or size, or graded. Prepping may include beheading, eviscerating, skinning, descaling, deboning, removing dark meat (known as "red meat"), debearding, cleaning, and picking out shell fragments. Large fish such as tuna and salmon are usually steamed first to make the job easier. (It is interesting to note that they are thus cooked twice, the second time during heat processing. Crab and oysters may also be cooked twice.)

Mussels are held in saltwater tanks to purge them of grit. Some fish, such as sardines, are brined to brighten their appearance and toughen the skin so it doesn't stick to the metal of the can. In the case of kippered herring, dye may be added to the brine because consumers prefer a mahogany color. For smoking, seafood is threaded onto rods, hung on hooks or laid out on mesh trays. The preparation work is done partly by hand, partly by machine.

In the Can

Seafood is then packed into cans. Some, like wee sprats, must be hand-packed or they will be mangled. Fish may be packed simply, with salt, in their own juices, water or oil (sardines are a good example). Or they may be treated with additives to preserve, retain moisture, thicken, sharpen flavor, maintain texture, enhance color and/or kill microbes. One additive prevents the formation of struvite crystals; these are not harmful, but they are alarming because they resemble glass (to test, struvite dissolves in warm vinegar). The more sensitive the seafood, such as crab or roe, the more likely it is to include unpronounceable additives. (My general shopping rule: the shorter and plainer the ingredient list, the better.)

The seafood is sealed and heated. Tuna, salmon, mackerel, shrimp, clams, oysters and mussels are sterilized under pressure. Crab may be packed in a can lined with parchment, then sterilized, or it may be pasteurized.

Tracking

Cans are coded to make batches traceable before being shipped to the shops. Codes identify the plant, packing date, batch and similar information. This is useful for tracking inventory and for dealing with recalls.

Anchovies Are Unique

The canning process differs for anchovies, which are "semi-preserved" or "partially preserved." They are actually cured, that is to say salted — a process that is often applied to meats to produce products such as prosciutto.

Anchovies are placed in buckets of brine to drain their blood, sorted and sized. Then they are cleaned, layered with salt, packed in barrels, covered with brine and pressed. The barrels are turned occasionally while the anchovies cure for many months. The fish are then rinsed, dried, skinned, descaled, trimmed, filleted and packed in tins or jars with oil. Both curing with salt and storage in oil make food inhospitable to microorganisms, but the food still has to be kept cold.

Storing Canned Fish

Nothing lasts forever — even in a can. Canning generally gives seafood a shelf life of about two years, depending on how it is stored. Check best-before dates on all canned seafood before purchasing and using it.

Keep shelf-stable cans in a cool, dry spot where the temperature doesn't fluctuate. If a can bulges or leaks or the seams look damaged, throw it out. Keep pasteurized seafood in the fridge. If you are not sure whether a can should be refrigerated, take your cue from the supermarket as well as reading the label. Do not put unopened cans or pouches in the freezer (unless, like some lobster, the product comes already frozen). Freezing can weaken the seams or even burst the container. If a can accidentally freezes (say it falls out of the grocery bag in your car in winter), inspect it for damage. If it looks okay, thaw the can in the fridge and use the seafood right away.

After opening a can, use the product immediately or transfer it to a storage tub with a tight lid and refrigerate. Depending on the seafood, leftovers can be kept for one to three days. I don't recommend freezing leftovers as a habit, as that may create an unpleasant texture. However, I also dislike waste. So, if necessary, you can freeze expensive leftover seafood in an airtight container. Use it in soups or cooked dishes, preferably saucy ones.

Greener Labels

Consumers drive change with their wallets. The dizzying array of canned seafood choices is expanding as manufacturers respond to the demands of environmentally concerned and health-conscious shoppers who want to know what they are eating. Vague labels are being replaced with more informative ones, and green brands are the latest thing. Some labels tell you what species you are eating and where and how it was caught. Premium boutique brands boast that they can track their fish from boat to can, identifying the vessel, captain, flag, harvest method, area of capture and trip dates.

Labels may also address the issue of "bycatch." This refers to species, ranging from sharks to turtles, that are killed or harmed incidentally by fishermen. Dolphins caught in tuna sweeps are the most famous bycatch. Many canned-fish labels are stamped "dolphin-safe." Low-bycatch fishing methods include pole, line and trap fishing and trolling. They are kinder to the environment than trawling or dredging, which damage the ecology of the sea bottom, or gill nets, which look like tennis nets and tangle fish by the gills. Purse-seining (in which a huge net is drawn around a school of fish) and longlines (many miles long and strung with branch lines with baited hooks) may or may not be harmful, depending on how and where they are used. Some seafood labels identify the fishing method that was used.

Aquaculture is another loaded topic, with too many pros and cons to debate here. If you are concerned about farmed seafood, look for the word "wild" on the label. There are plenty of greener choices in terms of canned seafood. For a full overview, check any of the sea-watch organizations online. Examples include SeaChoice (www.seachoice.org), Seafood Watch (www.montereybayaquarium.org/cr/seafoodwatch.aspx) and the Blue Ocean Institute (www.blueocean.org/seafood).

Healthy Options

Seafood is lower in calories and saturated fat than meat. It is rich in omega-3 fatty acids (the so-called heart-healthy fish oils that are essential to a sound metabolism) and the edible soft bones in some fish are a good source of calcium. Fatty coldwater fish — such as salmon, tuna, anchovies, herring, sardines and mackerel — are top sources of omega-3 fats.

Unfortunately, mercury levels in some seafood, both fresh and canned, is a concern. In fact, women of childbearing age and young children have been advised to minimize their intake of fish that are high in mercury.

Virtually all fish contain traces of mercury, but most do not contain amounts that are potentially harmful to your health. Contaminants such as mercury concentrate in fatty tissues such as belly flesh, skin and dark meat.

Fish are what they eat. Big predatory carnivores contain the most methylmercury, as the toxin is technically known. The larger, older and higher up in the food chain a fish is, the more contaminants it carries from years of gobbling up little fish. This means that smaller fish, such as skipjack, contain less mercury than larger ones, such as albacore tuna, and the little sardine and short-lived salmon will contain less mercury than a giant bluefin tuna. In general, anchovies, herrings, clams, shrimp, crabs, clams, oysters, mussels, squid and octopus are also lower in mercury. Certain species aren't as safe as their close relatives, however. For example, king mackerel is high in mercury while other mackerels are fine.

The bottom line: most experts say that the benefits of eating fish outweigh the risks, as long as you do not over-consume seafood that is high in contaminants.

Cooking with Canned Seafood

One of the great advantages to using canned seafood is that it is easy to upscale or downscale recipes; it simply depends upon the product you use. Canned tuna, salmon, crab and lobster, for instance, are interchangeable in many recipes but are miles apart psychologically. Even though you can buy high-end products such as tuna in extra virgin olive oil, canned fish is generally perceived as economical. On the other hand, canned crab and lobster are viewed as special-occasion seafood and have the price tags to match. Using substitutions, you can easily take recipes in this book from downtown to uptown. Check the chart on pages 272 to 278 for ideas on how to tailor recipes to suit your preference.

Using the Recipes

To help you choose and use my recipes according to your needs, I've added the following information to designate the special advantages of the dishes.

Fast: I'm not a fan of books that claim you can cook dinner in 10, 15 or even 20 minutes. Yes, you could do that maybe — if the butler collected all the ingredients, the sous-chef prepped them, the baby stopped crying, the dog stopped barking and the phone stopped ringing. However, I do admit that some dishes will be ready faster than others. So if a dish takes less than half an hour, I have noted it.

Kid-friendly: Well, that depends on the kid, the kid's age and the kid's ethnic background. So the "kid-friendly" designation is a gamble based on knowledge of what my kids (one a picky eater, the other an enthusiastic diner) and their friends appreciate. Generally kids like what they know. Even if a dish is not listed as kid-friendly, chances are there are plenty of kids who will like it. You'll never know if you don't try.

Healthy: Healthy cooking is not simply a matter of cutting fat. Dishes noted as healthy include lots of veggies or fiber and little fat except for a reasonable amount of extra virgin olive oil, which qualifies as a good fat.

Brown-bag: This speaks for itself. If you see this designation on a recipe, pack it for lunch and avoid the lineups at that fast-food place near the office.

Guest-worthy: You can serve practically anything to guests. People are grateful, not critical, when you feed them. However, I have designated some dishes, from appetizers to soups as well as main courses, as special-occasion foods. This may be because they have pricier ingredients, look pretty or appeal to the adventurous.

Water versus Oil

Should you choose seafood packed in water or in oil? It depends on your recipe. Are you going to add sauce or mayonnaise? Are you going to drain the oil anyway? Then choose water-packed seafood or the recently introduced "no-drain" type. However, be aware that fish packed in oil is superior because it has a silkier texture and richer flavor. It is especially good in salads. Choose fish packed in oil if you are planning to use the oil or are willing to spend the calories. Oil-packed tuna, for instance, has 25 to 50 percent more calories compared to the water-packed kind.

Extra virgin olive oil is the best of the available options. Strangely, anchovies and sardines are commonly packed in extra virgin olive oil, but not most tuna. It is usually packed in mere olive oil, a lower grade that includes refined oil stripped of antioxidants and flavor.

When fish is packed in olive oil, I recommend that you drain the oil from the can and use it in your recipe. For one thing, you've paid for it. For another, omega-3 fats leach from the fish into the oil, which is not the case with fish packed in water. Definitely don't discard the savory, salty oil from anchovies. In addition, oils from smoked fish, oysters or mussels are particularly tasty, even though they may be vegetable or seed oils.

I wonder about the worth of paying more for fish canned in refined soybean, seed or vegetable oils. The same goes for seafood packed in broth or broth and oil. Depending on which company is talking, the broth may add flavor or make the fish taste milder.

After Opening the Can

Gently drain and rinse canned fish or seafood with cold water whenever practical. This sloughs off some of the sodium and unwanted preservatives. It also refreshes the product, which can start to taste tinny in its liquid. I always rinse shrimp, lobster, crab and shellfish. This is not recommended for crab but I do it anyway, except when it comes in tiny flakes. I may rinse solid tuna, but not salmon — it gets too waterlogged. I rinse inexpensive caviar to get rid of some of the dye. Do not, of course, rinse seafood, plain or smoked, that is packed in oil. You may be able to use the oil, and anyway, it would be messy because oil and water don't mix.

Don't be afraid to gently squeeze seafood to remove excess moisture. This isn't necessary when you are adding seafood to a sauce, but it is probably crucial if you're making fish burgers or a pie. All my recipes specify squeezing the product when it is necessary for producing good results.

Whether you rinse them or not, canned lobster and crab may seem soggy because the meat is porous. Brief poaching in butter or oil, as part of the recipe, evaporates excess moisture and tenderizes the meat.

Watch the Salt

Be careful with the salt shaker, especially if you are adding seafood at the end of a recipe. Seafood is salted during canning — far too much, in my opinion. Choose seafood labeled "low-sodium" or check the labels and compare among brands to find those that have the least sodium.

I normally use coarse sea salt in seafood dishes, but I switched to table salt when testing the recipes for this book because it is standardized and more commonly used. If you want to substitute coarse sea salt or kosher salt, increase the quantities called for by a third to a half, or go by taste.

What about the Bones?

Some canned fish — including salmon, sardines, mackerel, herring and anchovies — contain small bones. Heat processing makes those bones soft, feathery and edible. I recommend that you eat the bones for the calcium they contain. I eat the tiny bones in salmon but usually pull out the backbone. The same goes for the skin, which is rich in omega-3 fats. If you don't like the skin or bones or if you want a smoother texture in your recipe (a dip, for example), discard them, or buy boneless, skinless fish.

Occasionally consumers find stray bones in tuna. These are not edible — discard them. Also, beware of shell fragments in canned crab, lobster and shellfish. The cannery tries to remove them all, but some do slip past inspection.

All these recipes were tested using a gas stove. If you're using an electric stove, you may have to adjust the heat up or down as needed, because the burners cycle on and off.

Working with Can Sizes

When developing the recipes in this book, I gave priority to using one or two cans per dish and stuck to sizes that are commonly available in supermarkets. However, there are regional differences, as well as odd sizes caused by disparities between metric and imperial measures. Also, some products are standardized while others come in a variety of sizes. In the case of crab and lobster, I usually specify both volume and weight.

Luckily, most canned seafood recipes are very forgiving. Just pick a size or weight that's close to the one in the ingredient list. (Note that some seafood labels state both net and drained weights. The latter is more accurate.) Dips, soups, pastas and the like should give you no problems. However, stick closely to the can size in the few cases where the amount used is crucial to the texture, such as crab cakes, fishballs and pâtés.

Using the Substitutions Chart

Each recipe in this book stars a specific seafood; the chart on pages 272 to 278 lists potential stand-ins. This will help you work with whatever you have in the pantry. It was impossible for me to test all the suggested substitutions. However, I did give careful consideration to each one, basing decisions on my decades of experience as an avid home cook, food writer and recipe tester. A lot of canned seafood is interchangeable in recipes, so don't be afraid to play around.

The Top 15 Classics

Vintage Tuna Salad

Tuna salad is a brown-bag, lunch counter and cafeteria mainstay for kids and grownups alike. This vintage version is made with tried-and-true ingredients. If you want to experiment, try the variations on pages 86 and 87.

Makes about 1 cup (250 mL)

- Fast
- Kid-friendly
- Brown-bag

Tips

You'd think tuna salad would be the perfect place to use the cheaper flaked tuna, since everything is smooshed together. Nope. I recommend chunk tuna because it's less likely to turn into a paste.

Weepiness is tuna salad's number one preventable problem. Before using, drain the tuna in a sieve, flake it with your fingers and gently squeeze out excess moisture. Avoid watery additions such as chopped tomato or cucumber. The mayonnaise you choose also plays a role. If you use lower-fat mayonnaise, the tuna salad will become a bit looser and more watery after sitting, but the calorie savings make it worthwhile.

I prefer to use the tender inner stalks of celery known as the heart. You can, however, tenderize an outside stalk by peeling it.

¼ to ⅓ cup	mayonnaise	60 to 75 mL
1 to 2 tbsp	finely chopped sweet pickles, patted dry	15 to 30 mL
1 tbsp	finely diced celery (see Tips, left)	15 mL
1 tbsp	finely diced red onion	15 mL
1	can (6 oz/170 g) chunk tuna in water, drained and broken into flakes	1
	Salt and freshly ground black pepper	

1. In a medium bowl, combine mayonnaise and pickles to taste, celery and onion. Gently squeeze tuna to remove excess moisture and add it to the bowl. Blend with a fork. Season to taste with salt and pepper.

2. Serve immediately or cover and refrigerate for up to 3 days.

Variations

Go upscale by using premium tuna in olive oil, drained. It is silkier and tastes richer, and you won't need as much mayonnaise.

Substitute an equal quantity of salmon, mackerel, sardines, sprats, shrimp, crab or lobster for the tuna.

Tuna Salad

Even if kids don't like fish, chances are they'll like tuna. Canned tuna was introduced to North Americans circa 1903, and tuna salad appeared not long afterward. It is the sandwich maker's Old Faithful — even more popular than its cousin, salmon salad. It is really a spread, of course, named back in the days when a few bits of chopped vegetables and mayonnaise made something a "salad." Versatile tuna salad is much more than a sandwich filling, however. You can mound it onto greens or rice to make a meal, spread it on crackers, or stuff it into celery boats or tomato cups.

Classic Salmon Salad

Salmon salad is lovely when the fish is mixed with its classic partners, lemon and dill. Spread it on toasted artisan bread, add a scoop to dressed salad greens or even warm noodles, or use it as a filling for baked potatoes.

Makes about 1 cup (250 mL)

- Fast
- Kid-friendly
- Brown-bag

Tip

Use lower-fat or regular mayonnaise, as you prefer.

¼ to ⅓ cup	mayonnaise	60 to 75 mL
1	green onion (white and light green parts), finely chopped	1
1 tbsp	finely chopped fresh dill fronds	15 mL
1 tbsp	sweet green relish	15 mL
1 tsp	finely grated lemon zest	5 mL
1	can salmon (7½ oz/213 g), drained, deboned and broken into flakes	1
	Salt and freshly ground black pepper	

1. In a bowl, mix mayonnaise to taste, onion, dill, relish and lemon zest. Gently squeeze salmon to remove excess moisture and add it to the bowl. Blend with a fork. Season to taste with salt and pepper.

2. Serve immediately or cover and refrigerate for up to 3 days.

Variations

Omit the dill and relish and add 2 tbsp (30 mL) finely chopped dill pickle, patted dry.

Substitute an equal quantity of lime zest for the lemon.

Substitute an equal quantity of tuna, mackerel, sardines, sprats, shrimp, crab or lobster for the salmon.

Caesar Salad Two Ways

Caesar salad must be North America's most popular restaurant, buffet and cafeteria salad. It gets its irresistible savoriness from anchovies and Parmesan cheese. When I crave Caesar salad, I start with this freeform recipe, then choose the dressing according to my mood. Add a topping and dinner is served.

Makes 4 servings

- Fast
- Kid-friendly
- Guest-worthy

Tip

Here's an easy way to cook crispy bacon with less mess: Place four slices of bacon in a single layer on a ribbed microwave grill pan. If you don't have one, place the bacon on a microwave-safe plate lined with a paper towel. Cover the bacon with another paper towel. Microwave it on High for 2 minutes. Turn, cover with a fresh paper towel and microwave until crispy, about 1 minute. For two slices of bacon, halve the time.

1	head romaine lettuce, leaves torn into bite-size pieces	1
	Creamy Caesar Dressing or Caesar Vinaigrette (page 29)	
4 to 8	slices bacon, cooked crisp and crumbled	4 to 8
¼ to ½ cup	freshly grated Parmesan cheese (½ to 1 oz/15 to 30 g)	60 to 125 mL
	Croutons	

1. In a large bowl, toss romaine with dressing to taste.

2. Add bacon, Parmesan and croutons to taste. Toss lightly and serve immediately.

Caesar Salad History

The Caesar salad was invented in 1924 in Tijuana, Mexico. Apparently Italian immigrant chef Caesar Cardini ran out of supplies and had to invent something to feed diners (this seems to be a common story in food history). The original Caesar was finger food that Cardini prepared tableside. He bathed whole leaves of romaine hearts with a dressing that included coddled egg, Parmesan cheese and Worcestershire sauce.

Creamy Caesar Dressing

If you crave a creamy Caesar salad without the fuss of making a mayonnaise dressing from scratch, here's a delicious compromise.

Makes about 1 cup (250 mL)

Tips

Using mayonnaise as a base instead of the traditional coddled egg is more convenient and safer if you have any concerns about your egg supply.

You can use lower-fat mayonnaise.

In dressings you can use 2 tbsp (30 mL) dry grated 100% Parmesan (sold in tubs) for ¼ cup (60 mL) of the freshly grated kind.

● **Food processor or blender**

3	cloves garlic	3
¾ cup	mayonnaise (see Tips, left)	175 mL
3	anchovy fillets	3
2 tbsp	extra virgin olive oil	30 mL
¼ cup	freshly grated Parmesan cheese (½ oz/15 g; see Tips, left)	60 mL
1 tbsp	freshly squeezed lemon juice	15 mL
1 tsp	Worcestershire sauce	5 mL
½ tsp	Dijon mustard	2 mL
4	capers, rinsed and drained	4

1. In food processor fitted with the metal blade, with the motor running, drop garlic through the feed tube to chop. (You can also do this in a blender.) Scrape down the sides of the bowl. Add mayonnaise, anchovies, olive oil, Parmesan, lemon juice, Worcestershire sauce, mustard and capers. Process until mixture is smooth.

Caesar Vinaigrette

For a lighter-tasting, crunchier Caesar salad, I sometimes opt for a vinaigrette dressing. This one has all the traditional Caesar flavors.

Makes about 1¼ cups (300 mL)

Tips

It's simpler and more efficient to mash anchovies with a fork instead of chopping them.

I prefer dry grated 100% Parmesan (the powdery kind sold in tubs) in vinaigrettes, as the result is less creamy. However, you can use ¼ cup (60 mL) freshly grated Parmesan if you prefer.

2	anchovy fillets, minced (see Tips, left)	2
2	cloves garlic, minced	2
1	small shallot, minced	1
1 tbsp	white wine vinegar	15 mL
1 tsp	Worcestershire sauce	5 mL
½ tsp	freshly ground black pepper	2 mL
¼ tsp	salt (approx.)	1 mL
⅛ tsp	hot pepper sauce	0.5 mL
1 cup	extra virgin olive oil	250 mL
2 tbsp	grated Parmesan cheese (½ oz/15 g; see Tips, left))	30 mL

1. In a bowl, whisk together anchovies, garlic, shallot, vinegar, Worcestershire sauce, pepper, salt and hot pepper sauce. Whisk in olive oil, then Parmesan. Add salt to taste, if necessary.

Salade Niçoise

This tuna and vegetable salad is the signature dish of the Mediterranean mecca Nice. It is authentic to use canned tuna in olive oil, not grilled fresh tuna. The French are adamant that the original included no cooked vegetables, but over the years potatoes have found their way in.

Makes 4 to 8 servings

- Kid-friendly
- Healthy
- Guest-worthy

Tips

Vinaigrette: In a large measuring cup, whisk together ¼ cup (60 mL) white wine vinegar, 1 minced shallot, 1 tbsp (15 mL) chopped parsley leaves, 1 tsp (5 mL) Dijon mustard and ½ tsp (2 mL) each salt and freshly ground black pepper. Gradually whisk in ½ cup (125 mL) extra virgin olive oil, until blended and thickened.

You can substitute oil from the tuna (about ¼ cup/60 mL) for some of the extra virgin olive oil in the Vinaigrette.

If you prefer, use thawed frozen artichoke hearts.

Slim French beans (called haricots) are standard in this salad, but regular green beans are fine. Don't trim the cute little squiggles off the ends.

Variations

Substitute an equal quantity of salmon, mackerel, cod, sardines, sprats, shrimp, crab, lobster or octopus for the tuna.

8 oz	green beans, trimmed and sliced in half crosswise (about 2 cups/500 mL)	250 g
8	mini red potatoes (about 12 oz/375 g) Vinaigrette (see Tips, left)	8
4	canned artichoke hearts, drained and quartered (see Tips, left)	4
1	head Boston lettuce, separated into leaves	1
2	small ripe tomatoes, cut in wedges	2
2	mini cucumbers, thinly sliced	2
1	small red bell pepper, cut in ¼-inch (0.5 cm) strips	1
1 cup	thinly sliced red onion	250 mL
4	cans (each 3 oz/85 g) solid tuna in olive oil, drained	4
2 tsp	capers, rinsed, drained and chopped	10 mL
1	small sprig basil	1
4	large eggs, hard-cooked and quartered	4
4	anchovy fillets, halved lengthwise	4
16	niçoise or small black olives, pitted	16

1. Bring a large pot of salted water to a boil over high heat. Add beans, reduce heat to medium and cook for 3 to 4 minutes, until tender-crisp. Using a mesh scoop, transfer beans to a colander and rinse under cold running water to stop the cooking. Set aside to cool.

2. Return heat to high and add potatoes to the cooking water. Bring to a boil, reduce heat to medium and cook for about 15 minutes, until potatoes are tender but firm. Drain and cut into quarters. Transfer to a bowl and toss warm potatoes with 1 tbsp (15 mL) vinaigrette.

3. In a small bowl, toss artichokes with 1 tbsp (15 mL) vinaigrette.

4. Line a large serving platter with lettuce. Arrange beans, potatoes, artichokes, tomatoes, cucumbers, red pepper and onion overtop, leaving a small space in the center. Mound tuna in the center. Scatter capers over tuna and garnish with basil. Place egg wedges at the corners and drape with anchovies. Scatter olives overtop. Serve immediately, with remaining vinaigrette alongside.

East Coast Lobster Rolls

A lobster roll is a simple thing: lobster chunks lightly bathed in mayonnaise and stuffed into a hot dog bun. A few extra elements may be added sparingly: celery, onion, a squeeze of lemon, salt and pepper. The bun should be toasted and well buttered. The sidekicks are pickles and potato chips. This classic roll is simply delicious. If you are craving a more sophisticated version, try Tarragon Lobster Rolls (page 111).

Makes 2 rolls

- Fast
- Kid-friendly
- Guest-worthy

Tips

Don't make globster rolls. Avoid a drippy mess by using a minimal amount of full-fat mayo, and lemon zest rather than juice. Leave the lobster in decent-sized chunks.

Purists start with live lobsters. Canned lobster, however, makes for almost instant gratification. It comes frozen in brine, pasteurized or heat processed, but it is not widely sold. The can sizes I have most often come across are 11.3 oz (320 g) and 6 oz (170 g), but they may be different in your area. You can use leftovers to make any of the other delicious recipes in this book (see chart pages 272 to 278).

Top-split hot dog rolls are traditional but may be hard to find in your area. Lightning won't strike if you use regular, side-split ones.

2 to 4 tbsp	mayonnaise	30 to 60 mL
2 tbsp	finely diced celery heart	30 mL
½ tsp	finely grated lemon zest	2 mL
¾ cup	canned lobster meat (about 4 oz/125 g), rinsed, drained and cut into large chunks	175 mL
	Salt and freshly ground white pepper	
2	hot dog buns, top- or side-split	2
4 tsp	unsalted butter, melted	20 mL

1. In a bowl, stir together 2 tbsp (30 mL) mayonnaise, celery and lemon zest. Gently squeeze lobster to remove excess moisture and add to bowl. Mix with a fork. Add more mayonnaise to taste, if desired. Season to taste with salt and pepper.

2. Brush cut sides of buns with half of the butter. Heat a skillet over medium-high heat and add buns, cut sides down. Cook, pressing very gently with a spatula, for about 2 minutes, until golden brown. Brush tops of buns with remaining butter, flip and cook for 1 to 2 minutes, until golden brown.

3. Fill buns with lobster mixture, dividing evenly, and serve immediately.

Variations

Make shrimp or crab rolls instead of using lobster.

New England Clam Chowder

It's white versus red in the clam chowder popularity contest, and the former, known as New England clam chowder, is winning. It appeared first, in the mid-1800s, and has a thick, creamy white base. I have sampled clam chowders all over Cape Cod and in Boston. They always seem bland, stodgy and — dare I say it? — gluey. This one is not. Many New England chowder recipes call for heavy cream, but I prefer to use lighter cream and less flour.

Makes 6 cups (1.5 L) 4 to 6 servings

- Kid-friendly
- Guest-worthy

Tips

You can make this soup in advance. Complete Steps 1 through 3, then cover and refrigerate overnight. When you're ready to serve, reheat the soup with the cream and dill (do not let it boil). Sprinkle with the bacon and serve.

Although you can use baby clams, surf or other meaty clams make a superior, heartier soup.

You can buy clams that are already chopped.

Waxy red spuds hold their shape in soup. You can add thickening power by substituting yellow-fleshed potatoes for some of the red ones.

Variations

Fool around with tradition — this recipe provides a fine base for all kinds of canned seafood. Substitute an equal quantity of tuna, salmon, mackerel, cod, kippers, shrimp, crab, lobster, oysters, mussels, squid or octopus for the clams. If you're substituting salmon or another flaky fish, add it at the end.

1 cup	water	250 mL
1	bottle (8 oz/240 mL) clam juice	1
4	red potatoes (about 1 lb/500 g), peeled and cut in ½-inch (1 cm) dice	500 g
1	can (5 oz/142 g) surf clams, rinsed, drained and chopped (see Tips, left)	1
1	bay leaf	1
4	slices bacon, chopped	4
1	onion, diced	1
1	stalk celery, cut in small dice	1
2	cloves garlic, minced	2
2 tbsp	all-purpose flour	30 mL
1 tbsp	dry sherry	15 mL
2 tsp	finely grated lemon zest	10 mL
½ tsp	salt (approx.)	2 mL
¼ tsp	freshly ground white pepper	1 mL
1 cup	table (18%) or half-and-half (10%) cream	250 mL
1 to 2 tbsp	chopped fresh dill fronds	15 to 30 mL

1. In a large saucepan over medium-high heat, bring water, clam juice, potatoes, clams and bay leaf to a simmer. Reduce heat to low, cover and simmer for 10 minutes, until potatoes are tender. Place a sieve over a bowl and drain, reserving broth and solids separately. Discard bay leaf.

2. In the same saucepan over medium heat, cook bacon for 5 minutes, until browned and crisp. Using a slotted spoon, transfer to a plate lined with paper towels. Drain off all but 2 tbsp (30 mL) bacon drippings.

3. Heat drippings over medium-low heat. Add onion, celery and garlic and cook, stirring often, for 4 to 5 minutes, until softened. Sprinkle in flour. Cook, stirring, for 1 minute. Gradually stir in reserved broth, mixing until no lumps remain. Add reserved solids, sherry, lemon zest, salt and pepper. Reduce heat to low and simmer for 5 minutes, until celery is tender-crisp.

4. Stir in cream and dill to taste. Add salt to taste if necessary. Sprinkle reserved bacon overtop and serve immediately.

Manhattan Clam Chowder

Tomatoey Manhattan clam chowder is more of an acquired taste than its New England relative — but also way less calorific. Culinary historians theorize that Portuguese immigrants created this classic, even though adding tomatoes to clam chowder was widely reviled. In 1939 a bill making the practice illegal was even introduced in the Maine legislature! Manhattan chowder was not actually invented in New York; it was so named because supposedly only New Yorkers were crazy enough to eat it. I beg to differ.

Makes about 8 cups (2 L) 6 to 8 servings

• Guest-worthy

Tips

Tangy clam-tomato cocktail is the not-so-secret ingredient in this recipe. It's sold in the supermarket's shelf-stable juice section.

Don't tell the clam chowder police I said so, but this tastes good with grated Parmesan.

Variations

Substitute an equal quantity of shrimp or lobster meat for the clams.

4	slices bacon, chopped	4
4	red potatoes (about 1 lb/500 g), cut in ½-inch (1 cm) dice	4
1	stalk celery, thinly sliced on the diagonal	1
1	carrot, cut into matchsticks	1
1	onion, diced	1
¼	bulb fennel, diced (about ¾ cup/175 mL)	¼
¼	green bell pepper, cut into matchsticks	¼
2	cloves garlic, minced	2
¼ cup	dry white wine	60 mL
2 cups	chicken stock	500 mL
1 cup	bottled clam-tomato cocktail	250 mL
1	bottle (8 oz/240 mL) clam juice	1
1	can (5 oz/142 g) surf clams, rinsed, drained and chopped	1
1 cup	canned diced tomatoes, with juice	250 mL
4	sprigs thyme	4
¼ tsp	salt (approx.)	1 mL
⅛ tsp	freshly ground black pepper	0.5 mL
¼ cup	chopped parsley leaves	60 mL
	Hot pepper sauce	

1. In a large saucepan over medium heat, cook bacon for 5 minutes, until browned and crisp. Using a slotted spoon, transfer to a plate lined with paper towels to drain.

2. You should have about 2 tbsp (30 mL) drippings in the pan. Add potatoes, celery, carrot, onion, fennel, green pepper and garlic. Cook over medium-low heat, stirring often, for 10 minutes, until softened. Stir in wine. Stir in stock, clam-tomato cocktail, clam juice, clams, tomatoes, thyme, salt and pepper. Bring to a simmer over medium-high heat. Reduce heat to low, cover and simmer until vegetables are tender, 15 to 20 minutes.

3. Remove thyme sprigs and discard. Adjust salt to taste. Add parsley and reserved bacon. Dash liberally with hot pepper sauce. Serve immediately.

Diner Tuna Melts

The tuna melt is so versatile it is more of an idea than a recipe. Here's an introductory version. You can experiment by using any type of bread or cheese, from marble rye to bagels and from Swiss to Brie. Made with pita bread, the tuna melt becomes a personal pizza. In the United Kingdom, melts are known as "toasties." For more tuna melts, see pages 110 and 111.

Makes 4 servings

- Fast
- Kid-friendly

Tip

Use lower-fat mayonnaise if you prefer.

- **Preheat oven to 400°F (200°C)**
- **Baking sheet, nonstick or lined with parchment**

2 tbsp	mayonnaise (see Tips, left)	30 mL
2 tbsp	finely diced celery heart	30 mL
1 tbsp	finely chopped onion	15 mL
1 tsp	finely chopped parsley leaves	5 mL
½ tsp	freshly squeezed lemon juice	2 mL
1	can (6 oz/170 g) chunk tuna in water, drained and broken into flakes	1
	Salt and freshly ground black pepper	
2	English muffins, split	2
4	thin slices tomato, optional	4
4	slices marble Cheddar cheese (each ¾ oz/22 g)	4

1. In a bowl, stir together mayonnaise, celery, onion, parsley and lemon juice. Add tuna and blend with a fork. Season to taste with salt and pepper.

2. Lightly toast muffins. Spread tuna mixture over each half, dividing equally. Place on prepared pan and top with tomato, if using, then the Cheddar. Bake in preheated oven for 5 to 10 minutes, until the cheese melts.

Variations

Substitute an equal amount of salmon, mackerel or shrimp for the tuna.

Pan Bagnat

This French sub is like a salade niçoise sandwich. Messy and delicious, it lives up to its name, which translates as "bathed bread." It makes a great meal, or, for something a little different, serve small slices as an appetizer.

Makes 4 to 6 servings

- Healthy
- Brown-bag

Tips

Olive dressing: In mini blender, combine olive oil from tuna plus enough extra virgin olive oil to make ¼ cup (60 mL). Add 12 pitted black olives, 1 tbsp (15 mL) rinsed, drained capers, 1 tbsp (15 mL) white wine vinegar, 1 tsp (5 mL) each anchovy paste and parsley leaves, ½ tsp (2 mL) Dijon mustard and ¼ tsp (1 mL) freshly ground black pepper. (If you don't have a small blender, chop or mash the ingredients finely, then whisk them together.)

Use a wider baguette, sometimes labeled "Parisian loaf," rather than a "French stick."

Cocktail tomatoes (such as Campari) are sold in most supermarkets. They are juicy and sweet, bigger than cherry tomatoes but smaller and rounder than plum tomatoes. You can substitute cherry or plum tomatoes in this sandwich.

- **Mini blender**

1	baguette (about 12 oz/375 g; see Tips, left)	1
	Olive dressing (see Tips, left)	
2	cans (each 3 oz/85 g) tuna in olive oil, drained (oil reserved) and broken into flakes	2
2 or 3	cocktail tomatoes, thinly sliced (see Tips, left)	2 or 3
	Salt	
1	piece (about 2 inches/5 cm) English cucumber, peeled, thinly sliced and patted dry	1
2	large eggs, hard-cooked and sliced	2
¼ cup	thinly sliced red onion	60 mL
2	canned or thawed frozen artichoke hearts, patted dry and thinly sliced	2
¼	small red bell pepper, thinly sliced	¼
6	small Boston lettuce leaves	6

1. Cut baguette in half lengthwise. Remove enough bread from the center of each half to make room for the filling. Lay bottom half, cut side up, on a long sheet of plastic wrap.

2. Smear half of the dressing over cut side of bottom layer. Add tuna and tomatoes and sprinkle lightly with salt. Layer on cucumber, eggs, onion, artichokes, red pepper and lettuce. Smear remaining dressing over cut side of top portion. Place on top of filled baguette and press down lightly.

3. Pull up the plastic around the loaf and wrap tightly. Refrigerate for 30 minutes before serving. To serve, cut on the diagonal into 4 to 6 sections.

Variations
Substitute an equal amount of salmon, sardines or sprats for the tuna.

Salmon Wiggle

The name of this dish is taken from the old expression "get a wiggle on," which means "hurry up." Early wiggles relied totally on canned ingredients — sometimes simply soup, salmon and peas — so the name is appropriate. This recipe is a bit fancier, but not by much. Salmon wiggle was a comforting childhood staple for many older folks, particularly in New England. Of course, there are plenty who recall tuna wiggle and shrimp wiggle too. Wiggle was ladled over toast, rice, noodles or even soda crackers. I prefer it over rice or noodles, but to each his or her own.

**Makes 3 cups
(750 mL)
2 to 4 servings**

• Fast
• Kid-friendly

Variations

Substitute an equal quantity of tuna, mackerel, cod, kippers or shrimp for the salmon.

2 tbsp	unsalted butter	30 mL
1	leek (white and light green parts), thinly sliced	1
½ tsp	salt (approx.)	2 mL
1	clove garlic, minced	1
¼ cup	dry white wine, optional	60 mL
1¼ to 1½ cups	whole milk	300 to 375 mL
2 tbsp	all-purpose flour	30 mL
1	can (7½ oz/213 g) sockeye salmon, drained, deboned and broken into chunks	1
1 cup	green peas, thawed if frozen	250 mL
	Freshly ground white pepper	
1 tbsp	chopped parsley	15 mL
4	lemon wedges	4

1. In a medium saucepan, melt butter over medium-low heat. Add leek and salt. Cook, stirring occasionally, for 8 to 10 minutes, until leek softens and turns golden. Stir in garlic for 20 seconds. Stir in wine, if using, and cook for 1 minute, until evaporated.

2. In a large measuring cup, whisk together 1¼ cups (300 mL) milk and the flour. Gradually add to leek, stirring constantly. When mixture comes to a simmer, reduce heat to low. Simmer for 2 minutes or until thickened. Stir in salmon and peas and season to taste with pepper. Cook, stirring often, for 5 minutes, until mixture is warmed through. Add some or all of the remaining milk to adjust the thickness, keeping in mind that the wiggle will loosen as it sits. Adjust salt to taste.

3. Sprinkle parsley overtop and serve immediately, with lemon wedges alongside.

Hot Crab Dip

Hot crab dip is usually baked, but you can make batches in the microwave. I recommend microwaving smaller batches for almost instant gratification. After all, how much hot crab dip can you consume before it gets cold?

Makes about 1 cup (250 mL) 4 appetizer servings

- Kid-friendly
- Guest-worthy

Tips

You can prepare the dip a day ahead. Cover and refrigerate until you're ready to serve.

It's okay to use less expensive flaked crab in this recipe.

Double or triple the quantity to suit your needs. If you're making a larger quantity, it is probably best to bake it in the oven (see Variations, below).

Be savvy about food safety — don't leave this dip lying around for hours. As a general rule, keep hot foods hot and cold foods cold. Never leave food at room temperature for more than two hours.

4 oz	block cream cheese, softened	125 g
3 tbsp	shredded Cheddar cheese	45 mL
1 tbsp	mayonnaise	15 mL
1 to 2 tsp	freshly squeezed lime juice, divided	5 to 10 mL
1/2 tsp	Worcestershire sauce	2 mL
1/2 tsp	hot pepper sauce	2 mL
1	green onion (white and light green parts), minced	1
1 tbsp	minced red bell pepper	15 mL
1	can (4.25 oz/120 g) crabmeat, rinsed and drained (see Tips, left)	1
	Salt and freshly ground white pepper	
	Sweet paprika	

1. In a microwave-safe bowl, using a fork, mash together cream cheese, Cheddar, mayonnaise, 1 tsp (5 mL) lime juice, Worcestershire sauce, hot pepper sauce, onion and red pepper. Gently squeeze the crab to remove excess moisture and add to the bowl. Fold in gently and season to taste with salt and pepper. Add remaining 1 tsp (5 mL) lime juice if you prefer a tangier dip.

2. Microwave on High for 1 to 2 minutes, until dip is bubbly at the edges. Stir well and return to microwave for 30 to 60 seconds, until hot and bubbly.

3. Scrape dip into a small serving bowl and sprinkle paprika generously overtop. Serve immediately.

Variations

If you wish to bake the dip, after completing Step 1, scrape the mixture into an ovenproof dish. Bake in a 375°F (190°C) oven until heated through and bubbly at the edges. Stir and sprinkle paprika overtop. Baking time depends on the amount and the size of dish. A triple batch of this recipe baked in a 4-cup (1 L) round casserole takes about 30 minutes.

Serve the dip in a bread bowl, with torn bread for dipping.

Experiment with other seafood such as tuna, salmon, mackerel, cod, kippers, shrimp, lobster, clams, oysters or mussels.

Crab Foo Yung with Soy Glaze

Egg foo yung is an iconic westernized Chinese dish. This version calls for crabmeat, but it's simple to substitute other types of seafood (see Variations, page 39).

Makes 4 to 6 servings

- Kid-friendly
- Healthy
- Guest-worthy

Tips

For the finest minced garlic, use a garlic press instead of chopping.

Shaoxing cooking wine is a salted Chinese rice wine.

I prefer to use lower-sodium soy sauce, to prevent oversalting.

Glaze

2 tsp	water	10 mL
½ tsp	cornstarch	2 mL
1 tbsp	oil	15 mL
1	shallot, chopped	1
1	clove garlic, minced	1
¼ cup	dry sherry, shaoxing wine or sake	60 mL
¼ cup	chicken stock	60 mL
2 tbsp	soy sauce (see Tips, left)	30 mL
1 tbsp	liquid honey	15 mL
	Asian chili sauce (such as sambal oelek or sriracha)	

Eggs

8	large eggs	8
½ cup	chicken stock	125 mL
¼ tsp	salt	1 mL
	Freshly ground white pepper	
1 tbsp + 1 tsp	oil, divided	20 mL
1½ cups	coarsely chopped oyster mushrooms (4 oz/125 g)	375 mL
2 cups	packed bean sprouts (4 oz/125 g)	500 mL
½ cup	thinly sliced chives	125 mL
1½ cups	canned crabmeat (8 oz/250 g), rinsed and drained (see Tips, page 39)	375 mL

1. *Glaze:* In a small bowl, stir together water and cornstarch.

2. In a small skillet, heat oil over medium heat until shimmery. Add shallot and garlic. Cook, stirring constantly, for 1 minute, until softened. Reduce heat to low. Stir in sherry and simmer for 1 minute. Stir in stock, soy sauce, honey and chili sauce to taste. Simmer for 2 minutes, until syrupy. Gradually stir in cornstarch slurry and cook for about 30 seconds, until thickened. Remove from heat and set aside.

3. *Eggs:* In a bowl, whisk together eggs, stock, salt and pepper to taste. Set aside.

Tips

You'll need two 4.25 oz (120 g) cans of shelf-stable crab or half a 1-lb (440 g) container of pasteurized crab. To use up leftovers, check the other delicious recipes in this book (see chart on pages 272 to 278).

If the crab is too wet, squeeze it gently to remove excess moisture before adding it to the pan.

4. In a large, nonstick skillet, heat 1 tbsp (15 mL) oil over medium-high heat until shimmery. Add mushrooms and cook, stirring often, for 4 to 5 minutes, until they release their liquid and turn golden. Stir in bean sprouts. Scrape mixture onto a large plate and sprinkle with chives. Cover the plate with foil and set aside.

5. Wipe the pan clean. Heat remaining 1 tsp (5 mL) oil over medium-high heat until shimmery. Reduce heat to medium-low. Add egg mixture and sprinkle crabmeat overtop. Cook for about 5 minutes, until bottom is golden brown and top is no longer wet, occasionally lifting the edges and tilting the pan to allow uncooked egg to flow underneath.

6. Transfer cooked egg mixture to a serving platter or individual plates. Drizzle with glaze and spoon the mushroom mixture overtop.

Variations

Substitute an equal amount of tuna, salmon, mackerel, shrimp, lobster or clams for the crab.

Spaghetti with White Clam Sauce

Fresh clams are good, but if you crave this Neapolitan favorite without the usual fuss and expense, you can make a very respectable version using canned clams. So now your choice is between white clam sauce (vongole bianco) or tomatoey clam sauce (vongole rosso). As with the New England versus Manhattan clam chowder rivalry (see pages 32 and 33), white has the edge. Which team are you on?

Makes 4 servings

- Fast
- Guest-worthy

Tips

You can use baby clams or meaty clams. If using the latter (my preference), chop them yourself or buy them already chopped.

For a pasta with bolder flavor, double the amount of clams.

Clam juice, sold in supermarkets, stands in for the liquor that the live clams release during cooking.

Use top-quality olive oil and fragrant dry white Italian wine, as they are essential flavorings in this simple dish.

12 oz	spaghetti	375 g
¼ cup	extra virgin olive oil	60 mL
4	large cloves garlic, minced	4
¼ tsp	hot pepper flakes	1 mL
½ cup	dry white wine	125 mL
½ cup	clam juice	125 mL
2 tbsp	heavy or whipping (35%) cream	30 mL
1	can (5 oz/142 g) chopped surf clams or baby clams, rinsed and drained	1
¼ cup + 1 tbsp	chopped parsley leaves, divided	75 mL
	Salt and freshly ground black pepper	
	Freshly grated Parmesan cheese, optional	

1. In a large pot of boiling salted water over medium heat, cook spaghetti for 10 to 12 minutes, until tender to the bite (al dente). Drain and set aside.

2. Meanwhile, in a large skillet, heat oil over medium heat until shimmery. Remove from heat, add garlic and hot pepper flakes and stir for 1 minute. Stir in wine, clam juice and cream. Return skillet to element and simmer mixture for 5 minutes or until reduced to about ¾ cup (175 mL). Stir in clams and ¼ cup (60 mL) parsley. Season to taste with salt and pepper. Remove from element.

3. Immediately add spaghetti to clam mixture and toss with tongs. Set aside for 5 minutes to absorb liquid.

4. Before serving, adjust the salt to taste, then sprinkle remaining 1 tbsp (15 mL) parsley overtop. Serve Parmesan alongside, if using.

Variations

Add oomph to this dish by including pancetta in Step 2. Sauté 2 oz (60 g) chopped pancetta in the hot oil until it is golden. Then remove the skillet from the heat and add the garlic and hot pepper flakes. Continue with the recipe.

Instead of using cream, stir in 2 tbsp (30 mL) cold butter after the sauce is reduced, before adding the clams.

Spaghetti with Red Clam Sauce

- Fast
- Guest-worthy

Tips

Buy canned diced tomatoes because they hold their shape better in pasta. I prefer the larger, 19-ounce (540 mL) can. If you use the smaller size, save some of the pasta cooking water and add a bit to the spaghetti if necessary.

If you don't have pancetta, omit it or use bacon. Pancetta is not traditional, but its smokiness complements the clams.

Parmesan is not traditionally served with fish or seafood pasta, but who cares? Add as much as you like.

12 oz	spaghetti	375 g
$\frac{1}{4}$ cup	extra virgin olive oil	60 mL
2 oz	pancetta, chopped (see Tips, left)	60 g
4	large cloves garlic	4
$\frac{1}{4}$ tsp	hot pepper flakes	1 mL
$\frac{1}{2}$ cup	dry white wine	125 mL
$\frac{1}{2}$ cup	clam juice	125 mL
1	can (14 to 19 oz/398 to 540 mL) diced tomatoes, with juices	1
1	can (5 oz/142 g) chopped surf clams or baby clams, rinsed and drained	1
$\frac{1}{4}$ cup + 1 tbsp	chopped parsley leaves, divided	75 mL
	Salt and freshly ground black pepper	
	Freshly grated Parmesan cheese, optional	

1. In a large pot of boiling salted water over medium heat, cook spaghetti for 10 to 12 minutes, until tender to the bite (al dente). Drain and set aside.

2. Meanwhile, in a large skillet, heat oil over medium heat until shimmery. Add pancetta and cook, stirring, for about 2 minutes, until golden and starting to crisp. Using a slotted spoon, transfer to a small bowl.

3. Remove skillet from heat, add garlic and hot pepper flakes and stir for 1 minute. Stir in wine, clam juice and tomatoes, with juice. Return skillet to element and simmer mixture for 10 minutes or until it is reduced to about $2\frac{1}{4}$ cups (300 mL). Stir in clams, $\frac{1}{4}$ cup (60 mL) parsley and salt and pepper to taste. Remove skillet from heat, add spaghetti and toss with tongs. Set aside for 5 minutes to absorb liquid.

4. Before serving, adjust the salt to taste, then sprinkle the pancetta and remaining 1 tbsp (15 mL) parsley overtop. Serve Parmesan alongside, if desired.

Tuna Tetrazzini

This casserole was named in honor of the plump and powerful 19th-century opera diva Luisa Tetrazzini. It was a rich dish, originally made with chicken or turkey. This tuna version cuts the fat by replacing most of the cream with stock and cream cheese.

Makes 4 servings

- Kid-friendly

Tip

Thank heavens for panko bread crumbs — they are light yet crunchy, and way better than standard dry crumbs for casserole toppings. Supermarkets stock panko, usually in the sushi section.

- **Preheat oven to 350°F (180°C)**
- **8-inch (20 cm) square baking dish**

8 oz	spaghettini	250 g
1½ cups	chicken stock	375 mL
¼ cup	all-purpose flour	60 mL
2 tbsp	unsalted butter, divided	30 mL
1 tbsp	extra virgin olive oil	15 mL
1	onion, diced	1
¼ cup	finely chopped red bell pepper	60 mL
2	cloves garlic, minced	2
12 oz	button mushrooms, sliced (4½ cups/1.125 L)	375 g
½ tsp	salt (approx.)	2 mL
½ tsp	freshly ground black pepper	2 mL
¼ cup	dry sherry	60 mL
1 tbsp	heavy or whipping (35%) cream	15 mL
2 oz	cream cheese (about ¼ cup/60 mL)	60 g
4 oz	freshly grated Parmesan cheese (about 2 cups/500 mL), divided	125 g
1	can (6 oz/170 g) tuna in water, drained and broken into chunks	1
½ cup	slivered almonds	125 mL
½ cup	panko bread crumbs (see Tip, left)	125 mL
4	lemon wedges	4

1. In a large pot of boiling salted water over medium heat, cook pasta for about 10 minutes, until just tender to the bite (al dente). Drain and set aside.

2. Meanwhile, in a large measuring cup, whisk together stock and flour. Set aside.

3. In a large skillet over medium heat, melt 1 tbsp (15 mL) butter with oil. Add onion and red pepper. Cook, stirring often, for 2 minutes, until softened. Stir in garlic for 20 seconds. Add mushrooms, salt and pepper. Cook for 5 minutes or until liquid from the mushrooms is released and evaporates. Stir in sherry. Cook, stirring occasionally, for 2 minutes.

4. Gradually stir in stock mixture. Reduce heat to low and simmer for 5 minutes, stirring often, until mixture thickens. Stir in cream and cream cheese. Add all but $\frac{1}{4}$ cup (60 mL) Parmesan and cook, stirring, until melted.

5. Remove pan from heat and stir in pasta and tuna. Add salt to taste, if necessary. Scrape into baking dish and sprinkle almonds evenly overtop.

6. In a microwave-safe bowl, melt remaining 1 tbsp (15 mL) butter in a microwave oven on High for 30 seconds. Add panko bread crumbs and remaining Parmesan and mix well. Sprinkle mixture evenly over surface of casserole.

7. Bake in preheated oven for 30 minutes, until bubbly and topping is golden brown. Remove from oven and let stand for 10 to 15 minutes before serving. Serve with lemon wedges alongside to squeeze overtop.

Variations

For a more substantial casserole, double the quantity of tuna.

Substitute salmon, mackerel, shrimp, lobster, clams or octopus for the tuna.

Old-Fashioned Tuna Noodle Casserole

A truly corporate recipe, the original tuna casserole was prepared completely from packages and cans. Culinary historians date the Campbell's recipe back to 1941. Tuna casserole is much beloved, and scores of diners (my children included) have succumbed to its allure over the passing decades. It is certainly easy to prepare and evokes a warm sense of nostalgia. This version is old-school comfort food. For a contemporary tuna casserole, see page 152.

Makes 4 servings

- Kid-friendly

Tips

Use the lower-sodium version of this soup.

Buy ripple chips (they're sturdier) and crush them with a rolling pin.

Variations

Substitute an equal quantity of salmon, mackerel, kippers, shrimp, lobster or clams for the tuna.

Instead of classic cream of mushroom soup, use condensed wild mushroom or garlic mushroom soup.

Top the casserole with crushed Ritz crackers or buttered cornflake crumbs.

- **Preheat oven to 350°F (180°C)**
- **8-inch (20 cm) square baking dish**

6 oz	broad egg noodles	175 g
1	can (10 oz/284 mL) condensed cream of mushroom soup (see Tips, left)	1
½ cup	whole milk	125 mL
1 cup	shredded Cheddar cheese (4 oz/125 g)	250 mL
1	can (6 oz/170 g) tuna in water, drained and broken into chunks	1
1 cup	green peas, thawed if frozen	250 mL
2 tbsp	chopped pimiento	30 mL
	Salt	
1 cup	crushed potato chips (see Tips, left)	250 mL

1. In a large pot of boiling salted water over medium heat, cook noodles for 10 to 12 minutes, until tender. Drain and set aside.

2. Meanwhile, in a saucepan over medium-low heat, cook soup, milk and Cheddar for about 5 minutes, until mixture is hot and cheese has melted. Add tuna, peas, pimiento and cooked noodles. Stir to combine and season to taste with salt.

3. Scrape mixture into baking dish and sprinkle chips overtop. Bake in preheated oven for 30 minutes, until sauce is bubbly and topping is golden. Remove from heat and set aside for 10 minutes before serving.

Appetizers and Snacks

Flavored Butters

Easy, fast and versatile, flavored butters are swanky enough to offer to company yet simple enough to serve as a snack. Spread them on crostini or crackers to make simple canapés, use them in fancy sandwiches, dollop them on meat, fish or steamed vegetables, or use them to spruce up potatoes, rice or pasta.

Makes about ½ cup (125 mL)

- Fast
- Guest-worthy

Anchovy butter goes well with a surprising number of foods. For instance, it makes an especially delicious finish for perfectly grilled steak.

Tips

Be careful not to discard the anchovy oil. It's an important flavoring agent.

For the finest minced garlic, push it through a press.

This bivalve butter is appealing and unusual. Take a Parisian specialty a step further and dip fresh, crunchy radishes in it. It's lovely in finger sandwiches too.

Instead of mixing with a fork, use a mini food processor for a smoother blend.

You can roll flavored butter into a log shape, wrap it in plastic, chill and then slice off coins. Some cooks spread the butter in a thin layer, chill it, then punch out shapes using cookie or fondant cutters.

Lip-Smacking Anchovy Butter

1	can (2 oz/50 g) anchovies in extra virgin olive oil, with oil, chopped	1
1 tsp	freshly squeezed lemon juice	5 mL
6 tbsp	unsalted butter, at room temperature (see Tips, page 47)	90 mL
1	small clove garlic, minced (see Tips, left)	1
2 tsp	capers, drained, rinsed and minced	10 mL

1. In a bowl, using a fork, mash anchovies with their oil and lemon juice. Mash in butter, garlic and capers until mixture is fluffy.

2. Serve immediately or cover and refrigerate for up to 1 week.

Variations

Substitute an equal quantity of shrimp or any kind of roe for the anchovies. If using roe, add it gently at the end, once the other ingredients are well combined.

Elegant Smoked Bivalve Butter

1	can (3 oz/85 g) smoked oysters or mussels, with oil	1
1 tsp	freshly squeezed lemon juice	5 mL
¼ tsp	salt	1 mL
Pinch	cayenne pepper	Pinch
¼ cup	unsalted butter, at room temperature	60 mL
1 tsp	finely chopped parsley leaves	5 mL

1. In a bowl, using a fork, blend oysters with oil, lemon juice, salt and cayenne. Mash in butter and parsley until fluffy.

2. Serve immediately or cover and refrigerate for up to 3 days.

Variation

Substitute regular canned oysters or mussels and, if desired, add a few drops of liquid smoke.

Bagna Cauda

Anchovies, garlic and oil are transformed into something marvelous in Piedmont, Italy, the home of bagna cauda. This mouthwatering partner for crusty bread and steamed or raw vegetables is a cross between a fondue and a dip. The name translates as "hot bath." Bagna cauda is decadently drippy, so it's easy to see why personal dipping plates have replaced the communal pots of yesteryear. Compatible veggies include baby squash and zucchini, artichoke hearts, cauliflower florets, grape tomatoes and green beans.

Makes about ³⁄₄ cup (175 mL)

- Fast
- Guest-worthy

Tips

It is important to mince the garlic as finely as possible. Better still, push it through a press.

Using unsalted butter is particularly important in recipes featuring anchovies, which are salty enough on their own.

Be aware that the amount of salt in salted butter varies by brand, and it contains more moisture, which may affect some recipes. Salt also masks rancidity, which means you can be more confident that you're using a fresh product when your butter isn't salted.

1	can (2 oz/50 g) anchovies in extra virgin olive oil, drained (oil reserved)	1
½ cup	extra virgin olive oil (approx.)	125 mL
4	large cloves garlic, minced	4
3 tbsp	unsalted butter (see Tips, left)	45 mL
	Freshly ground black pepper	

1. Soak anchovies for 10 minutes in a small bowl of cold water. Drain and pat dry, then chop coarsely. Transfer to a very small skillet or saucepan.

2. Pour reserved oil from the anchovies into a measuring cup and add enough extra virgin olive oil to equal ½ cup (125 mL). Add to anchovies and bring to a simmer over medium heat. Reduce heat to low and simmer for 5 minutes, until anchovies start to dissolve. Using a small, heatproof spatula, mash anchovies against the bottom of the pan. Stir in garlic. Cook for 1 minute, until garlic softens.

3. Remove from heat. Stir in butter until melted and blended. Season to taste with pepper. Serve warm, in individual dipping bowls.

Variation

Try using Bagna Cauda instead of oil or butter when making scrambled eggs. Yum!

Salsa Verde

Salsas verdes ("green sauces") are popular around the world, with different ingredients depending upon the location. This version is classic Italian. It is handy to have around — enjoy it as a tangy dip or spread or drizzle it over bruschetta. It is also delicious spooned over fish, vegetables, pasta or potatoes.

Makes about 1 cup (250 mL)

- Fast
- Guest-worthy

Tip

Capers come bottled in brine or dry-salted. The latter are less common but superior in pungency and firmness. You can use either type in this recipe.

● **Food processor**

2	cloves garlic	2
2 cups	parsley leaves (1 oz/30 g)	500 mL
½ cup	mint leaves (¼ oz/7 g)	125 mL
2	green onions (white and green parts) trimmed and cut into 1-inch (2.5 cm) segments	2
5	anchovy fillets	5
1 tbsp	capers, rinsed, drained and patted dry	15 mL
¼ tsp	salt (approx.)	1 mL
¼ tsp	freshly ground black pepper	1 mL
2 tbsp	white wine vinegar	30 mL
½ cup	extra virgin olive oil	125 mL

1. In food processor fitted with the metal blade, with the motor running, add garlic through the feed tube to chop. Scrape down the sides of the work bowl. Add parsley, mint, green onions, anchovies, capers, salt and pepper. Drizzle vinegar overtop. Process until mixture is minced, stopping the motor once and scraping down the sides of the bowl.

2. With the motor running, drizzle oil through the feed tube in a slow stream, processing until mixture is smooth but still showing tiny flecks of parsley. Add salt to taste, if necessary.

3. Serve immediately or cover and refrigerate for up to 1 week.

Variations

Add other fresh herbs, such as basil or thyme, instead of some or all of the mint.

Traditional optional additions include a couple of spoonfuls of canned tuna in olive oil or a bit of stale torn bread presoaked in the vinegar.

Stir salsa verde into mayonnaise, cream cheese or sour cream to make tangy green dips and spreads.

Taramosalata

This Greek dip is pretty in pink. It is made with tarama, which is salted and cured carp caviar. Tarama comes densely packed in jars, processed with salt, oil and (usually but not always) food coloring. Garnish this dip with cucumber and tomato and serve it with pitas.

Makes about 4 cups (1 L) 16 appetizer servings

- Fast
- Guest-worthy

Tips

Tarama (carp roe) is available in stores specializing in Greek provisions, and in some supermarkets. The color can vary from beige to pink, depending on the roe and the additives.

Greek grannies worked a mortar and pestle to make this dip creamy, but nowadays a food processor does the job. Avoid using the blender, because the roe mixture is dense and sticky at first.

One standard jar of tarama makes a party-sized bowl, but you can easily halve this recipe.

Grate the onion using the large holes on a box grater.

● **Food processor**

½	large loaf stale smooth white bread, crusts removed (about 8 oz/250 g)	½
1	jar (8 oz/250 g) tarama (about 1 cup/ 250 mL; see Tips, left)	1
¼ cup	grated red onion (see Tips, left)	60 mL
2 to 3 tbsp	freshly squeezed lemon juice	30 to 45 mL
¾ cup	extra virgin olive oil	175 mL
	Freshly ground white pepper	

1. Soak bread in a large bowl of cold water for 5 minutes. Using your hands, pull off chunks, squeeze out water and transfer bread to a sieve.

2. In food processor fitted with the metal blade, pulse tarama just until loosened. Scrape down the sides of the bowl. Add onion and 2 tbsp (30 mL) lemon juice. Process until tarama is broken down and color has lightened. Add bread gradually by the handful, processing after each addition until mixture is smooth. With the motor running, slowly pour oil through the feed tube and process until mixture is fluffy and looks like pink mayonnaise. Season to taste with pepper. Taste and, if a tangier dip is desired, add remaining lemon juice, then pulse once or twice to blend.

3. Cover and refrigerate for at least 2 hours or for up to 2 days.

Bread for Taramosalata

Use a white loaf such as the kind sold in Greek bakeries, with a fairly fine crumb but not spongy like sandwich bread. You may have to adjust the amount of oil, depending on the type of bread.

When making this recipe, it's best to measure the bread by weight. If you don't have a scale, you could double-check the amount by placing the soaked, squeezed bread into a large measuring cup (there should be about 3½ cups/875 mL). Then return the bread to the sieve until you are ready to use it.

Salmon and Green Onion Yogurt Dip

This tangy dip is a distant cousin of Greek tzatziki. It is great with toasted pita wedges or raw vegetables, and relatively easy on the waistline.

Makes about 1²/₃ cups (400 mL) 6 to 8 appetizer servings

- Fast
- Kid-friendly
- Healthy

Tips

Boneless, skinless salmon comes in smaller cans. You can substitute a 7½-oz (213 g) can of regular salmon and remove the skin and bones yourself.

Greek yogurt is perfect for dips because it is very thick. To keep the calories under control, use 2% Greek yogurt. As a substitute, spoon 1½ cups (375 mL) regular yogurt into a strainer lined with cheesecloth, place over a bowl, cover and refrigerate for about 2 hours, until drained and thick.

¼ cup	extra virgin olive oil	60 mL
6	green onions (white and green parts) thinly sliced	6
2	cloves garlic, minced	2
1	can (6 oz/170 g) boneless, skinless salmon, drained and broken into chunks	1
1 cup	Greek yogurt (see Tips, left)	250 mL
½ tsp	salt (approx.)	2 mL
	Freshly ground white pepper	
¼ tsp	ground cumin	1 mL

1. In a small skillet or saucepan, heat oil over medium heat until shimmery. Stir in onions and garlic. Reduce heat to medium-low and cook, stirring, for 3 minutes, until softened. Scrape mixture into a bowl and set aside to cool.

2. Gently squeeze salmon to remove excess moisture. Add to cooled onion mixture. Stir in yogurt, salt, pepper to taste, and cumin. Taste and add more salt if necessary.

3. Serve immediately or cover and refrigerate overnight.

> **Variations**
>
> Substitute an equal quantity of tuna, mackerel, cod, shrimp or lobster for the salmon. For a smoky dip, use drained smoked oysters, mussels or kippers. You will need two cans of oysters or mussels or one or two cans of kippers, according to taste.

Smoky Tuna Dip

Smoky accents give this dip added appeal. Enjoy it slathered on toasted pita wedges or sturdy crackers.

Tips

Use soft cream cheese (the kind scooped into tubs in supermarket delis) rather than the denser packaged blocks. You can cut calories by buying lower-fat cream cheese.

Liquid smoke is basically smoky water, usually hickory flavored. Add it in small increments, because too much will make your dip taste acrid. Liquid smoke is easy to find in the condiment section of most supermarkets. You can pick up bottled tomato-based chili sauce in the same place, near the ketchup. It is spiced but not spicy hot.

8 oz	soft cream cheese (1 cup/250 mL; see Tips, left)	250 g
½ cup	sour cream	125 mL
2 tbsp	bottled tomato-based chili sauce	30 mL
1 tbsp	freshly squeezed lime juice	15 mL
1	can (6 oz/170 g) tuna in water, drained and broken into flakes	1
¼ cup	finely chopped red onion	60 mL
¼ cup	finely chopped parsley leaves	60 mL
1	clove garlic, minced	1
¼ tsp	salt (approx.)	1 mL
	Freshly ground black pepper	
	Liquid smoke (see Tips, left)	

1. In a bowl, using a fork, mash together cream cheese, sour cream, chili sauce and lime juice until smooth and blended. Add tuna, onion, parsley, garlic, salt and pepper to taste. Add liquid smoke and more salt to taste, if necessary.

Variations

Substitute an equal quantity of salmon, mackerel, cod, kippers, shrimp, lobster, oysters or mussels for the tuna.

Omit the liquid smoke and mash in smoked oysters or mussels instead of the tuna. Alternatively, if you can find canned smoked tuna or salmon (sold in some specialty food shops), use it instead.

Clam, Bacon and Chive Dip

Clams and bacon go so well together. The clam juice punches up the flavor of this dip, which is delicious with toasted pitas or crackers.

Makes about 2 cups (500 mL) 8 appetizer servings

- Fast
- Guest-worthy

Tips

You can use lower-fat cream cheese and sour cream.

For convenience, make this dip up to 1 day ahead. Complete Steps 1 and 2 and cover and refrigerate the bacon and clam mixtures separately. When ready to serve, complete Step 3.

4	slices bacon, coarsely chopped	4
8 oz	soft cream cheese (1 cup/250 mL)	250 g
1 tbsp	bottled clam juice	15 mL
1 to 2 tsp	freshly squeezed lime juice	5 to 10 mL
1 tsp	Worcestershire sauce	5 mL
1	can (5 oz/142 g) baby clams, rinsed, drained and chopped	1
¼ cup	chopped chives	60 mL
2 tbsp	finely chopped red bell pepper	30 mL
2 to 4 tbsp	sour cream	30 to 60 mL
	Salt and freshly ground white pepper	

1. In a skillet, over medium heat, cook bacon, stirring often, for 5 minutes, until browned and crisp. Using a slotted spoon, transfer to a plate lined with paper towels to drain.

2. In a bowl, using a fork, mix cream cheese, clam juice, 1 tsp (5 mL) lime juice and Worcestershire sauce until blended. Stir in clams, chives and red pepper and just enough sour cream to reach dipping consistency. Season to taste with salt and pepper.

3. Crumble in the bacon and stir. Add remaining lime juice, if desired, to adjust the tartness. Taste and adjust salt, if necessary. Serve immediately.

> **Variations**
> Substitute an equal quantity of salmon, shrimp, crab or lobster for the clams.

Mussel Salad with Capers

Here's another one of those "salads" that isn't actually a salad. It's more of a spread — and it is darned tasty. Serve it with sturdy crackers or toast points or on a bed of greens, accompanied by artisan bread.

Makes about 1 cup (250 mL) 4 appetizer servings

- Fast
- Guest-worthy

Variations
Substitute an equal quantity of regular oysters, or smoked oysters or smoked mussels, for the regular mussels.

¼ cup	mayonnaise	60 mL
1 tbsp	freshly squeezed lemon juice	15 mL
¼ tsp	salt (approx.)	1 mL
⅛ tsp	freshly ground black pepper	0.5 mL
1 tbsp	finely chopped red onion	15 mL
1	small clove garlic, minced	1
1 tbsp	capers, rinsed, drained and chopped	15 mL
1 tbsp	chopped fresh dill fronds (approx.)	15 mL
1	can (7 oz/190 g) mussels, drained and coarsely chopped	1

1. In a small measuring cup, stir together mayonnaise, lemon juice, salt, pepper, onion, garlic, capers and 1 tbsp (15 mL) dill. Gently stir in mussels or, if you prefer, mash them in using a fork. Taste and adjust seasoning.

2. Sprinkle with additional dill and serve immediately.

Catalan Clams and Ham

Get in on the small-plates craze. Canned clams are the shortcut to enjoying this savory Spanish tapas dish. Mop up the sauce with crusty bread.

Makes 2 to 4 appetizer servings

- Fast
- Guest-worthy

Tip
You won't need salt because the ham and clams are already salty.

Variations
If you don't have Serrano ham, substitute prosciutto. Both are cured meats and sliced ultra-thin.

Substitute an equal quantity of lobster for the clams.

¼ cup	extra virgin olive oil	60 mL
2	large cloves garlic, minced	2
1	can (5 oz/142 g) surf or meaty clams, rinsed, drained and coarsely chopped	1
2 oz	sliced Serrano ham, cut in thin strips	60 g
½ cup	dry white wine	125 mL
2 tbsp	chopped cilantro leaves	30 mL
⅛ tsp	freshly ground black pepper	0.5 mL
¼ tsp	smoked sweet paprika	1 mL

1. In a skillet, heat oil over medium-high heat until shimmery. Remove from heat and stir in garlic for 30 seconds. Return to element and add clams and ham. Cook, stirring often, for 1 minute. Add wine, cilantro and freshly ground pepper. Cook, stirring often, for 2 to 3 minutes, until reduced and slightly thickened.

2. Just before serving, sprinkle paprika overtop.

Party Antipasto

I am dating myself when I say that back in the early eighties, antipasto meant one thing: tuna, veggies, olives and pickled things in a sweet-and-sour tomato sauce, scooped onto sturdy crackers. This was the trendy party food for young professionals. Antipasto still appeals, but I am not enamored of the ketchup base that is commonly used. Instead, my recipe relies on a combination of tomato paste, garden cocktail and tomato-based chili sauce.

Makes 4½ cups (1.125 L) 18 appetizer servings

• Guest-worthy

Tips

I prefer to use a tender inner stalk of celery for this. Inner stalks are called the heart.

Pickled pearl onions — the kind used in cocktails — are sold in supermarkets. You can buy sour or sweet versions, but I prefer the sour ones for this recipe.

2	cans (each 3 oz/85 g) tuna in olive oil	2
1 to 2 tbsp	extra virgin olive oil	15 to 30 mL
½ cup	tiny cauliflower florets (about 2 oz/60 g)	125 mL
1	small carrot (about 2 oz/60 g), cut into matchsticks	1
2	cloves garlic, minced	2
1	stalk celery heart, cut into matchsticks (see Tips, left)	1
½ cup	sliced (½ inch/1 cm) green beans (about 2 oz/60 g)	125 mL
¼ cup	coarsely chopped green bell pepper	60 mL
2 tbsp	tomato paste	30 mL
1½ to 2 cups	low-sodium bottled garden cocktail juice	375 to 500 mL
½ cup	bottled tomato-based chili sauce	125 mL
3 tbsp	white wine vinegar (approx.), divided	45 mL
2 tbsp	granulated sugar	30 mL
12	sour pickled pearl onions, coarsely chopped (about ⅓ cup/75 mL)	12
12	small black olives, pitted and coarsely chopped (about ¼ cup/60 mL)	12
6	large pimiento-stuffed green olives, coarsely chopped (about ¼ cup/60 mL)	6
2	canned or thawed frozen artichoke hearts, drained and coarsely chopped	2
4	anchovy fillets, chopped	4
½ cup	canned sliced mushrooms, rinsed and drained	125 mL
1 tbsp	capers, rinsed and drained	15 mL
	Salt and freshly ground black pepper	
	Hot pepper sauce	

1. Drain oil from the tuna into a small measuring cup. Set tuna aside. Add enough extra virgin oil to measuring cup to equal ¼ cup (60 mL). Transfer to a large saucepan and heat over medium heat until shimmery.

2. Add cauliflower and carrot. Cook, stirring often, for about 5 minutes, until vegetables are turning golden. Stir in garlic, celery, green beans and bell pepper and cook for 1 minute. Stir in tomato paste. Add $1\frac{1}{2}$ cups (375 mL) garden cocktail, chili sauce, 2 tbsp (30 mL) vinegar and sugar. Stir in pickled onions, two types of olives, artichokes, anchovies, mushrooms and capers. Bring to a simmer, reduce heat to low and simmer for 30 minutes.

3. Add reserved tuna. The mixture should be thick but easy to stir, to prevent scorching. If necessary, stir in enough of the remaining garden cocktail to loosen the mixture. Simmer for 15 minutes, until mixture is thick and vegetables are very tender. Season to taste with salt, pepper and hot pepper sauce. Remove from heat and set aside to cool to room temperature.

4. When mixture is cool, transfer to an airtight container and refrigerate overnight or for up to 1 week before serving. Taste and add remaining 1 tbsp (15 mL) vinegar and more salt and/or hot sauce, if desired (antipasto should be tangy and spicy).

The Grand Aïoli

When garlic season comes around in Provence, townsfolk sit down en masse for le grand aïoli. This feast of poached fish (usually cod), a cornucopia of cold vegetables and garlicky aïoli dip is also known as a Provençal platter. It's a fabulous appetizer or party platter, but it also makes a great meal. Use canned seafood and bottled mayonnaise as shortcuts. Just don't tell your happy guests that you slaved over a can opener and a pan of boiling water!

Makes 6 to 8 servings

- Kid-friendly
- Healthy
- Guest-worthy

Tips

Use drained canned artichokes or frozen artichokes, thawed.

Use canned chickpeas or cook your own.

You can make the aïoli a day ahead. Keep it covered and refrigerated.

Platter

8 oz	mini carrots	250 g
8 oz	cauliflower florets	250 g
4 oz	sugar snap peas, trimmed	125 g
8 oz	multicolored mini or fingerling potatoes, scrubbed	250 g
3	small beets, trimmed and scrubbed	3
4	artichoke hearts, quartered (see Tips, left)	4
1 cup	cooked chickpeas, rinsed and drained (see Tips, left)	250 mL
¾ cup	grape tomatoes	175 mL
½	large orange bell pepper, cut in strips	½
2	cans (each 4 oz/120 g) cod in olive oil (see Variations, page 57)	2
4	large eggs, hard-cooked and halved (see Tips, page 57)	4

Garnish

¼ cup	finely chopped parsley leaves	60 mL
2 tbsp	capers, rinsed, drained and chopped	30 mL

Aïoli

1 cup	mayonnaise	250 mL
4 cloves	garlic, minced	4
½ tsp	Dijon mustard	2 mL
	Salt and freshly ground black pepper	

1. *Platter:* In a saucepan over high heat, bring salted water to a boil. Lower the heat to medium, add carrots and cook for 5 minutes, until tender-crisp. Using a mesh scoop, transfer to a sieve and rinse under cold running water to stop the cooking. Drain and set aside.

2. Repeat the above sequence with cauliflower (3 to 4 minutes), peas (2 minutes), potatoes (15 minutes) and beets (30 minutes). After beets are cooked and cool enough to handle, slip off the skins and cut into quarters.

Tip

You don't need to boil eggs to cook them. Instead, place the eggs in a small pan and add enough water to cover them by $\frac{1}{2}$ inch (1 cm). Bring the water to a boil over high heat. Immediately cover the pan, turn off the element and let the eggs stand for 10 minutes. For the tidiest eggs with no pockmarks in the whites and no ugly dark rings around the yolk, as soon as they have finished cooking, run cold water over the eggs until they are cool enough to handle. Immediately peel the eggs, starting at the wide end where the air pocket is. If the shells start to stick, peel them under cold, running water. Use a wet knife to cut each egg in half.

3. Pat dry freshly cooked vegetables and arrange on a large serving platter with artichoke hearts, chickpeas, tomatoes, bell pepper and cod, with its oil. Position eggs among the vegetables.

4. *Garnish:* In a small bowl, stir together parsley and capers. Scatter evenly over platter.

5. *Aïoli:* In a medium measuring cup, stir together mayonnaise, garlic and mustard. Season to taste with salt and pepper. Transfer to a small serving bowl and place on or alongside the platter. Serve immediately.

Variations

There's no need to follow this recipe slavishly — you can use your favorite vegetables and fish. Canned cod is difficult to find, but don't worry, this dish is also excellent with tuna in olive oil. Other seafood that will work: salmon, mackerel, kippers, sardines, sprats, shrimp, crab, lobster, oysters, mussels or octopus. As for vegetables, asparagus and whole green onions are other tasty choices.

Brandade

Comfort food is in the eye of the beholder. Take this creamy potato and salt cod mash-up, for instance. For diners of all ages, it makes a surprisingly satisfying first course, side dish or mini meal. Pair it with steamed baby veggies, leafy greens or pickled beans. Brandade, which originated in the fish-loving nations of France and Spain, adapts well to canned seafood of all sorts.

Makes about 4 cups (1 L) 8 appetizer servings

- Fast
- Kid-friendly

Tips

The potatoes for brandade are usually puréed or beaten, but I hand-mash them because I prefer the rougher texture.

Evaporating the excess moisture in a dry pan makes for fluffier mashed potatoes.

Variations

Substitute an equal quantity of tuna, salmon, mackerel, kippers, shrimp, lobster, clams or octopus for the cod.

If you're substituting fish packed in brine or a nondescript oil, drain the can and add an extra 1 tbsp (15 mL) olive oil along with the cream mixture.

3	russet potatoes (about 2 lb/1 kg), peeled and quartered	3
¼ cup	heavy or whipping (35%) cream	60 mL
2	cloves garlic, minced	2
1	sprig fresh thyme	1
1	bay leaf	1
1	clove	1
¼ tsp	salt (approx.)	1 mL
⅛ tsp	freshly ground white pepper	0.5 mL
1	can (4 oz/120 g) cod in olive oil	1
2 tbsp	extra virgin olive oil, divided	30 mL
2 tbsp	chopped parsley leaves	30 mL

1. In a pot of salted water over high heat, bring potatoes to a boil. Reduce heat to medium and simmer for 15 to 20 minutes, until very tender.

2. Meanwhile, in a very small saucepan, bring cream, garlic, thyme, bay leaf, clove, salt and pepper to a simmer over medium heat. Reduce heat to low, cover and simmer for about 5 minutes, until garlic is tender. Remove from heat, cover and set aside. When ready to use, discard thyme sprig, bay leaf and clove.

3. When potatoes are cooked, drain and return to saucepan over low heat for 1 minute, shaking the pot a couple of times, to evaporate excess moisture (see Tips, left). Remove from heat. Add cream mixture and mash. Add cod and its oil, plus 1 tbsp (15 mL) extra virgin olive oil. Mix well. Adjust salt to taste.

4. Transfer to a serving bowl. Drizzle remaining 1 tbsp (15 mL) olive oil overtop and sprinkle with parsley. Serve immediately.

Tuna Tapenade

Tapenade is a versatile olive and anchovy paste from Provence. Adding tuna transforms it from a condiment to a spread. Whet your appetite by slathering it on crackers or crostini, liven up hard-cooked eggs by serving tapenade alongside, or dollop it on cheese pizza just before serving.

Makes about 1½ cups (375 mL) 6 appetizer servings

- Fast
- Healthy
- Guest-worthy

Tip

Niçoise olives are traditionally used in tapenade, but other black olives work well too.

- **Food processor**

2	cloves garlic	2
1 cup	pitted black olives (see Tips, left)	250 mL
1 cup	basil leaves (¼ oz/7 g)	250 mL
3	anchovy fillets	3
1 tbsp	capers, rinsed and drained	15 mL
2 tbsp	extra virgin olive oil	30 mL
2	cans (each 3 oz/85 g) tuna in olive oil, with oil	2
1 tsp	freshly squeezed lemon juice, optional Freshly ground black pepper	5 mL

1. In food processor fitted with the metal blade, with motor running, drop garlic through the feed tube to chop. Add olives, basil, anchovies and capers and process until puréed. Scrape down the sides of the bowl. With the motor running, drizzle olive oil through the feed tube and process until incorporated.

2. Transfer to a serving bowl. Add tuna with its oil and, using a fork, break into flakes and mix in well. Add lemon juice, if using, and season to taste with pepper.

Variations

Substitute an equal quantity of salmon, mackerel, sardines or sprats for the tuna.

Mix tapenade with hot pasta and serve as a main. Added to room-temperature pasta, it makes a salad.

To create a dip, stir tapenade to taste into 1 cup (250 mL) soft cream cheese.

Smooth out tapenade with mayonnaise, spoon it over a lettuce leaf and serve it with crusty bread alongside.

Caponata

Caponata is a rustic Sicilian relish. Add it to your next antipasto platter; serve it as a side dish, in sandwiches or tossed with pasta; or simply dollop it on baguette slices. It's good at any temperature.

Makes about 3½ cups (875 mL) 14 appetizer servings

- Healthy
- Guest-worthy

Tips

Use a serrated peeler to quickly strip the skin from the tomatoes.

If using tuna, you may substitute its oil for some of the extra virgin in this recipe.

Variations

Add raisins and/or pine nuts along with the vinegar.

Instead of tuna, stir in other fish such as mackerel. In Sicily, shrimp, octopus or tuna roe (bottarga) is sometimes used in this dish.

1	small Italian eggplant (about 1 lb/500 g), peeled and cut in ½-inch (1 cm) dice	1
1 tsp	salt (approx.)	5 mL
6 tbsp	extra virgin olive oil, divided	90 mL
1	small onion, diced	1
1	stalk celery, cut in ½-inch (1 cm) dice	1
1	clove garlic, minced	1
6	plum tomatoes (about 1½ lb/750 g), peeled, seeded and chopped	6
10	large green olives (about ½ cup/125 mL), pitted and coarsely chopped	10
2	anchovy fillets, chopped	2
2 tbsp	capers, rinsed and drained	30 mL
½ tsp	hot pepper flakes	2 mL
⅛ tsp	freshly ground black pepper	0.5 mL
1	can (3 oz/85 g) tuna in olive oil, drained, optional	1
½ cup	coarsely chopped parsley leaves	125 mL
2 tbsp	packed brown sugar	30 mL
1 tbsp	red wine vinegar	15 mL

1. In a large fine-mesh sieve, toss eggplant with salt. Set aside for 1 hour, shaking the sieve occasionally.

2. Meanwhile, in a wide, deep saucepan, heat ¼ cup (60 mL) olive oil. Add onion and celery and cook, stirring often, for about 5 minutes, until softened and golden. Stir in garlic for 10 seconds. Add tomatoes, olives, anchovies, capers, hot pepper flakes and black pepper. Reduce heat to low and simmer for 15 minutes, until mixture is sauce-like.

3. Meanwhile, in a separate large skillet, heat remaining 2 tbsp (30 mL) oil over medium-high heat. Add eggplant, in batches, if necessary, and sauté until it softens and starts to brown, tossing with a spatula and scraping the bottom of the pan.

4. Add eggplant to tomato mixture along with tuna, if using, parsley, brown sugar and vinegar. Return to a simmer over medium heat. Reduce heat to low, cover and simmer for 15 minutes, until eggplant is soft. Remove from heat and set aside to cool. Add salt to taste, if necessary.

Salmon Cheese Balls

You don't have to wait for a party to make cheese balls. These are great with crackers and wine, but they also make a tasty sandwich spread.

Makes 2 to 4 cheese balls 12 appetizer servings

- Brown-bag
- Guest-worthy

Tips

Sockeye salmon gives cheese balls a richer color and flavor than pink salmon.

Toast walnuts in a dry skillet over medium heat, shaking the pan often, for about 3 minutes, until fragrant and starting to brown. Transfer to a bowl to cool.

Variations

Add a dash of liquid smoke, or substitute an equal quantity of smoked oysters or mussels for the salmon. You can also substitute tuna, sardines, sprats, roe or shrimp.

Substitute an equal quantity of cilantro for the parsley.

Substitute an equal quantity of pecans for the walnuts.

Substitute ¼ cup (60 mL) well-drained prepared horseradish for the port.

Substitute an equal quantity of chopped green bell pepper for the olives.

2	packages (each 8 oz/250 g) block cream cheese, softened	2
¼ cup	port or Marsala wine	60 mL
1 tbsp	freshly squeezed lemon juice	15 mL
1	can (7½ oz/213 g) sockeye salmon, drained, deboned and broken into chunks (see Tips, left)	1
4 oz	medium Cheddar cheese, shredded (1 cup/250 mL)	125 g
½ cup	finely chopped pitted green olives (10 to 12 large)	125 mL
¼ cup	finely chopped red onion	60 mL
	Salt	
½ cup	walnut pieces, toasted and coarsely chopped (see Tips, left)	125 mL
½ cup	finely chopped parsley leaves	125 mL

1. In a large bowl, mash together cream cheese, port and lemon juice with a fork. Lightly squeeze salmon to remove excess moisture and add it to the bowl. Add Cheddar, olives and onion and mix well. Season to taste with salt. Mix in walnuts.

2. Place 2 or 4 sheets of plastic wrap on a work surface. Divide mixture into 2 or 4 portions. With moistened hands, shape each portion into a ball and wrap tightly in plastic. Refrigerate for at least 2 hours or preferably overnight to firm up and allow flavors to blend.

3. Before serving, place parsley on a large, flat plate. Pat cheese balls to round off their shape. Unwrap and, one at a time, roll in parsley to coat, lightly brushing off the excess. Serve immediately.

Salmon Pâté

Originally pâtés were en croûte *(wrapped in pastry), terrines were prepared in crockery or metal pans, and mousses were airy, with the help of whipped cream or egg whites. Nowadays these terms are used interchangeably.*

Makes about 3 cups (750 mL) 12 appetizer servings

- Guest-worthy

Tips

Seeing a pâté in a fish-shaped mold brings back memories. If you have one, by all means use it. Or make this in any 3- to 4-cup (750 mL to 1 L) pan or mold. If using a fish-shaped mold, grease it well and omit the parchment or waxed paper.

This pâté has a mild flavor. Stick to sockeye, which tastes more robust than pink salmon.

For proper texture, use full-fat (14%) sour cream in this recipe.

Variation

Herbes de Provence is a French dried herb blend that commonly includes dried basil, fennel, lavender, marjoram, rosemary, sage, savory and thyme. If you don't have some, substitute any of the individual herbs or a combination to taste.

- **Food processor**
- **3- to 4-cup (750 mL to 1 L) loaf pan, lightly oiled, bottom lined with lightly oiled waxed paper or parchment**

12	tiny dill sprigs	12
2 tbsp	cold water	30 mL
1	envelope unflavored gelatin powder (about 2½ tsp/12 mL)	1
¼ cup	boiling water	60 mL
1	can (7½ oz/213 g) sockeye salmon, drained, deboned and patted dry	1
½ cup	sour cream (see Tips, left)	125 mL
2 tbsp	freshly squeezed lemon juice	30 mL
1	green onion (white and light green parts), sliced	1
5	large green olives, pitted and chopped	5
¼ tsp	herbes de Provence	1 mL
½ cup	heavy or whipping (35%) cream	125 mL
	Salt and freshly ground black pepper	
1	jar (2 oz/50 g) red lumpfish caviar (roe)	1

1. Press dill sprigs in a decorative pattern onto the oiled paper in prepared pan.

2. Place cold water in a small bowl and sprinkle gelatin evenly overtop. Set aside for 1 minute. Add boiling water and stir until dissolved.

3. In a food processor fitted with the metal blade, process salmon, sour cream and lemon juice until puréed. Add green onion, olives and herbes de Provence and pulse to blend.

4. In a deep bowl, using an electric mixer, beat cream to soft peaks. Beat in the gelatin mixture. Fold in the salmon mixture and season to taste with salt and pepper.

5. Transfer to prepared pan, cover and refrigerate overnight or for up to 2 days.

6. To release the pâté, briefly dip the pan in a large container of hot water and run a thin knife around the edges. Place a serving plate over the pan and invert. Carefully peel off the paper. Using a small spatula, press the caviar decoratively around the bottom edges.

Avocado and Shrimp in New-School Marie Rose Sauce

Also known as ketchyo, maychup and ketchanaise, old-school Marie Rose sauce is a stodgy blend of mayonnaise, ketchup and Worcestershire sauce. I've lightened and brightened mine with crème fraîche. Slightly sweet and slightly sour, it complements both seafood and avocado. As the story goes, the original sauce was invented in 1981 by a Royal Navy chef catering to divers at the wreck of the Mary Rose *in Portsmouth Harbour, U.K. — he had prawns but no sauce for them. The misspelling began to appear in the 1990s.*

Makes 4 servings

• Fast

Tips

The sauce can be made ahead and refrigerated for up to 1 week.

Crème fraîche is sold in many supermarkets. If you can't find it, substitute an equal quantity of full-fat sour cream.

¼ cup	mayonnaise	60 mL
2 tbsp	crème fraîche (see Tips, left)	30 mL
1 tbsp	ketchup	15 mL
1 tsp	Worcestershire sauce	5 mL
1 tsp	freshly squeezed lime juice	5 mL
½ tsp	brandy or whisky	2 mL
1 tbsp	grated red onion, optional	15 mL
	Salt and freshly ground black pepper	
2	ripe avocados	2
1	can (4 oz/106 g) small shrimp, rinsed and drained	1
4	sprigs dill	4

1. In a measuring cup, stir together mayonnaise, crème fraîche, ketchup, Worcestershire sauce, lime juice and brandy. Stir in onion, if using. Season to taste with salt and pepper.

2. Just before serving, halve and pit the avocados and place on serving plates. Stir shrimp into the sauce and spoon into the avocado cavities, dividing equally. Garnish with dill.

Variations
Substitute an equal quantity of crab or lobster for the shrimp.

Devilish Angels on Horseback

The world calls these Angels on Horseback, but when I serve them every New Year's Eve I stubbornly call them Devils on Horseback, because they are spicy and dark. (Officially, devils are made with dried fruit such as dates or prunes.) I used to stick to a ratio of two oysters to one slice of bacon, but it's now three to one, thanks to changing tastes.

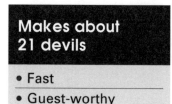

Makes about 21 devils

- Fast
- Guest-worthy

Tip

Buy thinly sliced bacon. It will cook more evenly and thoroughly.

- Preheat broiler, placing oven rack one level down from top position
- Rimmed baking sheet, lined with parchment or foil and topped with a wire rack

7	slices bacon (approx.)	7
1	can (3 oz/85 g) smoked oysters (about 21)	1
2	large lemon wedges	2
	Cayenne pepper	

1. Cut bacon slices crosswise into thirds. Using the blunt edge of a dinner knife, rub a bacon piece to stretch it thinly without breaking. Place 1 smoked oyster on the more ragged end. Squeeze lemon juice and sprinkle cayenne over the oyster. Roll up and secure with a toothpick speared sideways through the oyster. Place on rack in prepared pan. Repeat with remaining ingredients.

2. Place under preheated broiler and broil for 4 to 5 minutes, until bacon is golden brown. Turn with tongs and broil for 3 to 4 minutes, until bacon is nicely browned. Serve warm or at room temperature.

> ### Variation
> Substitute smoked mussels for the oysters. Mussels are smaller, so double up, using two per bacon piece.

Seafood Summer Rolls

Vietnamese summer rolls are so light compared to their fried cousins, spring rolls. Wrapped in thin rice paper, these uncooked rolls with greens are also known as salad rolls, fresh rolls or crystal rolls.

Makes 8 rolls

- Healthy

Tips

Dipping sauce: In a small bowl, stir together ¼ cup (60 mL) each freshly squeezed lime juice, fish sauce, water and granulated sugar, 1 tbsp (15 mL) shredded carrot and 1 thinly sliced Thai bird's-eye chile, if desired. Cover and refrigerate for at least 1 hour or overnight to develop flavors. (Makes about ⅔ cup/150 mL)

Thin, dry rice paper is tricky to work with. Soak it just until it is pliable but not ready to disintegrate. Run your fingers over the wrapper to help it soak evenly. You should be able to pick it up and place it on the work surface without it breaking. If the water cools too much, refill the container. You will ruin a few wrappers before you get the hang of it, but they are not expensive.

Instead of chopping the basil, you can shred it by piling the leaves on top of each other, rolling them up together like a cigar and then slicing crosswise.

Variations

Substitute an equal quantity of tuna, mackerel, shrimp, crab or lobster for the salmon.

- **Lightly greased baking sheet**

1 cup	peeled, julienned English cucumber (about ½)	250 mL
1 cup	watercress leaves	250 mL
½ cup	cilantro leaves	125 mL
½ cup	coarsely chopped or torn basil leaves (see Tips, left)	125 mL
½ cup	thinly sliced green onions (4 to 6; white and light green parts)	125 mL
¼ cup	shredded carrot	60 mL
8	rice paper wrappers, 8½ inches (22 cm) in diameter (see Tips, left)	8
	Salt and freshly ground black pepper	
2	cans (each 6 oz/170 g) boneless, skinless salmon, drained and broken into flakes	2
	Dipping sauce (see Tips, left)	

1. Place cucumber in a fine-mesh sieve and set aside to drain for at least 10 minutes. Pat dry just before using.

2. In a small bowl, toss together watercress, cilantro and basil. In another small bowl, stir together onions and carrot.

3. Fill a rimmed baking sheet or shallow container with warm water. Working with one wrapper at a time, submerge wrapper in water for 20 to 30 seconds, until softened all over. Lay flat on your work surface.

4. Place about 1½ tbsp (22 mL) onion mixture just below the centre of the wrapper. Top with about 1 tbsp (15 mL) cucumber. Season to taste with salt and pepper. Add about 2 tbsp (30 mL) salmon, spreading evenly over cucumber. Top with about ¼ cup (60 mL) watercress mixture. Fold edge of wrapper closest to you over filling. Fold sides toward the middle, then roll up tightly. Set, seam side down, on prepared baking sheet. Repeat with remaining wrappers and filling.

5. Serve immediately or place rolls under a damp cloth to keep moist (the wrappers tend to dry out quickly). To serve, cut each roll in half on the diagonal and serve dipping sauce alongside.

Chinese Takeout Egg Rolls

These are real old-school treats filled with cabbage, carrot and bean sprouts. Plum sauce is a must for dipping. In Chinese characters, egg rolls are actually "egg scrolls" — hence the rolling method you see here.

Makes 14 egg rolls

- Kid-friendly

Tips

Work more efficiently. Make the egg rolls in batches that will fit in your deep fryer or pot. While the first batch fries, roll the second batch, and so on. Don't let the uncooked egg rolls sit too long, or they may get soggy on the bottom.

You can save the shiitake soaking water for soups and stews.

- **Preheat oven to 200°F (100°C)**
- **Deep fryer or large, heavy pot**
- **Candy or deep-frying thermometer, if not using a deep fryer**
- **Rimmed baking sheet, topped with wire rack**

2	dried shiitake mushrooms (about 1/2 oz/15 g)	2
4 oz	green cabbage, finely shredded (about 1 1/2 cups/375 mL)	125 g
1	small carrot (2 oz/60 g), shredded (about 1/2 cup/125 mL)	1
1 tsp	oil	5 mL
1/2 cup	chopped celery	125 mL
1/2 cup	chopped green onions (white and light green parts)	125 mL
2 1/2 cups	bean sprouts (about 6 oz/175 g)	625 mL
1 tbsp	soy sauce	15 mL
1/2 tsp	granulated sugar	2 mL
1/2 tsp	salt	2 mL
1/8 tsp	freshly ground black pepper	0.5 mL
1/8 tsp	powdered ginger	0.5 mL
1	can (4 oz/106 g) small shrimp, rinsed, drained and patted dry	1
14	egg roll wrappers	14
	Vegetable oil	

1. In a small bowl, cover dried shiitakes with boiling water. Set aside to soak for 15 minutes to soften. Drain, squeeze out excess moisture and chop. Set aside.

2. In a pot of boiling salted water over medium heat, blanch cabbage and carrot for 3 minutes. Drain and rinse under cold running water to stop the cooking. Drain and set aside.

3. In a large skillet, heat oil over medium-high heat. Add celery and green onions and stir-fry for 1 minute. Add bean sprouts and stir-fry for 1 minute. Add reserved cabbage, carrot and soaked mushrooms and stir-fry for about 3 minutes, until vegetables are tender-crisp and not watery. Add soy sauce and stir for 10 seconds, until evaporated. Remove skillet from heat. Stir in sugar, salt, pepper and ginger. Transfer to a sieve and set aside until mixture cools to room temperature. Stir in shrimp.

Tip
If you're not using a deep-fryer you'll need to turn the egg rolls once.

4. Set a small bowl of water on work surface. In batches, place wrappers on work surface, corners pointing up to make a diamond shape. Place about $1/4$ cup (60 mL) loosely packed shrimp mixture in a horizontal line across the middle of each wrapper. Starting with the tip of the diamond closest to you, roll wrapper halfway over the filling. Tuck right and left corners over the filling. Roll almost to the end. Dip your finger in water and moisten the tip of the diamond. Finish rolling, pressing gently to seal. Set aside each roll, seam side down, on a large plate or baking sheet. Repeat until all the filling and wrappers are used up.

5. Place 1 inch (2.5 cm) vegetable oil in a large, heavy pot. Heat over medium-high heat until thermometer registers 375°F (190°C). (If you're using a deep fryer, follow the manufacturer's instructions.) In batches, fry rolls for about 4 minutes, until golden brown, turning if necessary (see Tip, left).

6. Serve immediately or transfer to prepared baking sheet and keep warm in preheated oven while preparing next batch.

Variations

Add barbecued pork bits and reduce the amount of shrimp.

Add 4 water chestnuts, chopped, for more crunch.

Substitute an equal quantity of coarsely chopped lobster for the shrimp.

Golden Purses

These dippable little Thai bundles are so cute. They make delightful cocktail snacks, dim sum items or appetizers. Unfortunately, they disappear all too quickly.

Makes 35 purses

- Kid-friendly
- Guest-worthy

Tips

Save the shiitake soaking liquid to flavor soups and stews.

Dumpling wrappers, also known as dumpling skins, resemble wonton wrappers, but they are round instead of square. Chinese wrappers are often sold in packages in the refrigerated section of supermarket produce departments. You can freeze any leftovers.

- **Food processor**
- **Deep fryer or large, heavy pot**
- **Candy or deep-frying thermometer, if not using a deep fryer**

2	dried shiitake mushrooms (about ½ oz/15 g)	2
1	large clove garlic	1
1	Thai bird's-eye chile, seeded and deveined, optional	1
1	can (4 oz/106 g) small shrimp, rinsed and drained	1
1	green onion (white and green parts) cut into 1-inch (2.5 cm) segments	1
2	water chestnuts	2
2 tsp	chopped cilantro leaves	10 mL
1 tsp	fish sauce	5 mL
1 tsp	soy sauce	5 mL
1 tsp	freshly squeezed lime juice	5 mL
⅛ tsp	freshly ground white pepper	0.5 mL
35	3¼-inch (8 cm) round dumpling wrappers (about 8 oz/250 g; see Tips, left)	35
	Vegetable oil	
35	chives	35
	Bottled Thai sweet chili sauce (see Tips, page 69)	

1. In a small bowl, cover dried mushrooms with boiling water. Set aside for 15 minutes to soften. Drain, squeeze out excess moisture and chop coarsely. Set aside.

2. In food processor fitted with the metal blade, with the motor running, add garlic and chile, if using, through the feed tube to chop. Scrape down the sides of the work bowl. Add shrimp, green onion, water chestnuts, cilantro, fish sauce, soy sauce, lime juice, pepper and reserved chopped mushrooms. Process until blended but mixture retains some texture.

Tips

Thai sweet chili sauce is sold in supermarkets. It is sweet and sour, with only a mild kick. Use it as a condiment or dip.

If you are not using a deep fryer, you will need to fry the purses on their sides, turning them once.

3. Place a small bowl of cold water on work surface. Working in batches of 12, lay wrappers on the surface. Moisten your finger and dampen the circumference of each wrapper. Place a generous 1 tsp (5 mL) filling in the center of each. Pull up sides of wrapper around the filling, then pinch it closed near the top to create a "neck" so that the dumpling resembles a drawstring bag. Push down gently to slightly flatten the bottom.

4. Place 1 inch (2.5 cm) oil in a large, heavy pot. Heat over medium-high heat until the thermometer registers 375°F (190°C). (If you're using a deep fryer, follow the manufacturer's instructions.) Add purses in batches and fry for 1 to 2 minutes, until golden, turning if necessary (see Tips, left). Lower the heat if they are browning too fast. Transfer to a plate lined with paper towels to drain.

5. For each purse, tie a loop in a chive, slip it over the neck and tighten carefully. If necessary, use scissors to trim the chives, particularly at the thicker ends, which are less flexible.

6. Serve immediately, with sweet chili sauce alongside.

Variations
Substitute an equal quantity of salmon, crab or lobster for the shrimp.

Salmon and Olive Puffs

Put the bite on these little puff pastries at cocktail hour or snack time. They gape open slightly as they bake so they look like little bivalves. Be careful — it's hard to stop eating these tasty tidbits.

Makes about 72 puffs

- Kid-friendly
- Guest-worthy

Tips

Puff pastry package sizes vary a great deal. If you can find 14 oz (397 g) packages, use two.

Work efficiently. Once you've filled a baking sheet with puffs, put it in the oven. While they're baking, prepare the next batch of puffs.

- **Two rimmed baking sheets, lined with parchment**

2 tbsp	extra virgin olive oil	30 mL
1	onion, diced	1
1/4 tsp	salt (approx.)	1 mL
1/2 cup	pimiento-stuffed green olives, chopped	125 mL
1	can (7 1/2 oz/213 g) salmon, drained, deboned and broken into flakes	1
	Freshly ground black pepper	
24 oz	puff pastry, thawed, divided (see Tips, left)	680 g

1. In a skillet, heat oil over medium-low heat until shimmery. Add onion and salt and cook, stirring often, for 5 to 7 minutes, until onion is tender and golden. Stir in olives for 10 seconds. Stir in salmon. Remove from heat and season to taste with pepper. Add salt to taste, if necessary. Set aside until mixture reaches room temperature.

2. Meanwhile, place a small bowl of cold water on your work surface. On a lightly floured surface, thinly roll out one-quarter of the pastry. Cut out circles using a 2 1/2-inch (6 cm) cookie cutter. Place a circle in your palm and, using a finger dipped in the water, moisten halfway around the circumference. Spoon about 1 tsp (5 mL) filling in the center of the round and fold over to make a half-moon shape. Press edges shut. Place on prepared baking sheet. Repeat with remaining pastry and filling, rerolling scraps (you will have leftover filling).

3. When you're ready to bake, preheat oven to 375°F (190°C). Bake pastries one sheet at a time (see Tips, left), for 20 minutes, until golden brown.

> ### Variations
> Substitute an equal quantity of tuna, mackerel, cod, kippers or shrimp for the salmon.

Soups

Salmon, Corn and Herb Chowder with Pepper Jack

Creamy chowders tend to be bland. The addition of pepper Jack cheese livens up this one.

Makes about 7 cups (1.75 L) 4 to 6 servings

• Kid-friendly

Tips

Yellow-fleshed potatoes are best for this recipe. They give the soup a pleasant creaminess without potentially becoming gluey, like waxy red potatoes, or grainy, like russets.

You can double the amount of salmon and enjoy this with crusty bread as a light dinner.

Variations

If you don't like spicy food, substitute your favorite melting cheese, such as Cheddar or fontina.

Substitute an equal quantity of tuna, mackerel, cod, kippers, shrimp, crab, lobster, clams, oysters, mussels or octopus for the salmon.

• **Blender or food processor**

1 tbsp	extra virgin olive oil	15 mL
1	onion, diced	1
2	potatoes (about 12 oz/375 g), peeled and cut in 1-inch (2.5 cm) chunks (see Tips, left)	2
4 cups	chicken or vegetable stock	1 L
1	can (7½ oz/213 g) salmon, drained, deboned and broken into chunks	1
1 cup	corn kernels	250 mL
2 tbsp	chopped parsley leaves	30 mL
2 tbsp	chopped chives	30 mL
1 tbsp	tarragon leaves, chopped	15 mL
1 tbsp	chopped dill fronds	15 mL
2 tsp	thyme leaves, chopped	10 mL
1 cup	half-and-half (10%) cream or whole milk	250 mL
	Salt	
1 cup	shredded pepper Jack cheese (4 oz/125 g)	250 mL

1. In a large saucepan, heat oil over medium heat until shimmery. Add onion and cook, stirring often, for 3 to 5 minutes, until softened. Stir in potatoes and stock. Increase heat to medium-high and bring to a simmer. Reduce heat to medium-low and simmer for about 15 minutes, until potatoes are tender.

2. In batches, transfer to a blender or food processor fitted with the metal blade (or use an immersion blender) and purée. Return soup to saucepan, if necessary, over medium-low heat and stir in salmon, corn, parsley, chives, tarragon, dill and thyme. Simmer for 5 minutes, stirring often. Stir in cream and simmer for 1 minute, until soup is very hot (do not allow it to boil). Season to taste with salt.

3. Ladle into warm bowls and sprinkle cheese overtop, dividing equally.

Smoked Salmon and Wild Rice Chowder

This meal-in-a-bowl is filling and has a lively Southwest vibe, thanks to the addition of ancho chile powder and sweet potato.

Makes about 8 cups (2 L) 4 to 6 servings

- Guest-worthy

Tips

Ancho chile powder is sold in supermarkets. Don't mistake it for the tired old chili powder blend shelved nearby.

Canned smoked salmon is sold in specialty shops.

For an even more substantial soup, use two cans of salmon.

Variations

Substitute smoked tuna for the salmon, or use regular canned salmon, tuna, mackerel, cod, kippers, shrimp or lobster and add liquid smoke.

3 cups	water	750 mL
	Salt	
¾ cup	wild rice, rinsed	175 mL
2 tbsp	extra virgin olive oil	30 mL
1	onion, diced	1
1	large clove garlic, minced	1
1	stalk celery, cut in ¼-inch (0.5 cm) dice	1
1	green bell pepper, cut in ¼-inch (0.5 cm) dice	1
1	small sweet potato (about 8 oz/250 g), cut in ¼-inch (0.5 cm) dice	1
4 cups	chicken or vegetable stock	1 L
1 tsp	ancho chile powder (see Tips, left)	5 mL
1	can (5 oz/150 g) smoked salmon, with liquid (see Tips, left)	1
¼ cup	heavy or whipping (35%) cream	60 mL

1. In a saucepan, salt water, to taste and bring to a boil over medium heat. Add wild rice and cook for 30 to 45 minutes, until tender yet firm. Drain and set aside.

2. Meanwhile, in a large saucepan, heat oil over medium heat until shimmery. Add onion, garlic and celery. Cook, stirring often, for about 5 minutes, until vegetables soften. Stir in green pepper and sweet potato and cook for 1 minute. Stir in stock and chile powder. Increase heat to high and bring to a boil. Reduce heat to medium-low and simmer for 8 to 10 minutes, until sweet potato is tender.

3. Stir in cooked wild rice, salmon, with liquid, and cream. Cook for 5 minutes, until heated through. Season to taste with salt.

4. Ladle into warm bowls and serve immediately.

Salmon and White Bean Soup with Oniony Croutons

This filling soup provides both nourishment and satisfaction. You can easily make a light meal of it.

Tips

Because the croutons are baked, they will get soggier faster than fried ones.

I use 19-ounce (540 mL) cans of beans. If you use a smaller size, the soup will be thinner. You can compensate by starting with 1½ cups (375 mL) water and adding more at the end if desired.

- **Preheat oven to 400°F (200°C)**
- **Rimmed baking sheet**
- **Blender or food processor**

Croutons

2 tbsp	extra virgin olive oil	30 mL
2 tsp	onion powder	10 mL
½ tsp	dried parsley	2 mL
½ tsp	salt	2 mL
⅛ tsp	freshly ground black pepper	0.5 mL
3 cups	diced (½ inch/1 cm) crusty bread	750 mL

Soup

2 tbsp	extra virgin olive oil	30 mL
1	onion, diced	1
1	carrot, coarsely chopped	1
1	stalk celery, diced	1
2	cloves garlic, chopped	2
2 cups	chicken or vegetable stock	500 mL
2 cups	water	500 mL
2	cans (each 14 to 19 oz/398 to 540 mL) cannellini (white kidney) beans, drained and rinsed (see Tips, left)	2
2 tbsp	chopped sage leaves, divided	30 mL
1	can (7½ oz/213 g) salmon, drained, deboned and broken into small chunks	1
	Salt and freshly ground black pepper	

1. *Croutons:* In a large bowl, stir together oil, onion powder, parsley, salt and pepper. Add bread cubes and toss until well coated. Spread evenly on baking sheet and bake in preheated oven for 8 to 10 minutes, shaking once or twice, until golden brown and crispy.

2. *Soup:* In a large saucepan, heat oil over medium heat until shimmery. Add onion, carrot, celery and garlic. Cook, stirring, for about 5 minutes, until vegetables soften and turn golden. Add stock, water, beans and half the sage. Bring the mixture to a simmer over medium-high heat. Reduce heat to low and simmer for 30 minutes, until vegetables are very soft.

3. Ladle out 2 cups (500 mL) of soup and set aside. In batches, transfer remainder to blender or food processor fitted with the metal blade (or use an immersion blender) and purée. Return to saucepan, if necessary. Add reserved soup and salmon and season to taste with salt and pepper. Bring to a simmer over medium heat and cook until heated through.

4. Ladle into warm bowls and scatter croutons overtop, dividing equally. Garnish with remaining sage and serve immediately.

Variations

Substitute tuna, mackerel or shrimp for the salmon.

Shortcut Shrimp and Sausage Gumbo

I hope lightning won't strike me if I say you can get a reasonable gumbo experience more quickly than traditional recipes suggest. Sure, this version is barely authentic, but you don't have to simmer it for hours either. While it doesn't strictly fit my definition of "fast," I have noted it as such because it is an abbreviated gumbo, plus you can multitask while it simmers. Gumbo is usually served over rice, so it makes a satisfying meal.

**Makes about
6 cups (1.5 L)
4 to 6 servings**

● Fast

Tips

Don't overcook the okra — it can get unpleasantly gummy. Firm okra gives this soup a fresher texture too.

Double the amount of shrimp if desired.

Variations

If you don't have andouille sausages, substitute an equal quantity of kielbasa.

Substitute an equal quantity of crab, lobster or clams for the shrimp.

¼ cup	vegetable oil	60 mL
¼ cup	all-purpose flour	60 mL
2	onions, finely chopped	2
1	red bell pepper, finely chopped	1
6	cloves garlic, minced	6
1	stalk celery, finely chopped	1
1 tbsp	Cajun seasoning	15 mL
4 cups	chicken or vegetable stock	1 L
1	bay leaf	1
2	andouille sausages (about 8 oz/250 g), thinly sliced	2
8 oz	okra, trimmed and cut in ½-inch (1 cm) slices (about 1½ cups/375 mL)	250 g
1	can (4 oz/106 g) small or medium shrimp, rinsed and drained	1
	Hot pepper sauce	
	Salt	
4	green onions (white and light green parts), thinly sliced	4

1. In a large saucepan, heat oil over medium heat until shimmery. Add flour and whisk constantly for 3 to 7 minutes, until mixture is a deep reddish brown (the time depends on the surface area of the pan). Remove from heat.

2. Add onions, red pepper, garlic, celery and Cajun seasoning. Return pan to medium heat and cook, stirring, for 5 minutes, until vegetables soften. Gradually whisk in stock. Add bay leaf and bring to a simmer over medium-high heat. Reduce heat to medium-low and simmer for 10 minutes. Stir in sausages and simmer for 15 minutes to meld flavors. Stir in okra and simmer for 5 minutes, until tender-crisp (see Tips, left). Remove bay leaf and discard. Stir in shrimp and hot sauce and salt to taste.

3. Ladle gumbo into warm bowls and serve immediately, garnished with green onions.

Crab, Watercress and Egg Drop Soup

This comfort food looks pretty, and when you are sick — or just sick of winter's cold — it really hits the spot.

Tips

Toasted sesame oil is often called Asian sesame oil.

Adding 1 tsp (15 mL) oil per egg prevents stringy, spongy blobs in your egg drop soup. Instead, the strands will be silky and even.

To grate or purée gingerroot, use a sharp-toothed rasp such as the kind made by Microplane.

Because the crab tends to make this soup salty, I specify low-sodium stock. You can add salt at the end, if necessary.

You can use less expensive crab leg and flaked crabmeat for this soup.

Hot chile oil is sold in the supermarket's Asian food section.

4 cups	low-sodium chicken or vegetable stock, divided	1 L
1 tbsp	cornstarch	15 mL
1	large egg	1
1 tsp	toasted sesame oil (see Tips, left)	5 mL
1	clove garlic, minced	1
1 tsp	finely grated gingerroot (see Tips, left)	5 mL
1	can (4.25 oz/120 g) crabmeat, rinsed and drained	125 g
2 cups	watercress leaves, coarsely chopped	500 mL
	Salt and freshly ground black pepper	
	Prepared hot chili oil, optional (see Tips, left)	

1. In a small measuring cup, stir together $\frac{1}{2}$ cup (125 mL) stock and the cornstarch.

2. In a small bowl, lightly whisk together egg and sesame oil.

3. In a saucepan over medium-high heat, bring remaining $3\frac{1}{2}$ cups (750 mL) stock, garlic and ginger to a simmer. Reduce heat to medium-low and simmer for 2 minutes. Give the cornstarch mixture a big stir and whisk into the stock mixture in a slow, steady stream. Heat, stirring often, for 1 to 2 minutes, until mixture returns to a simmer and thickens, raising the heat if necessary. Stir in crab and watercress.

4. Hold the bowl with the egg mixture a few inches above the surface of the soup. With one hand, slowly pour in the egg, using a fork in the other hand to draw wide circles on the surface of the soup, catching the egg mixture and separating it into thin threads. Season to taste with salt and pepper.

5. Ladle into warm bowls and serve with chili oil alongside, if using.

Variations

Use about 8 oz (250 g) asparagus instead of the watercress. Cut it into 1-inch (2.5 cm) segments and simmer it in the stock along with the garlic and ginger, until tender-crisp.

Substitute an equal quantity of salmon, shrimp, lobster or clams for the crab.

Lobster Mushroom Bisque

French bisque, a creamy, smooth seafood soup, is so civilized and indulgent. Here the lobster swims in a satiny base and the mushrooms add depth.

Makes 6 cups (1.5 L)
4 to 6 servings

- Guest-worthy

Tip

You can buy fish stock from a fishmonger or in gourmet food shops and some supermarkets.

Variations

Substitute salmon, shrimp, crab, clams, oysters or mussels for the lobster.

- **Blender**

6 tbsp	unsalted butter, divided	90 mL
1	can (11.3 oz/320 g) lobster meat, rinsed, drained and cut into small chunks	1
1½ cups	coarsely chopped cremini mushrooms (4 oz/125 g)	375 mL
1	leek, trimmed and thinly sliced	1
1	carrot, coarsely chopped	1
1	stalk celery, coarsely chopped	1
4 cups	fish stock, divided (see Tip, left)	1 L
1 tbsp	tomato paste	15 mL
2 tbsp	tarragon leaves	30 mL
½ tsp	salt (approx.)	2 mL
2 tbsp	all-purpose flour	30 mL
¾ cup	heavy or whipping (35%) cream	175 mL
¼ cup	dry sherry	60 mL
	Freshly ground white pepper	
¼ cup	crème fraîche or sour cream	60 mL
¼ cup	chopped chives	60 mL

1. In a large saucepan over medium-low heat, melt ¼ cup (60 mL) butter. Add lobster and poach for 5 minutes. Using a slotted spoon, transfer to a bowl, cover and set aside.

2. Increase heat to medium and add mushrooms, leek, carrot and celery. Cover and cook for 10 minutes, stirring often, until vegetables are tender. Stir in 2 cups (500 mL) of the stock, tomato paste, tarragon and salt. When mixture starts to simmer, reduce heat to low. Cover and simmer for 15 minutes, until vegetables are very soft. Transfer to blender and set pan aside. Purée until very smooth. Set aside.

3. Add remaining butter to pan and melt over medium-low heat. Whisk in flour and cook, stirring often, for about 2 minutes, until golden (do not let it brown). While whisking, gradually add remaining stock. Cook, whisking occasionally, for 5 minutes, until thickened and simmering. Stir in puréed vegetables, cream, sherry and pepper to taste. Stir in lobster, with juices. Add salt to taste.

4. Ladle into warm bowls and top each with a dollop of crème fraîche, dividing equally. Sprinkle with chives and serve immediately.

Faux Pho

Craving Vietnamese soup? This version is faster to make than traditional Vietnamese pho, which nowadays is a staple meal for college kids and diners on a budget.

Makes 4 large servings

• Healthy

Tips

Asian Stock: In a large saucepan, heat 1 tbsp (15 mL) vegetable oil over medium heat until shimmery. Add 1 small diced onion, 1 clove minced garlic and 4 thin (about $\frac{1}{8}$-inch/3 mm) slices of ginger. Cook, stirring, for about 3 minutes, until vegetables soften. Add 5 cups (1.25 L) chicken or vegetable stock and 1 cup (250 mL) water and bring to a boil over high heat. Reduce heat to medium-low and simmer for 10 minutes, until onion is tender. Remove and discard ginger. Stir in 2 tbsp (30 mL) soy sauce and 1 tbsp (15 mL) each fish sauce and hoisin sauce and season with salt to taste.

Rice noodles are sometimes labeled "rice sticks."

Variations

Substitute shrimp, lobster, or clams for the salmon. If using lobster or meaty clams, simmer in the stock with the onion and add equal amounts to the serving bowls along with the stock.

4 oz	snow peas, trimmed and halved lengthwise (about 1½ cups/375 mL)	125 g
8 oz	thin (⅛ inch/3 mm) rice noodles (see Tips, left)	250 g
1	can (6 oz/170 g) boneless, skinless salmon, drained and broken into chunks	1
6 oz	bean sprouts (about 2½ cups/625 mL)	175 g
2	green onions (white and light green parts), thinly sliced on the diagonal	2
¼ cup	loosely packed cilantro leaves	60 mL
¼ cup	loosely packed basil leaves, thinly sliced	60 mL
	Asian Stock (see Tips, left)	
	Asian chili sauce (such as sambal oelek or sriracha)	
1	lime, cut in 4 wedges	1

1. Bring a large pot of salted water to a boil over high heat. Add snow peas and blanch for 1 minute, until tender-crisp. Using a mesh scoop, transfer to a colander and rinse under cold running water to stop the cooking. Drain.

2. Add noodles to the boiling water and cook for about 5 minutes, until cooked through but not mushy. Drain. Rinse briefly under cold running water to stop the cooking. Drain.

3. Divide noodles among 4 warmed wide bowls. Top with equal amounts of salmon, snow peas, bean sprouts, green onions, cilantro and basil.

4. Reheat the stock over high heat until steamy but not boiling. Ladle into the bowls. Add a dollop of chili sauce to each bowl (or serve it alongside). Place a lime wedge on the edge of each bowl. Before eating, squeeze the lime into the soup and stir the ingredients together.

Salmon and Roasted Garlic Bisque with Cajun Croutons

Vampires need not apply for a bowl of this garlicky soup, which strikes a delicious balance between pungent and mellow. Almost any canned fish will work with the creamy base and crispy garnish.

Tips

For the creamiest result, use yellow-fleshed potatoes.

You can prepare this soup ahead of time. Once it's puréed, cover and refrigerate for up to 2 days. Just before serving, stir in the cream and salmon and heat until the soup is hot but not boiling.

- **Preheat oven to 400°F (200°C)**
- **Rimmed baking sheet**
- **Blender or food processor**

Croutons

1 tbsp	Cajun seasoning (see Tips, page 81)	15 mL
1 tsp	garlic powder	5 mL
2 tbsp	extra virgin olive oil	30 mL
1	small loaf ciabatta (about 6 oz/175 g) or demi-baguette, cut in $\frac{1}{2}$-inch (1 cm) dice	1

Soup

2	heads garlic	2
$\frac{1}{8}$ tsp	vegetable or olive oil	0.5 mL
2 tbsp	unsalted butter	30 mL
1	onion, diced	1
1	potato (about 8 oz/250 g), diced (seeTips, left)	1
1	bay leaf	1
1 tsp	thyme leaves	5 mL
3 cups	chicken or vegetable stock	750 mL
$\frac{1}{2}$ cup	half-and-half (10%) cream	125 mL
1	can (7$\frac{1}{2}$ oz/213 g) salmon, drained, deboned and broken into chunks	1
	Salt and freshly ground black pepper	

1. *Croutons:* In a small bowl, stir together Cajun seasoning and garlic powder. Set aside.

2. In a large skillet, heat oil over medium-high heat until shimmery. Stir in bread and cook, occasionally flipping with a spatula, for about 5 minutes, until golden brown. Remove from heat. Sprinkle reserved spice mixture evenly overtop and toss thoroughly. Transfer to baking sheet and spread evenly. Set aside to cool.

Cajun seasoning is a salt, spice, herb and vegetable blend. Mixtures vary by brand. It may include black pepper, cayenne, thyme and oregano, as well as dried garlic and brown sugar. Buy a kind that specifies no MSG has been added.

3. *Soup:* Meanwhile, remove any loose papery skin from the garlic heads. Cut a thin slice off the top of each head. Place each head on a square of foil and drizzle oil overtop. Wrap in foil and roast in preheated oven for about 45 minutes, until tender. Remove from oven and set aside to cool. Press roasted garlic cloves out of their skins and set aside. Discard skins.

4. In a saucepan over medium heat, melt butter. Add onion and cook 3 to 5 minutes, until softened. Stir in roasted garlic, potato, bay leaf and thyme. Add stock and bring to a simmer. Reduce heat to medium-low and cook for 20 minutes, until potato is very tender. Remove and discard bay leaf.

5. In batches, transfer to blender or a food processor fitted with the metal blade (or use an immersion blender) and purée until smooth. Return to saucepan, if necessary, over medium heat. Stir in cream and salmon and season to taste with salt and pepper. Heat for 2 to 3 minutes, until warmed through (do not allow the soup to boil).

6. Ladle into warm bowls and sprinkle with croutons to taste (you may have some left over). Serve immediately.

Variations

Substitute an equal quantity of tuna, mackerel, cod, shrimp, crab, lobster, oysters, mussels or octopus for the salmon.

Creamy Crab and Poblano Soup

In the Mexican collection of peppers, poblanos are relatively mild, but they still pack a punch in this addictive creation. You could add almost any seafood to the creamy base.

Makes about 5 cups (1.25 L)
4 servings

• Guest-worthy

Tips

To easily remove seeds from sticky roasted peppers, dip the pieces briefly into a bowl of cold water.

Yellow-fleshed potatoes are best for this recipe. They give the soup a pleasant creaminess without becoming gluey, like waxy red potatoes, or grainy, like russets.

Lump crabmeat is best in this recipe. You can use part of a 1 lb (440 g) container of pasteurized crab or a 4.25 oz (120 g) can of shelf-stable chunk crabmeat. If you have leftover crab, see the chart on pages 272 to 278 for other recipes in which to use it.

Variations

Substitute an equal quantity of tuna, salmon, mackerel, cod, kippers, shrimp, lobster, clams or octopus for the crab.

• **Preheat broiler**
• **Blender or food processor**

2	poblano peppers	2
2 tbsp	unsalted butter	30 mL
1	onion, diced	1
2	cloves garlic, chopped	2
1	potato, peeled and cut into 1-inch (2.5 cm) chunks (see Tips, left)	1
3 cups	chicken or vegetable stock	750 mL
½ cup	chopped red bell pepper	125 mL
½ cup	half-and-half (10%) cream	125 mL
¾ cup	canned lump crabmeat (about 4 oz/125 g), rinsed and drained	175 mL
	Salt and freshly ground black pepper	
¼ cup	chopped cilantro leaves	60 mL
4	lime wedges	4

1. Place poblano peppers on a baking sheet and broil, turning 2 to 3 times, until skin on all sides is blackened, about 25 minutes. Transfer to a paper bag and fold the top closed. When they are cool enough to handle, use a small, sharp knife to lift off the skins. Discard skins, core and seeds. Cut into ½-inch (1 cm) pieces. Set aside.

2. Meanwhile, in a saucepan, melt butter over medium heat. Add onion and garlic and cook, stirring often, for about 3 minutes, until softened. Stir in potato and stock and bring to a simmer over medium-high heat. Reduce heat to medium-low and simmer for about 15 minutes, until potato is tender.

3. In batches, transfer to blender or food processor fitted with the metal blade (or use an immersion blender) and purée. Return to saucepan, if necessary, and place over medium-low heat. Stir in bell pepper and simmer for about 5 minutes, until just tender. Stir in cream, reserved poblano peppers and crab. Heat the mixture for 1 minute but do not allow to boil. Season to taste with salt and pepper.

4. Ladle into warm bowls and garnish with cilantro. Serve with lime wedges to squeeze into the soup.

Thai Coconut Crab Soup

Thai soup made with coconut milk is deliciously popular and takes to all kinds of seafood.

Tips

You can use flaked crabmeat, but chunks are nicest in this soup. Buy shelf-stable crabmeat in a can or use part of a 1 lb (440 g) container of the better-quality pasteurized crabmeat.

I prefer the thick premium coconut milk, but you can use the "lite" kind. The result will be thinner.

Wild lime leaves, often called "Kaffir lime leaves," are sold in Asian grocery stores and well-stocked supermarkets. You can store leftover leaves in the freezer in zip-lock bags or plastic wrap. Nothing really substitutes for lime leaves, but in a pinch try 1 tsp (5 mL) grated lime zest instead.

To shred basil leaves, place them in a pile, roll them up like a cigar and slice thinly crosswise.

3 cups	chicken or vegetable stock	750 mL
4	fresh wild lime leaves (see Tips, left)	4
1	stalk lemongrass, trimmed and chopped	1
1 tbsp	chopped gingerroot	15 mL
1	can (14 oz/400 mL) coconut milk	1
2 tbsp	fish sauce (approx.), divided	30 mL
2	green onions (white and light green parts), sliced	2
1	Thai bird's-eye chile pepper, thinly sliced	1
2 tbsp	chopped cilantro leaves	30 mL
1 tbsp	shredded basil leaves (see Tips, left)	15 mL
1	can (4.25 oz/120 g) crabmeat, rinsed and drained	1
1 tbsp	freshly squeezed lime juice	15 mL
	Salt	

1. In a medium saucepan over medium-high heat, bring stock, lime leaves, lemongrass and ginger to a simmer. Reduce heat to medium-low and simmer, uncovered, for 15 minutes. Place a sieve over a large bowl and strain soup. Discard solids and return liquid to saucepan.

2. Add coconut milk, 1 tbsp (15 mL) fish sauce, green onions, chile pepper, cilantro and basil to pan. Bring to a simmer over medium heat. Reduce the heat to medium-low and simmer for 5 minutes. Stir in crab and simmer for 1 minute, until heated through. Stir in lime juice. Taste and add up to 1 tbsp (15 mL) additional fish sauce, if desired. Season to taste with salt.

Variations

Substitute an equal quantity of salmon, mackerel, cod, shrimp or lobster for the crab.

Clams in Herb Broth with Angel Hair Pasta

Is this a soup or a pasta? Well, it's both and neither. Definitions aside, you are sure to enjoy this vivid green, hot, comforting dish.

Makes 4 servings

- Fast
- Healthy

Tip

If you enjoy using chopsticks, get them out now to eat the noodles with. Wield a spoon for the broth.

Variations

Firm surf clams work best in this, but baby clams make an acceptable substitute.

Substitute an equal quantity of shrimp, crab, lobster, squid or octopus for the clams.

- **Mini blender or food processor**

1	clove garlic	1
1 cup	loosely packed coarsely chopped parsley leaves, divided	250 mL
½ cup	loosely packed coarsely chopped chives, divided	125 mL
¼ cup	loosely packed fresh dill fronds, divided	60 mL
2 tbsp	coarsely chopped tarragon leaves, divided	30 mL
1 tbsp	thyme leaves, divided	15 mL
¼ cup	extra virgin olive oil	60 mL
½ tsp	salt (approx.)	2 mL
⅛ tsp	freshly ground black pepper	0.5 mL
2¼ cups	chicken or vegetable stock	550 mL
1	bottle (8 oz/240 mL) clam juice	1
¼ tsp	hot pepper flakes	1 mL
1	can (5 oz/142 g) surf or meaty clams, rinsed, drained and coarsely chopped	1
4 oz	angel hair pasta	125 g

1. Bring a large pot of salted water to a boil over high heat.

2. In mini blender or food processor fitted with the metal blade, with the motor running, add garlic through the feed tube to chop. Scrape down the sides of the bowl. Add half each of the parsley, chives, dill, tarragon and thyme, and olive oil, salt and pepper. Process until smooth and light green. If necessary, add 2 tbsp (30 mL) stock to loosen the purée. Set aside.

3. In a saucepan, combine stock, clam juice, remaining parsley, chives, dill, tarragon, and thyme, and hot pepper flakes. Bring mixture to a simmer over medium-high heat. Reduce heat to medium-low and simmer for 10 minutes, until herbs are soft. Add clams and simmer for 5 minutes.

4. Meanwhile, add pasta to the boiling water and cook over medium heat for about 5 minutes, until tender to the bite (al dente). Drain.

5. Divide the pasta among 4 warmed large bowls and ladle soup overtop. Serve the garlic-herb purée alongside for diners to stir into the soup.

Salads

Tuna Salad with an Italian Accent

Globalization applies to culture and cuisine too. Tuna salad is a North American classic, but when I feel like updating and experimenting, I like to give it an international twist. For instance, pesto and sun-dried tomato add an Italian accent to this version. As with the original, it is very versatile.

Makes about 1 cup (250 mL)

- Fast
- Kid-friendly
- Brown-bag

Tips

I recommend using chunk tuna when making tuna salad because the end result is less likely to be pasty. Also, inexpensive flaked tuna sometimes tastes tinny.

Weepiness is tuna salad's number one preventable problem. Before using, drain the tuna in a sieve, flake it with your fingers and gently squeeze out excess moisture. Avoid watery additions such as chopped fresh tomato or cucumber. The mayonnaise you choose also plays a role. With lower-fat mayonnaise, tuna salad will be a bit looser and more watery after it sits, but the calorie savings are worthwhile.

¼ to ⅓ cup	mayonnaise	60 to 75 mL
4	large pimiento-stuffed green olives, finely chopped and patted dry	4
1	oil-packed sun-dried tomato, drained and finely chopped (about 1 tbsp/15 mL)	1
½ tsp	basil pesto	2 mL
1	can (6 oz/170 g) chunk tuna in water, drained and broken into flakes (see Tips, left)	1
	Salt and freshly ground black pepper	

1. In a bowl, combine mayonnaise to taste, olives, tomato and pesto. Gently squeeze tuna to remove excess moisture and add to the bowl. Blend with a fork and season to taste with salt and pepper.

2. Serve immediately or cover and refrigerate for up to 3 days.

Variations
In any tuna salad you can substitute an equal quantity of salmon, mackerel, sardines, sprats, shrimp, crab or lobster for the tuna.

Tuna Salad with an Indian Accent

Indian curry paste and mango chutney are among the many unusual ingredients you can add to tuna salad. Try spreading this version on warm naan bread or add a dollop atop rice for a quick meal.

Makes about 1 cup (250 mL)

- Fast
- Brown-bag

Tip

Supermarkets sell a wide variety of Indian curry pastes, from mild to hot. I prefer Patak's Madras hot curry paste, but you can use your favorite kind.

¼ to ⅓ cup	mayonnaise	60 to 75 mL
1 tbsp	finely diced yellow onion	15 mL
1 tsp	mango chutney	5 mL
½ tsp	prepared curry paste (see Tip, left)	2 mL
1 tsp	finely chopped cilantro leaves	5 mL
1	can (6 oz/170 g) chunk tuna in water, drained and flaked (see Tips, page 86) Salt and freshly ground black pepper	1

1. In a bowl, combine mayonnaise to taste, onion, chutney, curry paste and cilantro. Gently squeeze tuna to remove excess moisture and add to the bowl. Blend with a fork and season to taste with salt and pepper.

2. Serve immediately or cover and refrigerate for up to 3 days.

Tuna Salad with a Greek Accent

Classic Greek accents, including olives and mint, make this tuna salad deliciously different. Stuff it into pitas or add to Greek salad to make a meal.

Makes about 1 cup (250 mL)

- Fast
- Brown-bag

Tip

I recommend using chunk tuna when making tuna salad because the end result is less likely to be pasty. Also, inexpensive flaked tuna sometimes tastes tinny.

¼ to ⅓ cup	mayonnaise	60 to 75 mL
4	kalamata olives, pitted, chopped and patted dry	4
1 tbsp	finely chopped green bell pepper	15 mL
1 tbsp	finely diced red onion	15 mL
1 tsp	finely chopped mint leaves	5 mL
¼ tsp	finely grated lemon zest	1 mL
1	can (6 oz/170 g) chunk tuna in water, drained and broken into flakes (see Tip, left) Salt and freshly ground black pepper	1

1. In a bowl, combine mayonnaise to taste, olives, green pepper, onion, mint and lemon zest. Gently squeeze tuna to remove excess moisture and add to the bowl. Blend with a fork and season to taste with salt and pepper.

2. Serve immediately or cover and refrigerate for up to 3 days.

Tuna Salad Cream Cheese

When you replace the standard mayo in tuna salad with cream cheese, the result is a slightly tangy, firm and flavorful sandwich filling.

Tips

Use soft cream cheese in this recipe, not the kind sold in blocks. Soft cream cheese is the kind scooped into tubs at supermarkets and delis.

In this case, flaked tuna works fine because the cheese is dense and vibrant.

You can use any type of sweet pickle, including gherkins or sliced sweet pickles.

1	can (6 oz/170 g) flaked tuna in water, drained	1
4 oz	soft cream cheese (about 1/2 cup/125 mL)	125 g
2 tbsp	finely chopped sweet pickles (see Tips, left)	30 mL
2 tbsp	finely chopped sweet onion (such as Vidalia)	30 mL
	Salt and freshly ground black pepper	

1. In a bowl, combine tuna, cream cheese, pickles and onion. Mix with a fork and season to taste with salt and pepper.

2. Serve immediately or cover and refrigerate for up to 3 days.

> ### Variations
> Substitute an equal quantity of salmon, mackerel, sardines, sprats, kippers, shrimp, crab or lobster for the tuna.

Mediterranean Diet Tuna Salad

This mayo-free blend is an alternative to old-school tuna salads. With its lively flavor, better health profile and focus on premium tuna in olive oil, this is a simple but sophisticated tuna salad for the new millennium. Try it on crostini or atop salad greens, or stir it into cold pasta.

Variations

Substitute an equal quantity of salmon, mackerel, sardines, sprats, crab or lobster for the tuna.

2	cans (each 3 oz/85 g) solid tuna in olive oil, with oil, broken into flakes	2
4	small pimiento-stuffed green olives, finely chopped	4
1 tbsp	finely chopped red onion	15 mL
1 tsp	balsamic vinegar	5 mL
	Salt and freshly ground black pepper	

1. In a bowl, using a fork, blend tuna, with oil, olives, onion, vinegar and salt and pepper to taste.

2. Serve immediately or cover and refrigerate for up to 3 days.

Tuna Cobb Salad

Cobb salad is an iconic dish that originated at Hollywood's Brown Derby restaurant. It is a composed salad, which means it is artfully arranged in layers or sections rather than tossed. In this variation, canned fish replaces the usual chicken breast. It makes a good-looking light meal — show it off in a clear bowl. I like to use thin homemade French dressing because it's not gloppy.

Makes 4 to 8 servings

- Healthy
- Guest-worthy

Tips

Homemade French Dressing: Whisk together ⅓ cup (75 mL) white wine vinegar, 1 clove garlic, minced, 2 tsp (10 mL) granulated sugar, ½ tsp (2 mL) each Worcestershire sauce, sweet paprika, mustard powder and salt, ¼ tsp (1 mL) freshly ground pepper and ¾ cup (175 mL) vegetable oil.

For a retro flavor, use a neutral-tasting vegetable or seed oil such as canola. However, the dressing can be prepared with olive oil if desired. You can use olive oil drained from the tuna in place of some of the oil.

This makes about 1¼ cups (300 mL) dressing, which is more than you'll need. Cover and refrigerate leftovers for up to 1 week. You can use this dressing on any salad.

Cut up the avocado at the last minute. It will darken as it sits.

4	strips bacon, chopped	4
3 cups	coarsely chopped iceberg lettuce	750 mL
3 cups	coarsely chopped romaine lettuce	750 mL
1 to 1½ cups	watercress leaves	250 to 375 mL
1	small Belgian endive (about 3 oz/90 g), thinly sliced	1
4	cans (each 3 oz/85 g) solid tuna in olive oil, drained and broken into chunks	4
12	large cherry tomatoes (about 8 oz/250 g), quartered	12
1	ripe but firm avocado, cut in small dice (see Tips, left)	1
2	large eggs, hard-cooked and coarsely chopped	1
1 oz	blue cheese, crumbled (about ¼ cup/60 mL)	30 g
2 tbsp	chopped chives	30 mL
	Homemade French Dressing (see Tips, left)	

1. In a skillet over medium heat, cook bacon for about 5 minutes, until browned and crisp. Using a slotted spoon, transfer to a plate lined with paper towels. Set aside.

2. Toss lettuces, watercress to taste, and endive in a large serving bowl. Scatter tuna, then tomatoes overtop. Arrange avocado around the perimeter and scatter chopped egg in the center. Top with cheese, then chives. Scatter bacon overtop. Drizzle dressing over the salad or serve it alongside (you will have some left over).

Variations

Substitute salmon, mackerel, sardines, sprats, kippers, shrimp, crab or lobster for the tuna.

Thai Tuna Salad

One evening I was eating a classic Thai beef salad for dinner and thought, Wow, this would be great with seafood. *And it is, with only minimal changes.*

Makes 4 to 6 servings

- Healthy
- Guest-worthy

Tips

Toasted sesame oil is also known as Asian sesame oil.

Grate the ginger using a sharp-toothed kitchen rasp such as the kind made by Microplane.

Use red chiles so you can see them. The green ones would be like hidden bombs in this salad.

Dressing

2 to 3 tbsp	freshly squeezed lime juice	30 to 45 mL
2 tbsp	toasted sesame oil (see Tips, left)	30 mL
1 tbsp	fish sauce	15 mL
2 tsp	soy sauce	10 mL
2 tsp	finely grated gingerroot (see Tips, left)	10 mL
2	cloves garlic, minced	2

Salad

4	cans (each 3 oz/85 g) solid tuna in olive oil, drained and broken into chunks	4
1	English cucumber, scrubbed, halved lengthwise and sliced	1
1 lb	cherry tomatoes, halved	500 g
1 cup	sliced red onion	250 mL
2 to 4	red Thai bird's-eye chile peppers, thinly sliced	2 to 4
	Salt	
1 cup	lightly packed cilantro leaves	250 mL
1 cup	lightly packed torn basil leaves	250 mL
½ cup	roasted peanuts, coarsely chopped	125 mL

1. *Dressing:* In a small measuring cup, whisk together 2 tbsp (30 mL) lime juice, sesame oil, fish sauce, soy sauce, ginger and garlic. Taste and, if desired, whisk in remaining 1 tbsp (15 mL) lime juice. (The mixture should be tart.)

2. *Salad:* Place tuna in a small, airtight container. Add half of the dressing. Cover and refrigerate for 1 hour, turning or shaking the container occasionally.

3. In a large, shallow serving bowl, combine cucumber, tomatoes, onion and chile peppers to taste. Add remaining dressing to taste and toss. Season to taste with salt. Scatter tuna mixture overtop. Sprinkle cilantro and basil overtop, then sprinkle on peanuts.

> ## Variations
> Substitute an equal quantity of salmon or lobster for the tuna.

Tuna Taco Salad

Taco salad made with fish is better for you than one made with beef, because it is lower in saturated fat. This version makes a satisfying meal for both kids and grownups.

Makes 4 servings

- Kid-friendly
- Healthy

Variations

Substitute tortilla bowls for the tortilla chips. But instead of using fat-laden fried bowls, prepare baked ones. Brush large wheat tortillas with vegetable oil and sprinkle with salt and freshly ground black pepper to taste. Press into small, heatproof bowls (each about 2 cups/500 mL) and arrange the edges so they are evenly fluted. Bake on the second rack from the bottom in an oven preheated to 400°F (200°C), until crispy, about 10 minutes. Remove from bowls and turn upside down to cool and crisp. If you are using baked bowls, be aware that they will become soggy more quickly than fried bowls, so fill them at the last minute and serve immediately.

Substitute an equal quantity of salmon for the tuna.

2 tbsp	extra virgin olive oil, divided	30 mL
1	small onion, diced	1
1	clove garlic, minced	1
1 cup	chopped canned tomatoes, with juices	250 mL
1 cup	cooked red kidney beans, rinsed and drained	250 mL
1 tsp	chili powder	10 mL
1/2 tsp	ground cumin	2 mL
1/4 tsp	salt (approx.)	1 mL
	Freshly ground black pepper	
3 cups	shredded iceberg lettuce	750 mL
2	plum tomatoes, cut in 1/4-inch (0.5 cm) dice	2
1/4	English cucumber, quartered lengthwise and thinly sliced	1/4
1/4 cup	diced red onion	60 mL
1 tbsp	freshly squeezed lime juice	15 mL
8 cups	tortilla chips (about 6 oz/175 g)	2 L
1	can (6 oz/170 g) tuna in water, drained and broken into chunks	1
1 cup	shredded Monterey Jack cheese (4 oz/125 g)	250 mL
1/2 cup	sour cream	125 mL
2 tbsp	chopped pickled jalapeño peppers	30 mL

1. In a skillet, heat 1 tbsp (15 mL) oil over medium heat until shimmery. Add onion and garlic and cook, stirring, for 1 to 2 minutes, until onion softens. Stir in canned tomatoes, with juices, and cook for 1 minute. Add beans, chili powder, cumin, salt and freshly ground pepper. Reduce heat to medium-low, cover and simmer for 15 minutes, until mixture thickens.

2. Meanwhile, in a large bowl, combine lettuce, plum tomatoes, cucumber and red onion. Add lime juice, remaining 1 tbsp (15 mL) oil and salt, if necessary, and pepper to taste. Toss well.

3. Pile tortilla chips on individual serving plates. Top with lettuce mixture, tuna, cheese and warm bean mixture, dividing equally. Place a dollop of sour cream on each and scatter with jalapeños. Serve immediately.

Tuna and Bean Salad on Arugula

During the big blackout of August 2003, we didn't have power for almost a week. This was one of the nourishing no-cook meals I prepared during that challenging time.

Tips

If you are brown-bagging this salad, pack the arugula separately, then combine when you're ready to eat. Otherwise it will wilt.

Celery hearts are the tender inner stalks. They are best in salads.

Variations

Substitute an equal quantity of cranberry beans (also known as romano or borlotti beans) for the cannellinis.

Substitute chopped or baby spinach for the arugula.

Substitute an equal quantity of salmon for the tuna.

Dressing

2 tbsp	oil drained from tuna (approx.)	30 mL
1 tsp	oil drained from sun-dried tomatoes (approx.)	5 mL
1 to 2 tbsp	extra virgin olive oil	15 to 30 mL
2 tbsp	freshly squeezed lemon juice	30 mL
1	clove garlic, minced	1
2 tsp	chopped oregano leaves	10 mL
1/2 tsp	Dijon mustard	2 mL
1/4 tsp	salt (approx.)	1 mL
1/8 tsp	freshly ground black pepper	0.5 mL

Salad

1	can (14 to 19 oz/398 to 540 mL) cannellini (white kidney) beans, rinsed and drained	1
4	green onions, sliced	4
2	stalks celery heart with leaves, sliced on the diagonal	2
2	oil-packed sun-dried tomatoes, drained (oil reserved) and finely chopped	2
2	cans (each 3 oz/85 g) tuna in olive oil, drained (oil reserved) and broken in chunks	2
1	small bunch arugula, trimmed and torn into bite-sized pieces	1

1. *Dressing:* Pour oils from tuna and tomatoes into a measuring cup. Add extra virgin olive oil to equal 1/4 cup (60 mL). Add lemon juice, garlic, oregano, mustard, salt and pepper. Whisk well.

2. *Salad:* In a bowl, combine beans, onions, celery and sun-dried tomatoes. Pour dressing overtop and toss gently. Cover and marinate for 30 minutes at room temperature. Add tuna and toss. Adjust salt to taste.

3. Line a serving dish or individual bowls with arugula. Spoon bean mixture overtop. Serve immediately.

Smoked Tuna and Avocado on Baby Greens with Lemon Chervil Dressing

Smoked tuna does not make regular appearances at the supermarket but you can find it at specialty or gourmet food shops. It makes salads distinctively delicious.

Makes 4 small servings

- Fast
- Healthy
- Guest-worthy

Tips

This recipe makes about 1/3 cup (75 mL) dressing. You may have some left over — use it for other salads.

Slice the avocado at the last minute. It will darken as it sits.

Variations

Substitute an equal quantity of fresh tarragon if you can't find chervil.

Use regular tuna instead of the smoked version and add a dash of liquid smoke to the dressing.

Substitute an equal quantity of canned smoked salmon or kippers for the smoked tuna.

Dressing

1 tbsp	freshly squeezed lemon juice	15 mL
1/4 tsp	granulated sugar	1 mL
1/4 tsp	salt	1 mL
1/8 tsp	freshly ground black pepper	0.5 mL
1/8 tsp	Dijon mustard	0.5 mL
1 tbsp	chopped chervil	15 mL
2 tbsp	oil drained from tuna (approx.)	30 mL
1 tbsp	extra virgin olive oil (approx.)	15 mL

Salad

6 cups	mixed baby greens	1.5 L
1	can (5 oz/150 g) smoked tuna in oil, drained (oil reserved) and broken into chunks	1
1	ripe but firm avocado, sliced (see Tips, left)	1
1 cup	grape tomatoes, halved	250 mL
	Salt	

1. *Dressing:* In a small bowl, whisk together lemon juice, sugar, salt, pepper, mustard and chervil. Measure out tuna oil and add extra virgin olive oil to equal 3 tbsp (45 mL). Add to lemon mixture and whisk well. Add salt to taste, if necessary.

2. *Salad:* In a large bowl, toss greens with dressing to taste. Place on a serving platter or individual plates. Top with tuna. Arrange avocado overtop and surround the tuna with tomatoes. Sprinkle the tomatoes lightly with salt and serve immediately.

Mediterranean Roasted Peppers and Tuna

Pair this with toasted flatbread and enjoy it as a dinner salad.

Makes 4 servings

• Healthy

Tips

To roast peppers: Preheat broiler. Place peppers on a baking sheet and roast, turning three times, until skin on all sides is blackened, about 15 minutes. Place in a paper bag, fold the top closed and set aside until peppers are cool enough to handle. (Alternatively, instead of using a bag, place the peppers in a bowl and cover with a plate or plastic wrap.) When cool, using a sharp knife, lift off skins. Discard skins, stems and seeds and slice thinly.

This dressing recipe makes about ½ cup (125 mL). Use leftovers on any salad, steamed vegetables or poached chicken or fish.

The peppers can be marinated in the dressing for several hours prior to preparing the salad.

I use top-quality solid tuna for this salad, but chunk tuna will work.

Dressing

¼ cup	extra virgin olive oil	60 mL
2 tbsp	red wine vinegar	30 mL
1	shallot, minced	1
1 tbsp	chopped oregano leaves	15 mL
1	clove garlic, minced	1
1 tsp	honey	5 mL
½ tsp	salt	2 mL
½ tsp	freshly ground black pepper	2 mL

Salad

2	roasted red bell peppers, peeled, seeded and cut into strips, with juices (see Tips, left)	2
1	roasted yellow bell pepper, peeled, seeded and cut into strips, with juices	1
6 cups	arugula or mixed greens (3 oz/90 g)	1.5 L
2	cans (each 6 oz/170 g) solid tuna in water, drained and broken into chunks (see Tips, left)	2
16	black olives (about ¼ cup/60 mL), pitted if desired	16

1. *Dressing:* In a measuring cup, whisk together oil, vinegar, shallot, oregano, garlic, honey, salt and pepper. Set aside.

2. *Salad:* In a bowl, combine roasted pepper strips, with juices, and three-quarters of the dressing. Toss gently. (You will have dressing left over.)

3. Arrange arugula on four serving plates. Top each with one-quarter can of tuna, then one-quarter of the pepper mixture. Top peppers with one-quarter can of tuna each and scatter 4 olives overtop.

Variations

Substitute salmon, mackerel, cod, sardines or sprats for the tuna.

Marinated Tuna and Radicchio Salad

This simple, colorful salad has proven especially alluring to hungry diners surrounding a buffet table at my home.

Makes 4 servings

- Healthy
- Guest-worthy

Tips

You can buy pine nuts that are already toasted, or you can toast them yourself. Toast pine nuts in a dry skillet over medium heat, shaking the pan often, for 2 to 3 minutes, until fragrant and starting to brown. Transfer to a bowl to cool.

You will need ½ head of radicchio. To shred the radicchio, slice it thinly crosswise.

2 tbsp	extra virgin olive oil	30 mL
2 tbsp	freshly squeezed lemon juice	30 mL
1 tsp	granulated sugar	5 mL
¼ tsp	salt (approx.)	1 mL
¼ tsp	freshly ground black pepper (approx.)	1 mL
2	cans (each 3 oz/85 g) tuna in olive oil, with oil	2
1	small bay leaf	1
1	whole clove	1
4 cups	torn leaf lettuce	1 L
3 cups	shredded radicchio (see Tips, left)	750 mL
2	tomatoes, cut in wedges	2
2 tbsp	toasted pine nuts (see Tips, left)	30 mL
1 tbsp	chopped parsley or basil leaves	15 mL

1. In an airtight container, whisk together extra virgin olive oil, lemon juice, sugar, salt and pepper. Stir in tuna, with oil, bay leaf and clove. Cover and refrigerate for at least 1 hour or overnight. When you are ready to serve, remove and discard bay leaf and clove.

2. In a large serving bowl, toss lettuce and radicchio. Place tuna mixture in center of bowl, on top of the lettuces. Surround with tomatoes and sprinkle tomatoes with additional salt and pepper to taste. Scatter pine nuts and parsley overtop.

Variations
Substitute salmon, mackerel or lobster for the tuna.

Tuna, Egg and Fresh Bean Salad

Sometimes the simplest pleasures are the best, such as this down-to-earth, nourishing dinner salad.

Makes 4 servings

• Healthy

Tip

If you don't have a steamer, cook the beans in boiling salted water for about 5 minutes, until tender-crisp, or cook them in a microwave oven.

• **Steamer**

Dressing

2 tbsp	oil drained from tuna (approx.)	30 mL
2 tbsp	extra virgin olive oil (approx.)	30 mL
2 tbsp	white wine vinegar	30 mL
1 tbsp	chopped fresh basil leaves	15 mL
½ tsp	Dijon mustard	2 mL
¼ tsp	salt (approx.)	1 mL
¼ tsp	freshly ground black pepper	1 mL

Salad

1 lb	mixed green and yellow wax beans, trimmed	500 g
	Salt	
4	large leaves leaf lettuce	4
2	cans (each 3 oz/85 g) tuna in olive oil, drained (oil reserved) and broken into chunks	2
4	eggs, hard-cooked and halved or quartered	4
¼ cup	finely chopped red onion	60 mL

1. *Dressing:* Pour oil from the tuna into a small measuring cup. Add enough extra virgin olive oil to equal ¼ cup (60 mL). Whisk in vinegar, basil, mustard, salt and pepper.

2. *Salad:* Over a pan of simmering water, steam beans for about 10 minutes, until tender-crisp. Transfer to a colander and rinse under cold running water to stop the cooking.

3. Transfer beans to a medium bowl and add dressing. Toss well. Add salt to taste, if necessary.

4. Line a serving platter or individual bowls with lettuce. Arrange beans overtop, dividing equally. Scatter tuna over beans, dividing equally. Arrange eggs around the edges and scatter onion overtop. Serve immediately.

Variations

Substitute salmon, mackerel, cod or lobster for the tuna.

Salad Niçoise (page 30)

Golden Purses (page 68) and Salsa Verde (page 48)

Faux Pho (page 79)

Thai Tuna Salad (page 90)

Citrusy Crab and Sprouts (page 98)

Lobster, Avocado and Red Onion
Club Sandwiches (variation) (page113)

Fish Tacos (page 124)

Jerk Salmon Sliders (page 132)

California Salad, Starring Salmon

What is California salad, anyway? It usually involves tossing nuts and fruit with baby greens, but otherwise it seems to be a free-for-all. Walnuts and grapes add appealing texture and a pleasant sweet-and-sour effect to this surprising combination with salmon.

Makes 4 small servings

- Fast
- Brown-bag

Tips

The drier, less expensive pink salmon is fine for this because the mayonnaise moistens it.

If you're brown-bagging this salad, pack the greens separately and combine when you're ready to eat.

Toast walnuts in a dry skillet over medium heat, shaking the pan often, for about 3 minutes, until fragrant and starting to brown. Transfer to a bowl to cool.

Dressing

¼ cup	mayonnaise	60 mL
2 tbsp	extra virgin olive oil	30 mL
½ tsp	Dijon mustard	2 mL
⅛ tsp	salt	0.5 mL
⅛ tsp	freshly ground black pepper	0.5 mL
1 tbsp	chopped parsley leaves	15 mL
1 tbsp	chopped basil leaves	15 mL

Salad

1	can (6 oz/170 g) pink salmon, drained, deboned and broken into chunks	1
½ cup	walnut pieces, toasted (see Tips, left)	125 mL
½ cup	seedless red grapes, quartered	125 mL
3	green onions (white and light green parts), thinly sliced	3
	Salt	
4 cups	mixed baby greens	1 L

1. *Dressing:* In a measuring cup, whisk together mayonnaise, oil, mustard, salt, pepper, parsley and basil, until blended.

2. *Salad:* In a bowl, combine salmon, walnuts, grapes and onions. Add dressing and toss to coat. Season to taste with salt.

3. Place greens on a serving platter or four individual dishes. Spoon salmon mixture overtop. Serve immediately.

Variations

Stuff the salad into a pita or wrap and reduce the quantity of greens.

Substitute tuna for the salmon.

Tangerine Salmon Salad

This dish is pretty as well as being healthful. Serve it with crusty bread.

Makes 2 servings

- Fast
- Healthy

Tips

This recipe makes about ⅔ cup (150 mL) dressing. Use the leftover portion on other salads, or drizzle it on steamed fish or poached chicken.

Variations

Substitute tuna or crab for the salmon.

Dressing

6 tbsp	freshly squeezed tangerine juice	90 mL
¼ cup	extra virgin olive oil	60 mL
1	small clove garlic, minced	1
1 tsp	Dijon mustard	5 mL
½ tsp	finely grated tangerine zest	2 mL
¼ tsp	salt	1 mL
⅛ tsp	freshly ground black pepper	0.5 mL

Salad

4 cups	mixed baby greens	1 L
1	can (7½ oz/213 g) sockeye salmon, drained, deboned and broken into chunks	1
2	green onions (white and light green parts), thinly sliced	2

1. *Dressing:* In a small bowl, whisk together tangerine juice, oil, garlic, mustard, tangerine zest, salt and pepper.

2. *Salad:* Arrange the greens on serving plates, dividing equally. Scatter salmon overtop. Drizzle about 2 tbsp (30 mL) dressing over each. Sprinkle with onions.

Citrusy Crab and Sprouts

The fragrant orange accents in the dressing work well with delicate crab.

Makes 2 small servings

- Fast
- Guest-worthy

Tip

Use your favorite sprouts, such as pea, broccoli or onion sprouts, or try micro-greens — the tiny edible shoots of lettuces and vegetables — such as mizuna or kale. Micro-greens can be purchased individually or in blends. Look for them at greengrocers, specialty food shops and some supermarkets.

¼ cup	mayonnaise	60 mL
1	small clove garlic, minced	1
½ tsp	finely grated orange zest	2 mL
1½ tsp	freshly squeezed orange juice	7 mL
1	can (4.25 oz/120 g) chunk crabmeat, rinsed and drained	1
	Salt and freshly ground black pepper	
2	small leaves Boston lettuce	2
1½ cups	sprouts or micro-greens, coarsely chopped	375 mL
2	cocktail tomatoes (such as Campari), cut in wedges (see Tips, page 35)	2

1. In a bowl, stir together mayonnaise, garlic and orange zest and juice. Gently squeeze excess moisture from crab and add it to the bowl. Season to taste with salt and pepper.

2. Place lettuce on serving plates and mound crab mixture on top. Scatter sprouts overtop and finish with tomato wedges. Sprinkle additional pepper over the tomato.

Old-School Spinach Salad with Shrimp and Poppyseed Dressing

Adding seafood upgrades this popular bacon- and mushroom-studded spinach salad into a meal. I'm not crazy about sweet dressings, but my version of poppyseed vinaigrette hits the spot. It tastes like the classic kind but doesn't include the massive quantities of sugar used in older recipes.

Makes 4 to 6 servings

- Kid-friendly
- Guest-worthy

Tips

I use corn oil to give the dressing a classic flavor, but you can use any neutral vegetable or seed oil, such as canola. Olive oil, however, is too bold for this dressing.

This recipe makes about ¾ cup (175 mL) dressing. You can use the leftover portion on other hearty green or fruit salads. Poppy seed dressing is often paired with salads that include apples, pears and strawberries.

Variations

Substitute an equal quantity of salmon, crab or lobster for the shrimp.

● **Blender**

Dressing

2 tbsp	liquid honey	30 mL
2 tbsp	apple cider vinegar	30 mL
2 tbsp	diced onion	30 mL
½ tsp	Dijon mustard	2 mL
½ tsp	salt	2 mL
½ cup	oil (see Tips, left)	125 mL
2 tsp	poppy seeds	10 mL

Salad

4	slices bacon, chopped	4
8 cups	baby spinach leaves (about 4 oz/125 g)	2 L
½ cup	thinly sliced red onion rings	125 mL
1 cup	thinly sliced button mushrooms (about 2 oz/60 g)	250 mL
1	can (4 oz/106 g) small shrimp, drained	1
2	large eggs, hard-cooked and quartered	2
2 tbsp	dried cranberries, optional	30 mL
2 tbsp	slivered almonds, optional	30 mL

1. *Dressing:* In blender, combine honey, vinegar, onion, mustard and salt. With the motor running, gradually drizzle in oil through the hole in the lid, blending until smooth and creamy looking. Transfer to a small airtight container. Stir in poppy seeds.

2. *Salad:* In a skillet over medium heat, cook bacon for about 5 minutes, until browned and crisp. Using a slotted spoon, transfer to a plate lined with paper towels. Set aside.

3. Place spinach on serving plates, dividing equally. Scatter onion, mushrooms and shrimp evenly overtop and arrange egg wedges around the edges. Sprinkle cranberries and almonds, if using, and reserved bacon overtop. Drizzle with dressing or serve it alongside.

Sardines Caprese

Simple Caprese salad, which comes from the isle of Capri, is the epitome of sunny Mediterranean flavors. Sardines are also a favorite in the region, so why not combine the two? Serve this with crusty bread to mop up the tangy juices, of which there are plenty.

Makes 4 servings

- Fast
- Healthy
- Guest-worthy

Tips

If you have premium olive oil, now is the time to use it, to make the Mediterranean flavors shine.

Cut each sardine in half so you have two intact sides with the skin on.

2	ripe tomatoes (each 8 to 10 oz/250 to 300 g), cored and cut into $\frac{1}{2}$-inch (1 cm) slices	2
8 oz	buffalo mozzarella, drained and cut into $\frac{1}{4}$-inch (0.5 cm) slices	250 g
10	large basil leaves	10
1	can (3.75 oz/106 g) sardines, drained and cut in half lengthwise (see Tips, left)	1
2 tbsp	extra virgin olive oil	30 mL
1 tbsp	balsamic vinegar	15 mL
1	clove garlic, minced	1
$\frac{1}{4}$ tsp	salt	1 mL
$\frac{1}{8}$ tsp	freshly ground black pepper	0.5 mL

1. Place sliced tomatoes on platter or individual serving plates. Top each slice with a similar-sized piece of mozzarella, a basil leaf and a sardine half, skin side up.

2. In a small bowl, whisk together oil, vinegar, garlic, salt and pepper. Drizzle over the tomato stacks. Serve immediately.

Variations

Buffalo mozzarella is pricy. If you prefer, use less expensive alternatives such as fior de latte, which is made with cow's milk, or even the firmer bocconcini balls.

On a platter you can create a traditional overlapping pattern, alternating the ingredients in circles instead of stacking them.

Substitute an equal quantity of tuna, salmon, mackerel, cod, sprats or shrimp for the sardines. If substituting flaky fish such as tuna, break it into large chunks and put one chunk on top of each stack, or flake it and scatter over an overlapping pattern of the other ingredients.

Retro Tuna Salad Pasta

A pinch of nostalgia is the secret ingredient in this salad. I used to mix this up when I was a kid. It may be old-fashioned, but members of my family, both young and old, still gobble it up.

Makes 7 cups (1.75 L)
6 to 8 servings

- Fast
- Kid-friendly
- Brown-bag

Tips

I prefer to use the tender inner stalks of celery known as the heart. You can, however, tenderize an outside stalk by peeling it.

Cover and refrigerate leftovers for up to 3 days. The pasta will soak up the mayonnaise as it sits in the fridge. Revive leftovers by stirring in a tiny bit of cream or hot water.

8 oz	large pasta shells	250 g
1	can (6 oz/170 g) tuna in water, drained and broken into small chunks	1
1	stalk celery heart with leaves, cut in small dice (see Tips, left)	1
½	red bell pepper, cut in small dice	½
½ to ¾ cup	diced red onion	125 to 175 mL
½ cup	chopped sweet pickles	125 mL
½ cup	mayonnaise	125 mL
	Salt and freshly ground black pepper	
1 tbsp	chopped parsley leaves, optional	15 mL

1. In a large pot of boiling salted water, cook pasta over medium heat for about 12 minutes, until tender to the bite (al dente). Drain and rinse under cold running water until it cools to room temperature. Drain well.

2. Transfer to a large serving bowl. Add tuna, celery, red pepper, onion to taste, and pickles. Toss. Add mayonnaise and season to taste with salt and pepper. Mix well. Sprinkle parsley, if using, overtop. Serve immediately.

Variations

When tempted to embellish this salad, I add coarsely chopped pitted black olives.

If you think your family will eat all of this salad right after it is prepared, you can add diced tomato to taste. Do not add it if you expect to refrigerate the salad, because the tomato will develop an unappetizing texture.

Substitute an equal quantity of dill pickles for the sweet ones, and sliced green onions for the red ones.

Substitute an equal quantity of salmon, mackerel, sardines, sprats, kippers or shrimp for the tuna.

Cajun Pasta Salad

This addictive salad takes some cues from muffuletta, New Orleans' famous olive salad. It is a treat to eat and easy to make.

Tips

Cover and refrigerate leftovers for up to 3 days.

What with the olives, shrimp and Cajun seasoning, you probably won't need any salt.

Shake and toss pasta shells in the colander when draining them — the little cups hold water.

8 oz	small pasta shells	250 g
½ cup	mayonnaise	125 mL
1	clove garlic, minced	1
1 to 1½ tsp	Cajun seasoning	5 to 7 mL
15	small pimiento-stuffed green olives, sliced	15
10	black olives, pitted and chopped	10
2	stalks celery heart with leaves, chopped	2
1	can (4 oz/106 g) small shrimp, rinsed and drained	1
2 tbsp	chopped parsley leaves, divided	30 mL
	Salt, optional	

1. In a large pot of boiling salted water, cook pasta over high heat for about 7 minutes, until tender to the bite (al dente). Drain and rinse under cold running water until it cools to room temperature. Drain well.

2. In a bowl, combine mayonnaise, garlic and Cajun seasoning to taste.

3. In a serving bowl, combine pasta, olives, celery, shrimp and 1 tbsp (15 mL) parsley. Scrape mayonnaise mixture overtop and mix well. Season to taste with salt, if using (see Tips, left). Sprinkle remaining parsley overtop. Serve immediately.

Variations

Substitute an equal quantity of tuna, salmon, mackerel, cod, crab or lobster for the shrimp.

Thai Shrimp Noodle Salad

This noodle salad is so fresh and pretty. It's tough to stop eating it, but in this case overindulging won't break the calorie bank.

Tips

To shred basil leaves, stack them, roll them together like a cigar and slice thinly crosswise.

If you don't want to use peanut oil, substitute any neutral vegetable or seed oil.

Variations

You can use vermicelli or thin rice-stick noodles. Boil them for 2 to 3 minutes.

Substitute an equal quantity of salmon, crab or lobster for the shrimp.

Dressing

⅓ cup	peanut oil (see Tips, left)	75 mL
¼ cup	freshly squeezed lime juice	60 mL
2	cloves garlic, minced	2
1 tbsp	honey	15 mL
1 tbsp	fish sauce	15 mL
½ tsp	hot pepper flakes	2 mL
½ tsp	salt (approx.)	2 mL

Salad

3	mini cucumbers, unpeeled (6 to 8 oz/ 175 to 250 g total), thinly sliced	3
¼ tsp	salt (approx.)	1 mL
8 oz	rice noodles (⅛ to ¼ inch/3 to 5 mm wide)	250 g
4 cups	shredded leaf lettuce	1 L
1	carrot (about 2 oz/60 g), shredded	1
½ cup	thinly sliced red onion	125 mL
½	red bell pepper, thinly sliced (about ½ cup/125 mL)	½
1	can (4 oz/106 g) small shrimp, rinsed and drained	1
¼ cup	unsalted roasted peanuts, coarsely chopped	60 mL
¼ cup	shredded basil leaves (see Tips, left)	60 mL

1. *Dressing:* In a small saucepan, combine peanut oil, lime juice, garlic, honey, fish sauce, hot pepper flakes and salt. Bring to a boil over medium-high heat and boil for 2 minutes. Remove from heat and set aside to cool.

2. *Salad:* In a sieve, toss cucumbers with salt. Place over a large bowl and set aside to drain for 30 minutes.

3. Meanwhile, in a large pot of boiling salted water, cook noodles over medium heat for 5 minutes, until just tender. Drain and rinse under cold running water until they cool to room temperature. Drain well.

4. Line a serving platter with lettuce and top with noodles. Pat cucumber dry and scatter overtop. Scatter carrot, onion, red pepper and shrimp over cucumber. Drizzle with dressing and garnish with peanuts and basil.

Potato Salad with Smoked Oysters and Roasted Peppers

This isn't your grandma's potato salad — but she might enjoy it too.

Tips

To roast peppers: Preheat broiler. Place peppers on a baking sheet and broil, turning three times, until skin on all sides is blackened, about 15 minutes. Place in a paper bag, fold the top closed and set aside until peppers are cool enough to handle. (Alternatively, instead of using a bag, place the peppers in a bowl and cover with a plate or plastic wrap.) Using a sharp knife, lift off skins. Discard skins, stems and seeds and slice thinly.

Cover leftovers and refrigerate for up to 1 day.

Variations

The smoked oysters and charred roasted peppers make this salad pleasantly smoky. If you prefer, triple the smokiness factor by tossing the spuds with a bit of oil and grilling them instead of boiling.

This recipe works well with smoked mussels too. You can also substitute an equal quantity of smoked sprats or kippers for the oysters.

Dressing

2 tbsp	oil drained from smoked oysters (approx.)	30 mL
2 tbsp	extra virgin olive oil (approx.)	30 mL
2 tsp	freshly squeezed lemon juice	10 mL
1/2 tbsp	champagne or sherry vinegar	8 mL
1/8 tsp	Dijon mustard	0.5 mL
2 tsp	chopped fresh dill fronds	10 mL
1/4 tsp	salt	1 mL
1/8 tsp	freshly ground black pepper	0.5 mL

Salad

1 lb	mini red potatoes (1 to 1 1/2 inches/2.5 to 4 cm in diameter)	500 g
	Salt	
2	roasted red bell peppers, peeled, seeded and cut in 1/2-inch (1 cm) squares, with juices	2
1	can (3 oz/85 g) smoked oysters, drained (oil reserved)	1
1 tbsp	chopped fresh dill fronds	15 mL

1. *Dressing:* Pour oil from oysters into a small measuring cup. Add enough olive oil to make 1/4 cup (60 mL). Whisk in lemon juice, vinegar, mustard, dill, salt and pepper.

2. *Salad:* In a large pot of boiling salted water, cook potatoes for 10 to 15 minutes, until tender but firm. Drain and set aside to cool for 5 minutes.

3. Cut potatoes in half and transfer to a serving bowl. Toss with enough dressing to coat generously (you may have some dressing left over). Set aside until cooled to room temperature.

4. Add roasted peppers and their juices to potatoes. Season to taste with salt and stir gently. Scatter oysters over potato mixture and garnish with dill. Serve immediately.

Italian Tuna, Potato and Green Bean Salad

Europeans appreciate the many possibilities of canned tuna. Take this potato salad, for instance. The tuna makes it substantial, yet it still tastes light and fresh because it is tossed with dressing instead of mayonnaise.

Makes 4 to 6 servings

- Healthy
- Brown-bag
- Guest-worthy

Tips

Dressing: Drain the oil from the tuna into a small measuring cup. Add enough extra virgin olive oil to equal ¼ cup (60 mL). Whisk in 2 tbsp (30 mL) freshly squeezed lemon juice, 1 small clove garlic, minced, ½ tsp (2 mL) salt and ¼ tsp (1 mL) freshly ground black pepper.

I prefer to use yellow-fleshed potatoes in this recipe. They hold their shape but add a hint of creaminess, a welcome addition to a mayonnaise-free potato salad. However, waxy red potatoes will work. Avoid russets in potato salad because they are too floury.

Variations

Speed up the preparation by using mini potatoes, which will take less than 15 minutes to cook and needn't be peeled.

Substitute salmon, mackerel, cod, sardines or sprats for the tuna.

8 oz	green beans, trimmed and halved (about 2 cups/500 mL)	250 g
4	potatoes, scrubbed (about 1 lb/500 g)	4
	Salt	
	Dressing (see Tips, left)	
2	cans (each 3 oz/85 g) solid tuna in olive oil, drained (oil reserved) and broken into chunks	2
1	stalk celery heart, cut in small dice	1
2 tbsp	chopped celery leaves	30 mL
2 tbsp	chopped basil	30 mL
1 tbsp	chopped parsley leaves	15 mL
12	black olives, pitted and halved	12

1. In a pot of boiling salted water, cook beans over medium heat for about 5 minutes, until tender-crisp. Using a mesh scoop, transfer to a colander. Rinse under cold running water to stop the cooking. Drain.

2. Add potatoes to the same pot of water and return to a boil. Cook for 15 to 20 minutes, until tender but firm. Transfer to a colander and drain, then rinse under cold running water to stop the cooking. When potatoes are cool enough to handle, peel and slice into rounds ½ inch (1 cm) thick.

3. Arrange potato slices on a serving plate in overlapping rows. Drizzle with 2 tbsp (30 mL) dressing and sprinkle lightly with salt. Top with tuna, then celery, then beans. Drizzle with additional dressing.

4. In a small bowl, toss together celery leaves, basil and parsley. Scatter mixture over salad. Scatter olives overtop. Set assembled salad aside at room temperature for 10 minutes before serving, to meld flavors.

Basque-Style Shrimp, Ham and Potato Salad

Here's a hearty, colorful main-course salad. The smoked paprika and saffron push it to four-star status.

Tip

This salad should be served at room temperature, when the flavors and textures are at their best. Refrigeration toughens and dries out cooked potatoes.

Variations

Use fingerling potatoes when available.

If you can't find Serrano ham, substitute prosciutto.

Substitute an equal quantity of cod or clams for the shrimp.

1 lb	mini potatoes, scrubbed	500 g
¼ cup	extra virgin olive oil	60 mL
1	bunch green onions (white and green parts), sliced	1
½	green bell pepper, cut in small dice	½
½	red bell pepper, cut in small dice	½
½ tsp	saffron, crumbled	2 mL
½ cup	chopped parsley leaves	125 mL
1 tbsp	sherry vinegar	15 mL
½ tsp	salt (approx.)	2 mL
⅛ tsp	freshly ground black pepper	0.5 mL
4	slices Serrano ham (about 2 oz/60 g), chopped	4
1	can (4 oz/106 g) small shrimp, rinsed and drained	1
	Smoked hot or sweet paprika	

1. In a large pot of boiling salted water, cook potatoes over medium heat for 10 to 15 minutes, until tender but firm. Transfer to a colander and drain. Set aside to cool for 5 minutes.

2. Meanwhile, in a skillet, heat oil over medium heat until shimmery. Add green onions, bell peppers and saffron. Cook, stirring, for 1 minute, until vegetables soften slightly. Remove from heat and set aside to cool for 2 minutes. Stir in parsley, vinegar, salt to taste and pepper.

3. Cut potatoes into halves or quarters (depending on size) and transfer to a large serving bowl. Add onion and pepper mixture and toss gently. Set aside until cooled to room temperature, about 30 minutes.

4. Add ham and shrimp and toss gently. Season to taste with additional salt, if necessary. Sprinkle smoked paprika overtop.

Sandwiches and Wraps

Triple-Decker Triangle Sandwiches

No one, it seems, can resist the simple charm of dainty crustless tea sandwiches, also known as finger sandwiches or party sandwiches. The soft, spongy bread and savory fillings are reminiscent of childhood comfort food, but you still feel refined while indulging.

**Makes
32 triangles**

- Fast
- Kid-friendly
- Brown-bag
- Guest-worthy

Tips

Making tea sandwiches is not the time to experiment with rustic artisan bread. Buy old-fashioned sandwich bread with a moist, dense crumb. If you can find it, purchase a Pullman loaf, which is baked in a pan with a lid to create even, square edges. Because it doesn't have the standard indent near the top of the loaf, you'll end up with larger, neater slices and won't have to cut off as much crust.

When I arrange the bread in sets, I like to use a combination of white and whole wheat bread for each sandwich, for healthier and more attractive little bites.

Weighting the sandwiches makes them easier to cut and neater looking. The goal is to compress, not flatten. The softer and fresher the bread, the less time this will take. Whole wheat bread, which is firmer, takes a bit longer.

- **Baking sheets and light weights**

12	slices whole wheat sandwich bread	12
12	slices white sandwich bread	12
	Soft butter or mayonnaise	
3 cups	Vintage Tuna Salad (page 26) or Classic Salmon Salad (page 27) (approx.)	750 mL
16	pieces Boston lettuce leaves	16

1. Arrange bread slices on a baking sheet in eight sets of three (see Tips, left). Working with one set at a time, lightly smear two slices with butter on one side only, right to the edges. Smear the third slice on both sides, right to the edges. Spread about 3 tbsp (45 mL) tuna or salmon salad on bottom slice, leaving a narrow border. Top with a piece of lettuce. Cover with double-buttered slice of bread. Spread about 3 tbsp (45 mL) tuna or salmon salad on that slice, leaving a narrow border. Top with a piece of lettuce and the remaining slice of bread.

2. Repeat with remaining sets of bread and other ingredients.

3. Place a second baking sheet over the sandwiches and put light weights (such as cans) on top. Set aside until slightly compressed, about 5 minutes, depending on the texture of the bread.

4. Using a serrated knife, cut off the crusts and cut each sandwich into 4 triangles.

Variations

Inexperienced? For the fastest, easiest triangles, make regular double-decker sandwiches rather than triple-deckers, then quarter them.

If desired, you can use round cookie cutters to make perfectly circular sandwiches, or try other shapes. Alternatively, cut each sandwich into three or four fingers.

For the filling, instead of using tuna or salmon salad, you can substitute any fish or seafood salad, including mackerel, shrimp, crab or lobster. If desired, use an international variation of tuna salad (pages 86 to 87) or Tuna Salad Cream Cheese (page 88).

Pinwheel Sandwiches

Pinwheels are surely the ultimate party sandwich. They are suitable for occasions ranging from wedding showers to cocktail parties, and appeal to all ages.

Tips

When buying bread to make pinwheel sandwiches, ask the bakery to slice the loaf lengthwise for you. The alternative – doing it yourself – is a tricky job, even if you freeze the bread first.

Expect to end up with about seven usable lengthwise slices per loaf.

Coating the bread thinly to the edges with soft butter or full-fat mayonnaise before adding the filling prevents sogginess. For the thinnest coating, use whipped butter.

1	loaf white sandwich bread (about 1¼ lb/675 g), cut lengthwise into ½-inch (1 cm) thick slices, crusts removed	1
	Soft butter or mayonnaise	
3½ cups	Vintage Tuna Salad (page 26) or Classic Salmon Salad (page 27) (approx.)	825 mL

1. Working with one slice at a time, place bread on a clean work surface and, using a rolling pin, flatten slightly. Spread top lightly with butter, right to the edges. Spread about ½ cup (125 mL) tuna or salmon salad evenly over butter. Starting with the short edge closest to you, tightly roll up bread and filling, jelly-roll style. Place each roll seam side down and wrap tightly in plastic. Repeat with remaining bread and filling. Refrigerate for 1 hour to firm up.

2. Unwrap, using a serrated knife trim ragged edges if necessary, and slice each roll crosswise into 6 pinwheels.

Whipped Butter

You can buy whipped butter or make it yourself. To do so, use an electric mixer on medium-high speed to beat room-temperature butter in a bowl for 30 to 60 seconds, until the volume increases, the color lightens and the texture becomes fluffy.

Fishy Telescopes

These kid-pleasing cylinder-shaped sandwiches are fun for parties and sleepovers. A change from ordinary sandwiches, they are rolled and eaten whole.

10	slices white or whole wheat sandwich bread, crusts removed	10
1	recipe Tuna Salad Cream Cheese (page 88)	1

1. Working with one slice at a time, place bread on a clean work surface and, using a rolling pin, flatten slightly. Spread top with about 2 tbsp (30 mL) filling, right to the edges. Starting with the short edge closest to you, tightly roll up bread and filling, jelly-roll style. Place seam side down on a plate and serve immediately.

Tuna McMelts

In this twist on a certain fast-food chain's breakfast sandwiches, tuna replaces the ham. These are yummy, although the cheese is more wilted than melted.

Makes 4 servings

- Fast
- Kid-friendly

Tips

To maintain more control over the final result, I always use unsalted butter in recipes. With salted butter, the amount of salt varies by brand. And salted butter contains more moisture, which can affect some recipes. Salt also masks rancidity.

If you prefer, after adding the cheese, heat the muffin halves in a microwave oven on High for 10 to 15 seconds to slightly melt the cheese.

Use the individually packaged cheese singles labeled "Cheddar-style." Processed cheese is often called American cheese. It is produced from cheese and other ingredients.

If you don't have egg rings, use tuna or salmon cans with the tops and bottoms removed.

Here's a handy alternative to using egg rings if you are making just one or two of these sandwiches at a time: grease a 2-cup (500 mL) microwave-safe measuring cup. Crack an egg into it and pierce the yolk with a fork. Microwave the egg on Medium-High for 30 to 40 seconds, until the white is firm but the yolk is slightly wet, then let it sit for 10 seconds.

- **4 egg rings, greased**

1	can (6 oz/170 g) chunk tuna in water, drained and broken into flakes	1
2 tbsp	mayonnaise	30 mL
4	English muffins, split	4
2 tbsp	unsalted butter (approx.), softened	30 mL
4	large eggs	4
4	slices processed cheese singles (see Tips, left)	4

1. Gently squeeze excess moisture from tuna and place it in a bowl. Add mayonnaise and, using a fork, mash together. Set aside.

2. Toast muffin halves and spread with butter.

3. Heat a nonstick skillet over medium heat. Place egg rings in skillet and crack eggs into rings. Pierce yolks with a fork. Cook for about 3 minutes or until whites are firm but yolks are still slightly wet.

4. Meanwhile, spread tuna mixture over bottom halves of muffins. Lay cheese slices over tuna. Place on serving plates.

5. Slide a spatula under each egg ring, flip it and, if necessary, loosen edges with a knife to release the egg. Remove the rings and transfer eggs to muffins. Replace tops of muffins.

Variations

Substitute an equal quantity of salmon, mackerel or shrimp for the tuna.

Little Italy Tuna Melts

Focaccia and caponata relish push the tuna melt into the 21st century.

Tip

If you prefer, substitute store-bought caponata for the homemade version.

Variations

Substitute salmon, mackerel, sardines, sprats, shrimp or lobster for the tuna.

- **Preheat oven to 400°F (200°F)**
- **Baking sheet, nonstick or lined with parchment**

1	square rosemary focaccia loaf (about 12 oz/375 g), crusts trimmed	1
1	can (6 oz/170 g) chunk tuna in water, drained and broken into flakes	1
2 cups	Caponata (page 60)	500 mL
8	slices provolone cheese, cut in half	8

1. Cut focaccia into 8 slices, each about 1 inch (2.5 cm) thick. Toast lightly.

2. Gently squeeze excess moisture from tuna and transfer it to a bowl. Add caponata and blend with a fork.

3. Spread about ¼ cup (60 mL) tuna mixture evenly over each focaccia slice and transfer to prepared pan as completed. Top with equal quantities of cheese. Bake in preheated oven for 5 to 7 minutes, until cheese melts. Serve immediately.

Tarragon Lobster Rolls

When you are craving a more adventurous lobster roll, try this.

Makes 2 rolls

- Kid-friendly
- Brown-bag
- Guest-worthy

Tips

Use a tender inner stalk of celery for best results.

If you're serving more than two people, double or triple the quantity to suit your needs.

Variations

Turn this into a salad: Serve the lobster mixture on a bed of greens.

Substitute shrimp or crab for the lobster.

½ cup	mayonnaise	125 mL
2	green onions (white and light green parts), chopped	2
¼ cup	finely chopped celery	60 mL
2 tbsp	finely chopped red bell pepper	30 mL
2 tsp	finely chopped tarragon leaves	10 mL
1 tsp	freshly squeezed lime juice	5 mL
1½ cups	canned lobster meat (8 oz/250 g), rinsed, drained and coarsely chopped	375 mL
	Salt and freshly ground white pepper	
2	small whole-grain sub-shaped buns, split and toasted until golden	2
2 cups	baby greens or torn lettuce	500 mL

1. In a bowl, stir together mayonnaise, onions, celery, red pepper, tarragon and lime juice. Gently squeeze lobster to remove excess moisture. Add to bowl and blend with a fork. Season to taste with salt and pepper.

2. Spread lobster mixture over bottoms of buns and top with greens. Replace tops of buns and serve immediately.

CBLT

What could be better than a BLT? A CBLT — a crab, bacon, lettuce and tomato sandwich. Crab tossed with peppery lime mayonnaise puts this mainstay sandwich over the top.

**Makes
4 sandwiches**

- Fast
- Kid-friendly
- Guest-worthy

Tips

The oven is the best place to cook a large number of bacon slices without a big mess.

You can use two 4.25-oz (120 g) shelf-stable cans of chunk crabmeat or half of a 1-lb (440 g) container of pasteurized crab claw meat. To use up leftovers, check the chart on pages 272 to 278 for other delicious crab recipes.

- **Preheat oven to 450°F (230°C)**
- **Rimmed baking sheet**
- **Wire rack**

Lime Mayo

1/3 cup	mayonnaise	75 mL
1 tsp	finely grated lime zest	5 mL
1 tbsp	freshly squeezed lime juice	15 mL
1/8 tsp	salt	0.5 mL
1/4 tsp	freshly ground black pepper	1 mL

Sandwiches

12	slices bacon	12
8	slices white or whole wheat sandwich bread	8
4	small leaves Boston lettuce	4
2	tomatoes, thinly sliced	2
	Salt	
1 1/2 cups	crabmeat (8 oz/250 g), rinsed and drained (see Tips, left)	375 mL

1. *Lime Mayo:* In a measuring cup, stir together mayonnaise, lime zest and juice, salt and pepper.

2. *Sandwiches:* Lay bacon on wire rack and place on baking sheet. Bake in preheated oven for 15 to 20 minutes, turning halfway through, until crisp. Transfer to a plate lined with paper towels and drain.

3. Toast bread until it is golden but not crisp. Lay 4 slices on a work surface. Smear each with a thin layer of lime mayo. Place 3 slices of bacon on each slice of bread. Top with 1 lettuce leaf and tomato slices, dividing equally. Season to taste with salt.

4. Squeeze the crab gently to remove excess moisture and transfer to a bowl. Add remaining lime mayo and stir gently. Spoon mixture over tomato slices and spread evenly. Top with remaining bread.

5. Cut each sandwich into 2 triangles and serve immediately.

> ### Variations
> Substitute an equal quantity of chopped shrimp or lobster for the crab.

Salmon, Avocado and Red Onion Club Sandwiches

The iconic triple-decker club sandwich has evolved considerably beyond its standard chicken and bacon filling. This version calls for salmon, but it also works with other seafood. Culinary historians date the club back to the late 19th century. They think it originated in country clubs or men's social clubs, particularly one gambling establishment for gentlemen in Saratoga Springs, New York. The sandwich actually started as a double-decker, not a triple-decker. Add a retro touch by serving it with sweet gherkins and potato chips.

**Makes
2 sandwiches**

- Fast
- Guest-worthy

Variations

Substitute an equal quantity of tuna or chopped shrimp or lobster for the salmon.

4	slices bacon	4
¼ cup	mayonnaise	60 mL
1 tsp	freshly squeezed lemon juice	5 mL
2 tsp	chopped parsley leaves	10 mL
6	slices whole wheat bread	6
2	small leaves Boston lettuce	2
½	tomato, thinly sliced	½
	Salt and freshly ground black pepper	
½	ripe but firm avocado, thinly sliced	½
1	can (7½ oz/170 g) salmon, drained, deboned and broken into chunks	1
¼ cup	thinly sliced red onion	60 mL

1. In a skillet over medium-high heat, cook bacon for about 5 minutes, until browned and crisp. Transfer to a plate lined with paper towels to drain.

2. In a measuring cup, mix mayonnaise, lemon juice and parsley.

3. Toast bread until golden but not crisp. Arrange slices on a work surface in two sets of three. Lightly smear two slices with mayonnaise on one side only and smear the third slice on both sides. Repeat with second set.

4. Working with first set, with mayo side up, place lettuce leaf on bottom slice. Top with half of the bacon and 2 tomato slices (you will have some left over). Season to taste with salt and pepper. Top with half the avocado and the bread slice spread on both sides with mayo.

5. Mix salmon with remaining mayonnaise mixture. Spread half over top slice of bread. Arrange half the onion over salmon. Cover with third slice of bread, mayo side down, and press together gently. Repeat with second set of bread and remaining ingredients.

6. Cut each sandwich into 4 triangles and secure each with a toothpick. Serve immediately.

Nutty Salmon and Spinach Wraps

Nuts add a pleasant crunch to this herbed salmon salad, which is wrapped in a whole wheat tortilla. The result has a wholesome appeal.

Makes 2 wraps

- Fast
- Brown-bag

Tips

You can use lower-fat mayonnaise to keep the calorie count down.

Toast walnuts in a dry skillet over medium heat for about 3 minutes, until fragrant and turning golden.

Slice the spinach by stacking the leaves in a pile, rolling them up like a cigar and then cutting crosswise.

1/4 cup	mayonnaise (see Tips, left)	60 mL
2	green onions (white and green parts), finely chopped	2
1/2 tsp	Dijon mustard	5 mL
1 tbsp	chopped basil leaves	15 mL
1 tbsp	chopped parsley leaves	15 mL
1	can (7 1/2 oz/213 g) salmon, drained, deboned and broken into chunks	1
1/4 cup	walnuts or pecans, toasted and chopped (see Tips, left)	60 mL
2 tbsp	dried cranberries, optional	30 mL
	Salt and freshly ground black pepper	
2	small whole wheat tortillas (6 1/2 inches/ 17 cm in diameter)	2
1 cup	finely sliced spinach leaves	250 mL

1. In a bowl, using a fork, stir together mayonnaise, green onions, mustard, basil and parsley. Gently squeeze salmon to remove excess moisture and add it to the bowl. Add walnuts and cranberries, if using, and mix well. Season to taste with salt and pepper.

2. Lay tortillas on a work surface and spread with salmon mixture, leaving a 2-inch (5 cm) border on the right. Top with spinach leaves. Fold up about 1 inch (2.5 cm) of bottom edge of each tortilla, then roll tightly from left to right. Lay seam side down on work surface.

3. Wrap each tightly in a napkin, leaving top exposed. Serve immediately.

Variation

Substitute an equal quantity of tuna for the salmon.

Tuna Muffuletta Sandwiches

Fish goes wonderfully well with olive salad, which means you can easily transform the famous New Orleans muffuletta into a healthier dish by substituting fish for the traditional salami and ham. The hearty muffuletta sandwich was invented in 1906 by a Sicilian who ran Central Grocery, an Italian-American store in the city's French Quarter.

Makes 4 to 6 sandwiches

• Healthy

Tips

Although kalamatas are traditionally used in the olive salad, I prefer the richness of crinkly black olives.

You can buy green olives that are already pitted, but black olives tend to be sold unpitted because they are riper and softer. Avoid the canned pitted black olives.

Don't overdo the chopping — you want olive salad, not paste.

Variations

Go upscale by choosing tuna in olive oil. Drain and reserve the oil and substitute it for some of the extra virgin olive oil in the salad.

You can make this using individual rolls instead of a whole loaf of bread.

Hot pepper flakes are good in this olive salad, or try chopped peperoncini for a kick. Add them to taste.

Substitute an equal quantity of salmon or mackerel for the tuna.

Olive Salad

2/3 cup	black olives, pitted and finely chopped	150 mL
2/3 cup	green olives, pitted and finely chopped (see Tips, left)	150 mL
1/4 cup	pimientos, drained and chopped	60 mL
1/4 cup	finely chopped red onion	60 mL
3	cloves garlic, minced	3
1	anchovy, minced	1
1/3 cup	chopped parsley leaves	75 mL
2 tbsp	chopped fresh oregano leaves	30 mL
1 tbsp	capers, rinsed, drained and chopped	15 mL
1/4 tsp	freshly ground black pepper	1 mL
1/2 cup	extra virgin olive oil	125 mL

Sandwiches

1	foccacia loaf (about 6½ by 10½ inches/ 16 by 27 cm), cut in half horizontally	1
4 oz	provolone cheese, sliced (6 slices)	125 g
2	cans (each 6 oz/170 g) tuna in water, drained and broken into flakes	2

1. *Olive Salad:* In an airtight storage container, using a fork, stir together black and green olives, pimientos, onion, garlic, anchovy, parsley, oregano, capers, pepper and olive oil. Cover and refrigerate for several hours or overnight to meld flavors.

2. *Sandwiches:* Moisten bottom half of the loaf with a thin layer of olive salad. Layer on provolone, then tuna. Spread remaining olive salad overtop. Replace the top half of the loaf.

3. Cut into 4 or 6 segments and serve immediately.

Tuna and Artichoke Panini

Add fish to your panini-press repertoire with these easy sandwiches. Brown-baggers, take note: this sandwich is surprisingly fine the day after it's made. You can eat it cold or heat it up in a microwave or toaster oven.

Makes 4 panini

- Fast
- Brown-bag

Tips

If you don't have a panini press, heat the sandwiches in a large skillet or grill pan. Preheat the pan and weigh the sandwiches down by placing a second hot skillet on top. If the sandwich is not toasting evenly, flip it.

Use crusty rolls with a soft crumb.

You can use lower-fat mozzarella.

Save the oil from the marinated artichoke hearts to make salad dressing.

- **Panini press, preheated to High**

4	cans (each 3 oz/85 g) tuna in olive oil, drained (oil reserved)	4
4	crusty rolls, split	4
4	slices mozzarella (about 4 oz/125 g), each cut in half, divided	4
¼ cup	parsley leaves	60 mL
¼ cup	chopped basil leaves	60 mL
1	jar (6 oz/170 g) marinated artichoke hearts, drained and chopped	1

1. In a bowl, using a fork, lightly mash tuna.

2. Brush cut surfaces of rolls with oil from the tuna. Place bottoms on a work surface. Layer with half the mozzarella, all the parsley, basil, tuna and artichokes, and then the remaining mozzarella. Replace tops.

3. Place sandwiches on preheated panini press and cook for 3 to 5 minutes, until toasted and golden. Cut in half before serving.

> ## Variations
> Substitute an equal quantity of salmon or mackerel for the tuna.

Tuscan Sandwiches

Load up on flavor and healthful fiber with these wholesome sandwiches. They feature signature Tuscan ingredients, including cannellini beans and extra virgin olive oil.

Makes 3 sandwiches

- Fast
- Healthy
- Brown-bag

Tip

I use a 19-ounce (540 mL) can of beans. If using a smaller can, you will end up with less filling. In that case, try filling two buns instead of three.

1	can (14 to 19 oz/398 to 540 mL) cannellini (white kidney) beans, drained and rinsed (see Tip, left)	1
3 tbsp	extra virgin olive oil, divided	45 mL
1 tbsp	white wine vinegar	15 mL
	Salt and freshly ground black pepper	
3	crusty Italian sub-shaped buns (each about 6 inches/15 cm long), split	3
1	can (6 oz/170 g) tuna in water, drained and broken in small chunks	1
1/3 to 1/2 cup	thinly sliced red onion	75 to 125 mL
2 cups	torn arugula leaves	500 mL

1. In a bowl, using a potato masher, mash beans, 1 tbsp (15 mL) oil, vinegar and salt and pepper to taste. (Do not mash the beans into a paste — you want some texture in the sandwich.)

2. Brush remaining 2 tbsp (30 mL) oil over cut sides of buns. Arrange bottom halves on a work surface and spread with bean mixture. Gently squeeze tuna to remove excess moisture and place equal amounts over the beans. Add onion to taste and arugula, dividing equally. Replace tops, cut in half and serve immediately.

Variations

Go upscale with tuna in olive oil and substitute the oil it is packed in for the extra virgin olive oil.

Make 4 small sandwiches with smaller buns.

Increase your fiber intake by using whole wheat buns.

Substitute an equal quantity of salmon, mackerel, sardines or sprats for the tuna.

Parmesan Tuna Sandwiches

Here's another great Italian twist on the iconic tuna salad sandwich.

Tips

If you're brown-bagging this sandwich, pack the tomatoes separately.

Use a rasp to grate the Parmesan so it is fluffy.

¼ cup	mayonnaise	60 mL
3 tbsp	freshly grated Parmesan cheese (about ½ oz/15 g)	45 mL
1 tbsp	chopped basil leaves	15 mL
1 tsp	freshly squeezed lemon juice	5 mL
1	can (6 oz/170 g) tuna in water, drained and broken into chunks	1
2	small kaiser rolls (about 4 inches/10 cm in diameter) split	2
4	slices tomato	4
	Salt and freshly ground black pepper	
	Extra virgin olive oil	

1. In a bowl, stir together mayonnaise, Parmesan, basil and lemon juice. Gently squeeze tuna to remove excess moisture and add it to the bowl. Mix with a fork.

2. Lightly toast rolls. Slather tuna mixture over bottom halves. Top with tomato slices, dividing equally, and season to taste with salt and pepper. Brush olive oil over cut sides of tops and replace.

3. Cut sandwiches into halves and serve immediately.

Variation

Substitute an equal quantity of salmon for the tuna.

Shrimp and Cuke Croissants

These refined sandwiches are easy to make and easy to eat.

Tips

You don't have to peel the cucumber.

If you're brown-bagging this sandwich, pack the cucumber separately.

2	cans (each 4 oz/106 g) small shrimp, rinsed, drained and chopped	2
2 tbsp	finely chopped green bell pepper	30 mL
1 tsp	chopped fresh dill fronds	5 mL
1/4 cup + 1 tbsp	mayonnaise	75 mL
1/2 tsp	Dijon mustard	2 mL
4	large croissants, split	4
24	thin slices English cucumber (see Tips, left)	24
	Salt and freshly ground black pepper	
4	leaves Boston lettuce	4

1. In a bowl, using a fork, mash together shrimp, green pepper, dill, 1/4 cup (60 mL) mayonnaise and mustard.

2. Place bottom halves of croissants on a work surface. Spread with shrimp mixture and lay cucumber overtop, dividing equally. Season to taste with salt and pepper and top with lettuce. Lightly smear remaining 1 tbsp (15 mL) mayonnaise on cut sides of croissant tops, dividing equally, and place them over lettuce.

3. Cut into halves and serve immediately.

Variations

Substitute an equal quantity of crab or lobster for the shrimp.

Anchovy Egg Salad, Tomato and Sprouts in Pitas

The anchovy and the egg are true soul mates. Together they make a lip-smacking savory sandwich filling.

**Makes
8 sandwiches**

- Fast
- Brown-bag

Tips

Here's a carefree way to hard-cook eggs: Place the eggs in a small pan and cover with about ½ inch (1 cm) water. Heat on medium-high. When the water comes to a full boil, cover and immediately remove the pan from the heat. Let it stand for 10 minutes. Run cold water over the eggs until they are cool enough to handle. Peel them immediately (the shell is less likely to stick that way).

If you're brown-bagging this sandwich, prevent sogginess by packing the tomatoes separately.

8	large eggs, hard-cooked and coarsely chopped (see Tips, left)	8
¼ cup	mayonnaise	60 mL
8	anchovy fillets, minced	8
1 tsp	Dijon mustard	5 mL
¼ tsp	sweet paprika	1 mL
⅛ tsp	freshly ground black pepper	0.5 mL
4	whole wheat pocket pitas (about 6 inches/15 cm in diameter), halved	4
2	tomatoes, thinly sliced	2
1	package (2½ oz/70 g) onion sprouts	1

1. In a bowl, using a fork, mash eggs, mayonnaise, anchovies, mustard, paprika and pepper. You will have about 2¼ cups (550 mL) filling.

2. Place pitas on work surface. Spread a generous ¼ cup (60 mL) filling in each pita half. Insert tomato slices and stuff in sprouts. Serve immediately.

> **Variations**
> Use your favorite type of sprouts, such as broccoli, alfalfa or onion sprouts, or substitute micro-greens such as broccoli, kale, radish or cabbage shoots.

Körözött Cheese on Rye

This classic Austro-Hungarian cheese spread is tangy and bold, thanks to the addition of anchovies. It is better known by its German name, Liptauer cheese, although there are many versions in different parts of Europe. Mine is modernized with lemon juice to brighten the flavor and a lot less butter than my mom uses. Rating körözött as kid-friendly may seem odd, but I loved this as a kid, and so did my own children.

Makes 10 to 12 servings
About 1 1/3 cups (325 mL)

- Fast
- Kid-friendly
- Brown-bag
- Healthy

Tips

In this recipe, do not use the large-curd, creamy cottage cheese sold in tubs, which is too wet. For the best texture and richer flavor, I use dry cottage cheese with 10% milk fat, but lower-fat versions will work too.

If you can't wait, you can enjoy körözött immediately after making it. However, it is best once chilled.

Körözött keeps well in the fridge for a week, so you don't have to make all the sandwiches at once. Enjoy this spread at breakfast or lunch.

1	package (8 oz/250 g) pressed dry cottage cheese (see Tips, left)	1
2 tbsp	unsalted butter, softened	30 mL
3	green onions (white and light green parts), minced	3
4	anchovy fillets, minced	4
2 tbsp	capers, rinsed, drained and finely chopped	30 mL
1 tsp	Dijon mustard	5 mL
1 1/2 tsp	sweet paprika (approx.)	7 mL
1/4 tsp	caraway seeds	1 mL
1 to 2 tsp	freshly squeezed lemon juice	5 to 10 mL
	Salt	
10 to 12	slices rye bread	10 to 12

1. In a bowl, using a fork, mash together cottage cheese and butter. Add green onions, anchovies, capers, mustard, paprika and caraway seeds. Add 1 tsp (5 mL) lemon juice and blend well. Add salt and additional lemon juice, if desired, to taste.

2. Transfer to an airtight container, cover and refrigerate for at least 1 hour to meld the flavors, or for up to 7 days. When you are ready to serve, toast bread until golden brown. Smear about 2 tbsp (30 mL) körözött over each slice. Sprinkle additional paprika lightly overtop.

3. Cut each slice in half and serve immediately.

Variations

If you don't like caraway seeds, add a pinch of ground caraway.

Spread körözött on crackers for snacks and canapés.

You can substitute pickle juice for the lemon juice.

Scandinavian Dilled Shrimp on Party Pumpernickel

Shrimp salad, known in Sweden as skagen, *is usually served on white bread that has been fried in butter, but I prefer to use sturdy pumpernickel rye.*

Tips

Don't use lower-fat mayonnaise in this recipe. You need thick, full-fat mayonnaise to hold everything together.

Substitute chopped lobster for the shrimp.

Caviar is delicate. To pat it dry, place it on a paper towel and dab gently.

2 tbsp	mayonnaise (see Tips, left)	30 mL
2 tbsp	crème fraîche	30 mL
$\frac{1}{4}$ tsp	Dijon mustard	1 mL
2 tbsp	finely chopped red onion	30 mL
2 tsp	chopped fresh dill fronds	10 mL
1	can (4 oz/106 g) tiny shrimp, rinsed and drained	1
	Salt and freshly ground black pepper	
14	slices party pumpernickel rye (approx.) (2½ inches/6 cm square)	14
1	jar (2 oz/50 g) red lumpfish caviar (roe), rinsed, drained and patted dry (see Tips, left)	1
14	small sprigs fresh dill	14
1	lemon, sliced into thin wedges	1

1. In a bowl, stir together mayonnaise, crème fraîche, mustard, onion and dill. Stir in shrimp. Season to taste with salt and pepper.

2. Toast pumpernickel slices and place on a serving platter. Dollop about 1 tbsp (15 mL) shrimp mixture on each slice. Top each with ¼ to ½ tsp (1 to 2 mL) caviar (you will have some left over). Garnish with dill. Serve immediately with lemon wedges to squeeze overtop.

Sardines on Toast with Drizzle

Turning sardines into a light meal is simple. As a kid in a Hungarian family, I happily munched on rye bread and sardines with a spritz of lemon. This is a tad more sophisticated but still fast and easy.

Makes 2 servings

- Fast
- Healthy

Tip

This recipe makes about 1/4 cup (60 mL) dressing. You can spoon leftovers over other canned or fresh fish or steamed vegetables.

- **Mini food processor**

1 cup	parsley leaves	250 mL
1/2 cup	fresh dill fronds	125 mL
1 tbsp	freshly squeezed lemon juice	15 mL
1/4 tsp	salt (approx.)	1 mL
2 tbsp	extra virgin olive oil	30 mL
2	slices rye bread	2
	Softened unsalted butter, optional	
2	leaves Boston lettuce	2
2	cans (each 4 oz/120 g) boneless, skinless sardines, drained	2

1. In a 2-cup (500 mL) measure, combine parsley and dill. Add boiling water to cover. Immediately transfer to a fine-mesh sieve, drain and rinse under cold running water. Drain well and use the back of a spoon to squeeze out remaining moisture.

2. In mini food processor, pulse parsley and dill until chopped and blended. Add lemon juice, salt and oil and process until smoothly blended. Adjust salt to taste.

3. Lightly toast the bread until golden and butter lightly, if desired. Place toast on individual serving plates and top each with a lettuce leaf. Arrange whole sardines overtop. Drizzle 1 to 2 tbsp (15 to 30 mL) herb dressing over each, to taste.

Variations

Substitute an equal quantity of tuna, salmon, mackerel, sprats, kippers, crab or lobster for the sardines.

Fish Tacos

These are less calorific but just as messy cousins of Baja fish tacos. Usually made with fried battered fish and tortillas that are either fried or doubled up to prevent leaks, Baja fish tacos are San Diego's most famous dish. They were popularized in 1983 by chain restaurateur Ralph Rubio, who first enjoyed them a decade earlier in Mexico.

Makes 12 tacos

- Kid-friendly

Tips

Go upscale by using top-quality solid white albacore tuna. Squeeze the tuna gently with your hands to remove excess moisture before using it.

These tacos are not rolled but rather presented open-faced, to be folded by the diner.

Bonus: This fresh salsa is also delightful with quesadillas, enchiladas or nachos, or served alongside grilled fish or chicken. Do not make the salsa ahead of time — refrigeration is disastrous for it because the cold ruins the texture of the tomatoes.

● **Preheat oven or toaster oven to 350°F (180°C)**

Dressing

½ cup	sour cream	125 mL
½ cup	mayonnaise	125 mL
2 tbsp	chopped cilantro leaves	30 mL
1 tbsp	minced chipotle chile pepper in adobo sauce	15 mL
	Salt	

Salsa

3	small tomatoes (about 12 oz/375 g total), cut in ¼-inch (0.5 cm) dice	3
⅓ cup	chopped sweet onion (such as Vidalia)	75 mL
⅓ cup	loosely packed cilantro leaves	75 mL
1	small jalapeño pepper, seeded and chopped	1
1	clove garlic, minced	1
1 tbsp	freshly squeezed lime juice	15 mL
½ tsp	salt (approx.)	2 mL
¼ tsp	freshly ground black pepper	1 mL

Tacos

12	small corn tortillas (about 5½ inches/ 14 cm in diameter)	12
1½ cups	finely shredded green cabbage (about 3 oz/90 g)	375 mL
2	cans (each 6 oz/170 g) tuna in water, drained, excess moisture removed and broken into flakes (see Tips, left)	2

1. *Dressing:* In a measuring cup, stir together sour cream, mayonnaise, cilantro, chipotle pepper and salt to taste. You will have about 1 cup (250 mL) dressing.

2. *Salsa:* In a bowl, stir together tomatoes, onion, cilantro, jalapeño, garlic, lime juice, salt and pepper. Taste and adjust salt if necessary. You will have about 2 cups (500 mL) salsa.

3. *Tacos:* Divide tortillas into two batches and wrap each in foil. Place in preheated oven and heat for 10 to 12 minutes, until warm.

4. Place warm tortillas on a work surface. Smear each with about 1½ tbsp (22 mL) dressing and top with about 2 tbsp (30 mL) cabbage. Add about 2 tbsp (30 mL) tuna and, using a slotted spoon, about 2 tbsp (30 mL) salsa. (You will have some salsa left over.) Serve immediately.

Variations

Substitute flour tortillas for the corn ones.

Substitute an equal quantity of salmon for the tuna.

Salmon and Sprout Quesadillas

You can't go wrong with quesadillas when the family's mealtime looms. These are fast, easy and popular with all ages.

Makes 4

- Fast
- Kid-friendly
- Healthy

Tip

You can also cook quesadillas in a panini press preheated to Medium.

8	whole wheat flour tortillas (7 inches/ 18 cm in diameter)	8
2 cups	shredded smoked mozzarella (8 oz/250 g)	500 mL
1	can (7 1/2 oz/213 g) salmon, drained, deboned and broken into flakes	1
2 cups	loosely packed onion or broccoli sprouts, divided	500 mL
	Vegetable oil or spray	
1/4 to 1/3 cup	prepared salsa	60 to 75 mL
1/4 to 1/3 cup	sour cream	60 to 75 mL
	Hot pepper sauce	

1. Place 4 tortillas on a work surface. Scatter with half the mozzarella, dividing equally. Gently squeeze salmon to remove excess moisture and scatter it evenly overtop. Set aside a small portion of sprouts for garnishing and scatter the remainder over salmon. Top with remaining cheese. Place remaining tortillas overtop.

2. Heat a large skillet or griddle over medium heat. Brush or spray lightly with oil. Using a wide spatula, transfer quesadillas to pan and cook, in batches if necessary, for about 2 minutes per side, until cheese melts and tortillas are slightly crisp and marked by brown spots. If they are browning too quickly, reduce heat to medium-low. Transfer each to a serving plate as completed and keep warm.

3. When all the quesadillas are cooked, top each with a dollop each of salsa and sour cream and finish with a dash of hot sauce (you can also serve it alongside). Garnish with reserved sprouts and serve immediately.

Variations

Use any kind of sprouts or micro-greens you like.

Replace salmon with an equal quantity of tuna or shrimp.

Fish Burgers, Fish Cakes, Fishballs and More

Salmon Burgers with Honey Ginger Mayo

The touch of sweetness in this fragrant honey-spiked mayonnaise complements the salmon.

Tips

It can be tricky to prepare burgers with canned fish. Since it is already cooked, the mixture doesn't naturally adhere together when heat is applied, so binders are necessary. I prefer to use egg and bread crumbs, fresh or dry, or sometimes mashed potato. Some cooks turn to dried potato flakes or cooked rice. You need to find a balance – just enough binder to make fish burgers, not bread burgers.

I like to use a kitchen rasp, such as the kind made by Microplane, to grate the ginger into a purée.

- Preheat broiler, placing oven rack one level down from top position
- Broiling pan, covered with generously greased foil
- Food processor

Honey Ginger Mayo

¼ cup	mayonnaise	60 mL
2 tsp	soy sauce	10 mL
1 tsp	honey	5 mL
1	small clove garlic, minced	1
½ tsp	finely grated gingerroot (see Tips, left)	2 mL

Burgers

2	slices stale whole wheat bread (about 2½ oz/70 g), torn into chunks	2
1	large egg	1
2 tbsp	mayonnaise	30 mL
2 tsp	soy sauce	10 mL
2 tsp	chopped chives	10 mL
1 tsp	finely grated lime or lemon zest	5 mL
⅛ tsp	freshly ground black pepper	0.5 mL
2	cans (each 7½ oz/213 g) pink salmon, drained, deboned and broken into chunks	2
4	multigrain flatbread burger buns, about 4½ inches (11 cm) in diameter (see Tips, page 129)	4
¼ cup	thinly sliced red onion	60 mL
½ cup	watercress leaves or baby greens	125 mL

1. *Honey Ginger Mayo:* In a measuring cup, stir together mayonnaise, soy sauce, honey, garlic and ginger. Set aside.

2. *Burgers:* In food processor fitted with the metal blade, pulse bread 10 times, until medium crumbs form. You should have about 1½ lightly packed cups (375 mL; see Tips, page 129).

Tips

Fresh bread crumbs can vary wildly in volume, depending on how you put them in the measuring cup and how long they sit. As time passes the volume diminishes because the crumbs dry out and settle. So if you have a kitchen scale, go by weight. I pulse the torn bread into medium crumbs — neither too coarse nor too fine. For a volume measure I scrape the crumbs into a measuring cup but do not pack them down or rap the cup to get them to settle.

Flatbread burger buns, split horizontally, are sold in many supermarkets. You can, however, use any bun you like.

3. In a bowl, using a fork, mix egg, mayonnaise, soy sauce, chives, lime zest and pepper. Gently squeeze salmon to remove excess moisture and add to the bowl. Add bread crumbs and mix well.

4. Divide salmon mixture into 4 portions, each a generous $\frac{1}{2}$ cup (125 mL), and shape each into a patty about 4 inches (10 cm) in diameter. Place on prepared pan as completed.

5. Place patties under preheated broiler for about 5 minutes, until tops are golden brown. Carefully turn over and broil for about 4 minutes, until flipside is golden brown. Remove from oven and set aside for 2 minutes to firm up.

6. Place patties on bottoms of buns and slather with the mayo. Top with onion and watercress, replace tops and serve immediately.

Making Fish Burgers

- To counteract dryness I add a bit of mayonnaise, oil or butter to the mix when making fish burgers. Salmon needs less than tuna. Full-fat mayo is preferable but the lower-fat kind will work. Another potential moistener is sour cream.

- When making fish burgers, it's important to squeeze excess moisture from the fish to ensure that the mixture won't be too wet to handle. You should be able to gently pat the mixture into patties.

- I prefer to cook fish burgers under the broiler or on the grill rather than in a skillet, which increases the chances that they will crumble. If you're using the barbecue, place the burgers on greased foil rather than directly on the grate, which is a recipe for disaster.

- Be gentle with the patties. Use a spatula to lift them from your work surface or plate to the pan, and turn them carefully as they cook. I use two short-handled spatulas to turn them.

Open Sesame Salmon Burgers

Sesame lovers can get their fix with this Asian-inspired fish burger.

Makes 4 burgers

- Kid-friendly
- Healthy

Tips

Sesame Mayo: In a measuring cup, stir together ¼ cup (60 mL) mayonnaise, 2 tsp (10 mL) each toasted sesame oil and toasted sesame seeds (see Tips, below), ½ tsp (2 mL) each finely grated lime zest and freshly squeezed lime juice, and ¼ tsp (1 mL) each soy sauce and Asian chili sauce, such as sambal oelek or sriracha.

Toast sesame seeds in a dry skillet over medium heat, shaking the pan often, for 2 to 3 minutes, until seeds start to clump and turn golden and fragrant. Immediately transfer to a bowl. Even easier, buy toasted sesame seeds, which are available in many supermarkets. For an attractive presentation, use toasted mixed white and black sesame seeds.

Panko is Japanese-style bread crumbs. Light yet crunchy, panko straddles the gap between standard dry bread crumbs and fresh bread crumbs. I highly recommend it. Most supermarkets sell panko, often in the sushi section.

See page 129 for additional tips on making fish burgers.

- Preheat broiler, placing oven rack one level down from top position
- Broiling pan, covered with generously greased foil

1	large egg	1
2 tbsp	mayonnaise	30 mL
1 tbsp	toasted sesame oil	15 mL
2 tsp	soy sauce	10 mL
2	cans (each 6 oz/170 g) boneless, skinless salmon, drained and broken into chunks	2
½ cup	panko bread crumbs (see Tips, left)	125 mL
4	leaves leaf lettuce	4
4	sesame seed buns	4
	Sesame Mayo (see Tips, left)	
4	slices tomato	4
¼ cup	thinly sliced red onion	60 mL

1. In a bowl, using a fork, mix egg, mayonnaise, sesame oil and soy sauce. Gently squeeze salmon to remove excess moisture and add to the bowl. Add panko crumbs and mix well.

2. Divide salmon mixture into 4 portions and shape each into a patty approximately 4½ inches (11.5 cm) in diameter. Place each on prepared pan as completed.

3. Place patties under preheated broiler for about 5 minutes, until tops are golden brown. Carefully turn over and broil for about 4 minutes, until flipside is golden brown. Remove from oven and set aside for 2 minutes to firm up.

4. Place lettuce on bottoms of buns and place patties on top. Slather patties with sesame mayo and top with tomato and onion. Replace tops of buns and serve immediately.

Thai Curry Salmon Burgers

Curry accents work nicely with the salmon in these fish burgers. The topping, a Thai version of tartar sauce, puts them over the top.

Makes 4 burgers

- Healthy
- Guest-worthy

Tips

Basil Mayo: In a measuring cup, stir together ¼ cup (60 mL) mayonnaise, 1 tbsp (15 mL) sour cream, 1 small green onion, minced, 2 tsp (10 mL) chopped basil leaves, ½ tsp (2 mL) freshly squeezed lemon juice, and salt and freshly ground black pepper, to taste.

Coconut cream is richer and denser than coconut milk, but it is not widely sold. If you don't have coconut cream, scoop the separated "cream" off the top of a can of non-emulsified coconut milk or substitute thick premium coconut milk. Do not mistake coconut cream for creamed coconut, which is sweetened and sold in blocks.

I enjoy fish burgers in the thin specialty buns sold in many supermarkets. These small, round flatbreads, split horizontally, don't overwhelm the patty. You can, however, use any bun you like.

For additional tips on making fish burgers, see page 129.

- **Preheat broiler, placing oven rack one level down from top position**
- **Broiling pan, covered with generously greased foil**

1	large egg	1
2 tbsp	mayonnaise	30 mL
2 tbsp	coconut cream (see Tips, left)	30 mL
2 tsp	Thai green curry paste	10 mL
1	small clove garlic, minced	1
¼ tsp	dried basil	1 mL
⅛ tsp	freshly ground black pepper	0.5 mL
2	cans (each 7½ oz/213 g) salmon, drained, deboned and broken into chunks	2
½ cup	panko bread crumbs (see Tips, page 130)	125 mL
4	leaves leaf lettuce	4
4	whole-grain flatbread burger buns, about 4½ inches (11.5 cm) in diameter (see Tips, left)	4
	Basil Mayo (see Tips, left)	

1. In a bowl, using a fork, mix egg, mayonnaise, coconut cream, curry paste, garlic, basil and pepper. Gently squeeze salmon to remove excess moisture and add to the bowl. Add panko crumbs and mix well.

2. Divide salmon mixture into 4 portions, each a generous ½ cup (125 mL), and shape each into a patty about 4 inches (10 cm) in diameter. Place on prepared pan as completed.

3. Place patties under preheated broiler for about 5 minutes, until tops are golden brown. Carefully turn over and broil for about 4 minutes, until flipside is golden brown. Remove from oven and set aside for 2 minutes to firm up.

4. Place lettuce on bottoms of buns and place patties on top. Slather patties with the Basil Mayo, replace tops and serve immediately.

Jerk Salmon Sliders

Sliders are miniature burgers that make great party fare. These sliders are tasty morsels for fans of spicy food.

Tips

Toasted sesame oil, also known as Asian sesame oil, is made from toasted or roasted seeds. Dark and aromatic, it is sold in small bottles as a flavoring agent. Do not confuse toasted sesame oil with yellow sesame oil pressed from raw seeds.

Jamaican jerk sauce is made with hot peppers (particularly Scotch bonnet chiles) and aromatic spices. You can buy small jars at the supermarket.

For additional tips on making fish burgers, see page 129.

- **Preheat broiler, placing oven rack one level down from top position**
- **Broiling pan, covered with generously greased foil**

Herb Lime Mayo

¼ cup	mayonnaise	60 mL
1	small clove garlic, minced	1
2 tsp	finely chopped parsley leaves	10 mL
2 tsp	finely chopped chives	10 mL
1 tsp	finely grated lime zest	5 mL
	Salt	

Burgers

1	large egg	1
2 tbsp	mayonnaise	30 mL
1 tbsp	toasted sesame oil (see Tips, left)	15 mL
2	green onions (white and light green parts), minced	2
2 tsp	soy sauce	10 mL
1 tsp	finely grated lime zest	5 mL
1 tsp	finely chopped cilantro leaves	5 mL
2	cans (each 7½ oz/213 g) salmon, drained, deboned and broken into chunks	2
½ cup	panko bread crumbs (see Tips, page 133)	125 mL
¼ cup	prepared jerk sauce (see Tips, left)	60 mL
8	slider buns, each about 2½ inches (6 cm) in diameter	8
8	slices plum tomato	8

1. *Herb Lime Mayo:* In a measuring cup, stir together mayonnaise, garlic, parsley, chives, lime zest and salt to taste. Set aside.

2. *Burgers:* In a bowl, using a fork, mix egg, mayonnaise, sesame oil, green onions, soy sauce, lime zest and cilantro. Gently squeeze salmon to remove excess moisture and add to the bowl. Add panko crumbs and mix well.

Tips

Panko is Japanese-style bread crumbs. Light yet crunchy, panko straddles the gap between standard dry bread crumbs and fresh bread crumbs. I highly recommend it. Most supermarkets sell panko, often in the sushi section.

If you prefer, grill fish burgers on the barbecue. For best results, mimic the broiling method, placing the burgers on greased foil, not directly on the grate.

3. Divide salmon mixture into 8 portions, each a generous $\frac{1}{4}$ cup (60 mL), and shape each into a patty about $2\frac{1}{2}$ inches (6 cm) in diameter. Place on prepared pan as completed.

4. Place patties under preheated broiler for 3 to 4 minutes, until tops look golden and dry. Brush with half the jerk sauce and broil for 1 minute. Carefully turn over and broil until flipside looks golden and dry, about 2 to 3 minutes. Brush with remaining jerk sauce and broil for 30 to 60 seconds. Remove from oven and set aside for 2 minutes to firm up.

5. Place patties on bottom halves of buns and top with tomato slices. Slather cut sides of tops with the mayo, replace tops and serve immediately.

Niçoise Tuna Burgers

The fixings put these fish burgers over the top, but you can also use the recipe to make generic tuna burgers and add your own touches.

Tips

Panko is Japanese-style bread crumbs. Light yet crunchy, panko straddles the gap between standard dry bread crumbs and fresh bread crumbs. Most supermarkets sell panko, often in the sushi section.

To counteract dryness I add a bit of mayonnaise to fish burgers. Tuna needs more than salmon. Full-fat mayo is preferable but the lower-fat kind will work.

- **Preheat broiler, placing oven rack one level down from top position**
- **Broiling pan, covered with generously greased foil**

Niçoise Mayo

¼ cup	mayonnaise	60 mL
1 tbsp	chopped marinated artichoke hearts	15 mL
2 tsp	finely chopped red onion	10 mL
2 tsp	finely chopped black olives (3 small)	10 mL
½ tsp	capers, drained and finely chopped	2 mL
¼ tsp	anchovy paste	1 mL
1	large basil leaf, chopped	1
	Salt	

Burgers

1	large egg	1
¼ cup	mayonnaise (see Tips, left)	60 mL
1	clove garlic, minced	1
1 tbsp	prepared tomato-based chili sauce	15 mL
1 tsp	finely grated lemon zest	5 mL
1 tsp	finely chopped parsley leaves	5 mL
2	cans (each 6 oz/170 g) tuna in water, drained and broken into chunks	2
½ cup	panko bread crumbs	125 mL
2 tbsp	extra virgin olive oil, divided	30 mL
4	small crusty buns, about 3½ inches (9 cm) in diameter, split	4
4	slices tomato	4
2	eggs, hard-cooked and sliced	2

1. *Niçoise Mayo:* In a measuring cup, stir together mayonnaise, artichokes, onion, olives, capers, anchovy paste, basil and salt to taste. Set aside.

2. *Burgers:* In a bowl, using a fork, mix egg, mayonnaise, garlic, chili sauce, lemon zest and parsley. Gently squeeze tuna to remove excess moisture and add to bowl. Add panko crumbs and mix well.

Be gentle with the patties. Use a spatula to lift them from your work surface or plate to the pan, and turn them carefully as they cook. I use two short-handled spatulas to turn them.

3. Divide tuna mixture into 4 portions, each about $\frac{1}{2}$ cup (125 mL), and shape each into a patty approximately $3\frac{1}{2}$ inches (9 cm) in diameter. Place on prepared pan as completed.

4. Brush tops of patties with half of the oil. Place under preheated broiler for about 5 minutes, until tops look golden and dry. Carefully turn over and brush with remaining oil. Return to broiler and broil for about 4 minutes, until flipsides look golden and dry. Set aside for 2 minutes to firm up.

5. Place patties on bottoms of buns and top with tomato and eggs. Slather Niçoise Mayo on cut sides of the top halves of buns and replace. Serve immediately.

Crab Cakes

Canned crab is worth buying just for these tasty little treats. Crab cakes can be tricky to prepare, as they are best with as little binder as possible. I've added just enough egg and crumbs to hold them together.

Tips

Buy small lump crabmeat, as the flaked kind is not substantial enough for making patties. I prefer pasteurized claw meat because it has a fuller flavor and firmer texture. Coarsely chop any long claw pieces. You'll need half of a pound (500 g) container. If desired, double this crab cake recipe or use the remainder in other dishes. See the chart on pages 272 to 278 for ideas.

For the finest minced garlic, push the clove through a garlic press.

Toasted sesame oil, also known as Asian sesame oil, is made from toasted or roasted seeds. Dark and aromatic, it is sold in small bottles as a flavoring agent. Do not confuse toasted sesame oil with yellow sesame oil pressed from raw seeds.

- **Food processor**

2	slices stale white bread (about 2½ oz/70 g), torn into chunks	2
1	large egg	1
1 tbsp	toasted sesame oil	15 mL
1 tbsp	freshly squeezed lime juice (see Tips, page 137)	15 mL
1	small shallot, minced	1
1	clove garlic, minced (see Tips, left)	1
1 tbsp	finely chopped red bell pepper	15 mL
1 tsp	chopped parsley leaves	5 mL
¼ tsp	ground ginger	1 mL
¼ tsp	salt	1 mL
1½ cups	canned crab claw meat (8 oz/250 g), rinsed and drained (see Tips, left)	375 mL
	Cornstarch	
1 tbsp	unsalted butter, optional	15 mL
¼ cup	oil for frying	60 mL
	Minty Cucumber Dip (page 139)	

1. In food processor fitted with the metal blade, pulse bread 10 times, until medium crumbs form. You should have about 1½ lightly packed cups (375 mL).

2. In a bowl, using a fork, mix egg, sesame oil, lime juice, shallot, garlic, red pepper, parsley, ginger and salt. Gently squeeze crab to remove excess moisture and add to bowl along with bread crumbs. Mix well.

3. Scatter cornstarch evenly and liberally over a large plate. Divide crab mixture into 8 portions. With greased hands, pat each mound into a ball, roll in the cornstarch to coat, then flatten slightly. Refrigerate, uncovered, for 15 to 30 minutes to firm up.

Tips

I use two small spatulas to carefully turn the crab cakes.

Adding a pat of butter to the frying oil adds buttery flavor to fish cakes.

To maintain more control over the final result, I always use unsalted butter in recipes. With salted butter, the amount of salt varies by brand. And salted butter contains more moisture, which can affect some recipes. Salt also masks rancidity.

Bottled reconstituted lemon and lime juices usually contain additives. That's why I always use freshly squeezed juice. I squeeze the whole lemon or lime and immediately store the leftover juice in a small tub in the fridge or freeze it in 1 tbsp (15 mL) portions in an ice cube tray.

4. In a large skillet, melt butter, if using, with oil over medium heat. Using a spatula, and with greased hands, transfer a patty to your palm. Gently flatten to $\frac{1}{2}$ to $\frac{3}{4}$ inch (1 to 2 cm) and place in the hot oil. Repeat, in batches, with remaining patties, frying for 3 to 4 minutes a side and turning carefully when bottoms are golden brown and firm (lower the heat if they are browning too quickly).

5. Set aside for 2 minutes to firm up. Serve warm, with Minty Cucumber Dip alongside.

Variations

The cornstarch makes the patties easier to work with, but if you prefer, use dry crumbs such as panko instead. Note that crab cakes with a panko coating will brown faster.

Substitute an equal quantity of full-fat mayonnaise for the sesame oil.

Substitute an equal quantity of coarsely chopped lobster for the crab.

Tuna Croquettes

Fish cakes aren't pretty to look at but they taste pretty good. My family snatches them up before I can even get them onto serving plates. Minty Cucumber Dip is a refreshing accompaniment.

Tips

Tuna croquettes are a fine way to use up leftover mashed potatoes.

Before refrigeration, the tuna mixture should just hold together. To test it, press a small amount lightly in your hand — it should not crumble.

If your mashed potatoes are very moist, very dry or very buttery, you may have to experiment with the quantity of bread crumbs you add to the tuna mixture.

2	large eggs	2
1	can (6 oz/170 g) tuna in water, drained and broken into chunks	1
1 cup	packed cold mashed potatoes (about 8 oz/250 g; see Tips, left)	250 mL
1 tbsp	honey Dijon mustard	15 mL
1 tsp	freshly squeezed lemon juice	5 mL
1	large green onion (white and green parts), minced	1
1 tsp	finely chopped fresh dill fronds	5 mL
1/4 tsp	sweet paprika	1 mL
1/4 tsp	salt	1 mL
1/8 tsp	freshly ground black pepper	0.5 mL
3/4 cup	panko bread crumbs, divided (see Tip, page 139)	175 mL
1 tsp	dry Italian seasoning	5 mL
1 tbsp	unsalted butter, optional	15 mL
1/4 cup	vegetable oil	60 mL
	Minty Cucumber Dip (page 139)	

1. In a bowl, lightly whisk eggs. Gently squeeze tuna to remove excess moisture and add to bowl. Add potatoes, mustard, lemon juice, green onion, dill, paprika, salt and pepper. Mix well with a fork. Add 1/4 cup (60 mL) panko crumbs. Refrigerate, uncovered, for 15 to 30 minutes.

2. Place remaining panko crumbs and Italian seasoning in a wide, shallow bowl. Crumble together with fingers.

3. Divide croquette mixture into 8 portions. With greased hands, shape each into a rough ball and roll in the crumbs to coat thoroughly. Pat into a disk about 3 inches (7.5 cm) in diameter.

4. In a skillet over medium heat, melt butter, if using, with oil. In batches, fry croquettes for 2 to 3 minutes a side, turning carefully when bottoms are golden brown and firm (turn down heat if they are browning too quickly).

5. Set aside for 2 minutes to firm up. Serve warm, with Minty Cucumber Dip alongside.

Minty Cucumber Dip

Yogurt dips go well with fried foods such as crab cakes and tuna croquettes. This one is similar to tzatziki.

Makes about 1½ cups (375 mL)

Tip

If you don't have Greek yogurt, spoon 1½ cups (375 mL) regular yogurt into a strainer lined with cheesecloth, place over a bowl, cover and refrigerate for 2 hours or until thickened and reduced to 1 cup. Discard liquid in bowl.

½ cup	finely chopped cucumber	125 mL
¼ tsp	salt (approx.)	1 mL
1 cup	Greek yogurt	250 mL
1 tbsp	freshly squeezed lime juice	15 mL
1 tbsp	chopped mint leaves	15 mL

1. In a fine-mesh sieve, toss cucumber with salt. Place over a bowl and set aside to drain for 10 to 15 minutes.

2. Squeeze excess moisture from cucumber and transfer to a small serving bowl. Add yogurt, lime juice and mint and stir to blend. Taste and adjust salt. Cover and refrigerate until chilled or for up to 2 days.

Salmon Kofta in Tomato Almond Curry Sauce

Kofta are spicy Indian meatballs — or in this case, fishballs — swimming in a tangy sauce. For an irresistible meal, serve this dish over rice or set out warm naan bread alongside to mop up the sauce.

Makes 4 servings

- Guest-worthy

Tips

Panko is Japanese-style bread crumbs. Light yet crunchy, panko straddles the gap between standard dry bread crumbs and fresh bread crumbs. I highly recommend it. Most supermarkets sell panko, often in the sushi section.

For the finest grated lemon zest, use a kitchen rasp.

This recipe will work with pink salmon but I prefer using sockeye salmon because it is moister and more flavorful.

- **Preheat oven to 350°F (180°C)**
- **Rimmed baking sheet, lined with generously greased foil**

Kofta

2	cans (each 7½ oz/213 g) salmon, drained, deboned and broken into chunks	2
2	large eggs	2
¼ cup	panko bread crumbs	60 mL
1	green onion (white and light green parts), finely chopped	1
1	clove garlic, minced	1
1 tbsp	unsalted butter, melted and cooled, optional (see Tips, page 141)	15 mL
1 tbsp	finely chopped cilantro leaves	15 mL
2 tsp	finely grated lemon zest (see Tips, left)	10 mL
½ tsp	ground cumin	2 mL
⅛ tsp	salt	0.5 mL
⅛ tsp	freshly ground black pepper	0.5 mL

Sauce

1 tbsp	vegetable oil	15 mL
¼ cup	ground blanched almonds	60 mL
1	can (14 oz/398 mL) tomato sauce	1
½ tsp	ground cardamom	2 mL
½ tsp	ground cumin	2 mL
¼ tsp	salt	1 mL
⅛ tsp	cayenne pepper	0.5 mL
½ cup	heavy or whipping (35%) cream	125 mL

1. *Kofta:* Gently squeeze salmon to remove excess moisture and place in a bowl. Add eggs, panko crumbs, green onion, garlic, butter, if using, cilantro, lemon zest, cumin, salt and pepper. Using a fork, mash salmon and mix well.

2. With greased hands, shape salmon mixture into 1-inch (2.5 cm) balls and place on prepared baking sheet as completed (you should have about 35). Bake in preheated oven for 10 minutes. Turn and bake for 10 minutes more. Remove from oven and set aside for 5 minutes to firm up.

Tips

Fishballs have a tendency to become dry. The butter makes them moister, but this recipe will work fine without it.

You need to use a 12-inch (30 cm) skillet so all the fishballs will fit.

3. *Sauce:* In a 12-inch (30 cm) skillet (see Tips, left), heat oil over medium heat until shimmery. Add almonds and cook, stirring, for 1 minute, until golden. Stir in tomato sauce, cardamom, cumin, salt and cayenne and bring to a simmer. Reduce heat to medium-low and simmer for 5 minutes. Stir in cream.

4. Add kofta to pan, stirring gently to coat. Simmer for 1 minute, until heated through. Serve immediately.

Variation

Replace some of the cream with thick yogurt. Do not allow it to boil, or it will curdle.

Fishballs

Who needs meatballs? Fishballs are healthier, and I have found many uses for them. Try my versions on pages 140, 142 and 144 before experimenting on your own. You can start with the fishball basics — salmon, eggs, panko, zest, garlic or onion, salt, pepper and butter (if desired) — in the amounts shown in the recipes. Then customize with your own herbs, spices and flavorings.

Fishballs Braised in Tomato Wine Sauce

Forget spaghetti and meatballs — try spaghetti and fishballs. This saucy dish is your ticket to a variety of meals. Serve it over pasta or rice, or slice up some crusty bread to serve alongside.

Makes 4 to 6 servings

- Healthy

Tips

To purée the tomatoes, pulse them, with their juices, for a few seconds in a food processor.

This recipe will work with pink salmon but I prefer using sockeye salmon because it is moister and more flavorful.

Fishballs have a tendency to become dry. The butter moistens them, but this recipe will work fine without it.

- **Preheat oven to 350°F (180°C)**
- **Rimmed baking sheet, lined with generously greased foil**
- **8-inch (20 cm) square baking dish**

Fishballs

2	cans (each 7½ oz/213 g) salmon, drained, deboned and broken into chunks	2
2	large eggs	2
¼ cup	panko bread crumbs	60 mL
1	clove garlic, minced	1
1 tbsp	unsalted butter, melted and cooled, optional (see Tips, left)	15 mL
2 tsp	finely chopped parsley leaves	10 mL
1 tsp	finely grated lemon zest	5 mL
½ tsp	hot pepper flakes	2 mL
⅛ tsp	salt	0.5 mL
⅛ tsp	freshly ground black pepper	0.5 mL

Sauce

2 tbsp	extra virgin olive oil	30 mL
1	onion, diced	1
1	clove garlic, finely chopped	1
1	carrot (about 2 oz/60 g), chopped	1
½ cup	dry white wine	125 mL
1	can (28 oz/796 mL) plum tomatoes, with juice, puréed (see Tips, left)	1
¾ cup	chicken stock	175 mL
1 tbsp	granulated sugar	15 mL
2 tbsp	chopped basil leaves	30 mL
1 tbsp	chopped fresh oregano leaves	15 mL
1	bay leaf	1
¼ tsp	salt (approx.)	1 mL
⅛ tsp	freshly ground black pepper	0.5 mL
	Freshly grated Parmesan cheese	

Variation

Add 2 tbsp (30 mL) dry grated Parmesan cheese to the fishball mixture in Step 1.

1. *Fishballs:* Gently squeeze excess moisture from salmon and place it in a bowl. Add eggs, panko crumbs, garlic, butter, if using, parsley, lemon zest, hot pepper flakes, salt and pepper. Mash with a fork until blended.

2. With greased hands, shape salmon mixture into 1-inch (2.5 cm) balls and place on prepared baking sheet as completed. (You should have about 35.)

3. Bake in preheated oven for 10 minutes. Turn and bake for 10 minutes more. Remove from oven and set aside for 5 minutes to firm up. Lower oven temperature to 325°F (160°C).

4. *Sauce:* Meanwhile, in a skillet, heat oil over medium heat until shimmery. Add onion, garlic and carrot and cook, stirring often, for 5 minutes, until vegetables soften. Stir in wine, scraping brown bits from bottom of pan. Stir in tomatoes, stock, sugar, basil, oregano, bay leaf, salt and pepper. Bring to a boil. Reduce heat and simmer for 10 minutes, until slightly thickened.

5. Transfer fishballs to baking dish. Ladle sauce overtop, shaking dish gently to distribute evenly. Bake in preheated oven for 1 hour, until sauce is thick. Discard bay leaf and gently stir together fishballs and sauce. Taste and adjust the salt.

6. Sprinkle Parmesan, to taste, evenly overtop and serve immediately.

Soba Noodles with Fishballs and Snow Peas

This Japanese-style soup tastes good, looks good and is good for you.

Tips

Soba are thin buckwheat noodles, which are very popular in Japan and catching on in other parts of the world. Ponzu is a citrus soy sauce. Both are sold in specialty shops and supermarkets with a good Asian section.

Fishballs have a tendency to become dry. The butter makes them moister, but this recipe will work fine without it.

• **Preheat oven to 350°F (180°C)**
• **Rimmed baking sheet, lined with generously greased foil**

Fishballs

1	can (7½ oz/213 g) salmon, drained, deboned and broken into chunks	1
1	egg	1
2 tbsp	panko bread crumbs	30 mL
1	small clove garlic, minced	1
1½ tsp	unsalted butter, melted and cooled, optional	7 mL
1 tsp	finely grated lemon zest	5 mL
1 tsp	finely chopped cilantro leaves	5 mL
½ tsp	finely grated gingerroot	2 mL
Pinch	salt	Pinch
Pinch	freshly ground white pepper	Pinch

Soup

8 oz	soba noodles (see Tips, left)	250 g
6 cups	chicken or vegetable stock	1.5 L
4 oz	snow peas, trimmed and halved lengthwise (about 1½ cups/375 mL)	125 g
1	small carrot (about 2 oz/60 g), shredded (about ½ cup/125 mL)	1
4	shiitake mushrooms (about 2 oz/60 g), stemmed and sliced (see Tip, page 145)	4
4	slim green onions (white and light green parts), cut in 1-inch (2.5 cm) segments	4
2 tbsp	ponzu sauce (see Tips, left)	30 mL

1. *Fishballs:* Gently squeeze salmon to remove excess moisture and place in a bowl. Add egg, panko crumbs, garlic, butter, if using, lemon zest, cilantro, ginger, salt and pepper. Using a fork, mash salmon and mix well.

2. With greased hands, shape salmon mixture into 1-inch (2.5 cm) balls and place on prepared baking sheet as completed (you should have about 18). Bake in preheated oven for 10 minutes. Turn and bake for 10 minutes more. Remove from oven and set aside for 5 minutes to firm up.

Tip

Shiitake mushroom stems are too fibrous and tough to be edible. To remove them, just twist, pinch and pull them gently off the cap. If "waste not" is your mantra, use the stems to flavor stock before discarding them.

3. *Soup:* In a large pot of boiling salted water over medium heat, cook noodles until tender but firm, about 10 minutes. Drain and rinse briefly under cold running water to remove excess starch. Drain.

4. Meanwhile, in a saucepan, bring stock to a simmer over high heat. Reduce heat to medium, add snow peas and carrot and simmer for 3 minutes, until tender-crisp. Add mushrooms and onions. Simmer for 1 minute, until just tender. Remove from heat and stir in ponzu.

5. Divide noodles among 4 warmed serving bowls. Add fishballs and ladle hot soup overtop.

Variations

Substitute an equal quantity of shelled edamame for the snow peas. Simmer for 5 minutes.

Substitute Japanese udon (thicker wheat noodles) for the soba. Adjust the cooking time by following the package instructions.

Fishloaf

Here's the canned-fish equivalent of meatloaf. For an easy family dinner, serve it with mashed potatoes and salad. Enjoy any leftovers by turning them into fishloaf sandwiches.

Tips

Lining the pan with a parchment sling allows you to lift out the loaf in one neat piece. Tear off a sheet of parchment wide enough to cover the bottom and long sides of the pan (about 8 inches/20 cm) and let it hang over the sides. Don't worry about lining the ends of the pan — the fishloaf isn't that sticky.

Oven temperatures vary quite a bit, which may affect the cooking time of this loaf. Look for signs of doneness: when you lightly press the loaf in the center, the indentation should slowly spring back. A slice cut from the middle while warm should hold together rather than breaking. Quick fix: if your slice of fishloaf isn't quite done, zap it in the microwave for 20 to 30 seconds. This works for fish burgers and fish cakes too.

For a smaller, faster fishloaf, halve the ingredients. Toast the bread crumbs for about 5 minutes and cook the fishloaf for about 30 minutes.

Variation

Substitute an equal quantity of tuna for the salmon.

- **Preheat oven to 325°F (160°C)**
- **Food processor**
- **Rimmed baking sheet**
- **9- by 5-inch (23 by 12.5 cm) loaf pan, greased and lined with parchment sling (see Tips, left)**

4	slices stale white bread (about 5 oz/150 g), torn	4
4	cans (each 7½ oz/213 g) salmon, drained, deboned and broken into chunks	4
4	large eggs	4
¼ cup	mayonnaise	60 mL
2 tsp	finely grated lemon zest	10 mL
2 tbsp	freshly squeezed lemon juice	30 mL
2 tsp	Dijon mustard	10 mL
½ cup	chopped chives	125 mL
2 tsp	chopped fresh dill fronds	10 mL
½ tsp	salt	2 mL
¼ tsp	freshly ground black pepper	1 mL

1. In food processor fitted with the metal blade, pulse bread 10 to 12 times, until medium crumbs form. You should have about 3 cups (750 mL). Transfer to a rimmed baking sheet and toast in preheated oven for 15 minutes, stirring twice, until crumbs start to turn golden and crisp. Remove from oven and set aside to cool.

2. Meanwhile, gently squeeze salmon to remove excess moisture and place in a bowl. Add eggs, mayonnaise, lemon zest and juice, mustard, chives, dill, salt and pepper. Using a fork, mash salmon and mix gently. Add crumbs and mix well.

3. Scrape mixture into prepared loaf pan and pat with fork to even and smooth top. Bake in preheated oven for 1 to 1¼ hours or until top looks dry and loaf slowly springs back when lightly pressed.

4. Remove from oven and place on a wire rack. Set aside to firm up for 15 minutes. Loosen at the ends by pushing a thin knife between the loaf and the pan. Using the parchment sling, lift out loaf and transfer to a cutting board. Slice and serve warm or allow to cool to room temperature.

Curries, Casseroles and More

Lobster Tikka Masala

Tikka masala is a British takeout curry rather than a true Indian dish. Red food dye usually gives this popular dish its lurid hue, while paprika creates a subtler tint. It is traditionally made with chicken but there are also fish, lamb and vegetable versions. The fragrant, creamy tomato sauce is heavenly with chunks of lobster. Serve this dish over rice or with warm naan alongside.

Makes 4 servings

- Fast
- Guest-worthy

Tips

Ghee is a kind of clarified butter. It is sold in many supermarkets, particularly those with a good Asian foods section. If you don't have it, substitute an equal quantity of clarified butter or a mixture of butter and oil.

There aren't a lot of choices in can sizes when it comes to lobster. If you obtain a 11.3-oz (320 g) can, increase this recipe by 50% or use the remaining lobster in other dishes. For delicious lobster recipe ideas, check the chart on pages 272 to 278.

Adding the yogurt after the pan is off the heat prevents curdling.

1 tsp	sweet paprika	5 mL
¾ tsp	ground cumin	3 mL
¾ tsp	ground coriander	3 mL
½ tsp	salt (approx.)	2 mL
¼ tsp	cayenne pepper	1 mL
¼ tsp	ground fenugreek	1 mL
2 tbsp	ghee (see Tips, left)	30 mL
1	onion, finely chopped	1
3	cloves garlic, minced	3
2 tsp	finely chopped gingerroot	10 mL
6	canned plum tomatoes, puréed (about 1⅓ cups/325 mL)	6
⅓ cup	heavy or whipping (35%) cream	75 mL
2 tbsp	unsweetened desiccated coconut	30 mL
1½ cups	canned lobster meat (8 oz/250 g), rinsed, drained and coarsely chopped	375 mL
½ cup	plain yogurt	125 mL
2 tbsp	chopped cilantro leaves	30 mL

1. In a small bowl, stir together paprika, cumin, coriander, salt, cayenne and fenugreek. Set aside.

2. In a saucepan over medium heat, melt ghee. Add onion and cook, stirring often, for 3 to 5 minutes, until it softens and turns golden. Add garlic and ginger and cook, stirring, for 1 minute. Add paprika mixture and cook, stirring, for 30 seconds. Stir in tomatoes, cream, coconut and lobster. Bring to a simmer, reduce heat to low and simmer for 5 minutes.

3. Remove from heat and set aside for 30 seconds. Stir in yogurt and add salt to taste, if necessary. Garnish with cilantro and serve immediately.

Variations

Substitute an equal quantity of tuna, salmon or shrimp for the lobster. Stir it in gently after adding the yogurt.

Express Coconut Tuna and Pea Curry

This is not an authentic curry and the heat is an afterthought, but the creamy coconut sauce makes it comfort food for young and old. It is good, fast food for a light dinner. Serve it over rice or toast.

Makes 4 small servings

• Fast

Tip
Use "lite" coconut milk if you prefer.

1 tbsp	vegetable oil	15 mL
1	small onion, diced	1
1	clove garlic, minced	1
2 tsp	curry powder	10 mL
1	can (14 oz/398 mL) coconut milk	1
3 tbsp	chopped cilantro leaves, divided	45 mL
$\frac{1}{2}$ tsp	salt (approx.)	2 mL
1	bay leaf	1
1 cup	green peas, thawed if frozen	250 mL
1	can (6 oz/170 g) tuna in water, drained and broken into chunks	1
1 tbsp	freshly squeezed lime juice	15 mL
	Hot pepper sauce	

1. In a saucepan, heat oil over medium heat until shimmery. Add onion and cook, stirring often, for 3 to 5 minutes, until it softens and starts to turn golden. Add garlic and cook, stirring, for 20 seconds. Stir in curry powder. Add coconut milk, 2 tbsp (30 mL) cilantro, salt and bay leaf. Bring to a simmer. Reduce heat to medium-low and simmer for 5 minutes, until onion is soft and the sauce thickens. Remove and discard bay leaf.

2. Add peas and tuna and stir well. Simmer for 2 minutes, until heated through. Stir in lime juice. Add salt to taste, if necessary, and season to taste with hot pepper sauce.

3. Garnish with remaining cilantro and serve immediately.

Variations
Substitute an equal quantity of salmon, mackerel, shrimp, crab or lobster for the tuna.

Jamaican Crab and Okra Curry

Give okra a chance. When properly cooked, this unfairly maligned vegetable is tender-crisp and delightfully peppery, not limp and slimy. Okra adds tasty texture to this Caribbean-style curry. Serve it over rice.

Makes 4 small servings

- Fast
- Healthy

Tips

The crab should be chunky rather than flaky. For best results, buy pasteurized lump crabmeat. You can use the remainder of a pound (500 g) container in other dishes. Check the chart on pages 272 to 278 for good recipes.

Use thawed frozen okra if you can't find fresh. Add it with the crab and cook just until it's heated through.

2 tbsp	extra virgin olive oil	30 mL
2 tbsp	curry powder	30 mL
1	onion, diced	1
1	large clove garlic, minced	1
1/3 cup	chopped red bell pepper	75 mL
1/2 tsp	hot pepper flakes	2 mL
1/2 tsp	salt (approx.)	2 mL
1/4 tsp	freshly ground black pepper	1 mL
3 tbsp	tomato paste	45 mL
1 cup	chicken or vegetable stock, divided	250 mL
1 cup	trimmed, sliced (1/4 inch/0.5 cm) okra (about 4 oz/125 g)	250 mL
1	green onion, trimmed and sliced	1
1 1/4 cups	canned crabmeat, rinsed and drained (6 oz/175 g)	300 mL
1/2 cup	water, optional	125 mL

1. In a saucepan, heat oil over medium heat until shimmery. Add curry powder and cook, stirring constantly, for 30 to 60 seconds, until dark brown but not burned. Add onion, garlic, red pepper, hot pepper flakes, salt and pepper. Cook, stirring constantly, for 2 to 3 minutes. Stir in tomato paste and 1/2 cup (125 mL) stock. Cook, stirring often, for 3 minutes.

2. Stir in remaining stock along with okra and green onion. Reduce the heat to medium-low, cover and cook for about 3 minutes, until okra is tender-crisp. Stir in crab and cook for 1 minute, until heated through. If necessary, add some or all of the water to adjust the consistency (the sauce should be like thick gravy). Adjust salt to taste and serve immediately.

Variations

Replace the hot pepper flakes with some Scotch bonnet or habanero pepper. These are among the hottest peppers in the world, so start with a 1/4-inch (0.5 cm) slice, minced.

Substitute an equal quantity of shrimp or lobster for the crab.

Cheesy Tuna, Broccoli and Rice

This makes a tasty workaday meal, and without a can of condensed soup in sight.

Tip

You can use economical flaked tuna in this recipe. Double the amount of tuna if desired.

Variations

Substitute an equal quantity of salmon, mackerel, cod, shrimp or clams for the tuna.

- Preheat oven to 400°F (200°C)
- 8-inch (20 cm) square baking dish

1 cup	long-grain white rice, rinsed	250 mL
1 cup	chicken or vegetable stock	250 mL
1⅓ cups	water, divided	325 mL
4 cups	tiny broccoli florets (about 8 oz/250 g)	1 L
1	can (6 oz/170 g) tuna in water, drained and broken into chunks	1
2 tbsp	extra virgin olive oil	30 mL
1	onion, finely chopped	1
1	clove garlic, minced	1
2 tbsp	all-purpose flour	30 mL
1½ cups	whole milk	375 mL
1 tsp	finely grated lemon zest	5 mL
8 oz	sharp (old) Cheddar cheese, shredded (about 2 cups/500 mL)	250 g
	Salt and freshly ground black pepper	
1	recipe Uptown Crumb Topping or Quick Crumb Topping (page 178)	1

1. In a saucepan, bring rice, stock and ¾ cup plus 2 tbsp (200 mL) water to a boil over high heat. Reduce heat to low, cover and cook for 15 minutes, until rice is barely tender and water is absorbed. Remove from heat and set aside for 5 minutes.

2. Meanwhile, in a large microwave-safe bowl, combine broccoli and remaining water. Place in microwave oven and cook, covered, on High for about 2 minutes, until tender-crisp. Drain. Return broccoli to bowl, add rice, then scatter tuna overtop.

3. In a saucepan, heat oil over medium heat until shimmery. Add onion and cook, stirring, for 2 to 3 minutes, until it softens and turns golden. Stir in garlic. Add flour and cook, stirring, for 1 minute. Gradually whisk in milk. Cook, stirring, for 1 to 2 minutes, until thickened. Stir in lemon zest and cheese.

4. Pour cheese sauce over rice mixture and stir gently to blend. Season to taste with salt and pepper. Scrape mixture into baking dish and sprinkle topping evenly overtop.

5. Bake in preheated oven for about 15 minutes, until casserole is bubbling at the edges and topping is golden. Let casserole rest for 10 minutes before serving.

Updated Tuna Noodle Casserole

Want to modernize your tuna noodle casserole? This is a step up from the vintage version on page 44: instead of canned soup it relies on béchamel sauce and fresh mushrooms. It still has, however, an old-fashioned comfort food vibe that your family will appreciate.

Makes 4 servings

• Kid-friendly

Tips

I prefer to use whole milk to give this sauce a creamier consistency.

To maintain more control over the final result, I always use unsalted butter in recipes. With salted butter, the amount of salt varies by brand. And salted butter contains more moisture, which can affect some recipes. Salt also masks rancidity.

• **Preheat oven to 350°F (180°C)**
• **8-inch (20 cm) square baking dish**

1 cup	trimmed green beans cut in thirds (4 oz/125 g)	250 mL
6 oz	broad egg noodles	175 g
2 cups	whole milk	500 mL
1/4 cup	all-purpose flour	60 mL
1 tsp	fresh thyme leaves	5 mL
1 tsp	finely grated lemon zest	5 mL
2 tbsp	unsalted butter	30 mL
1	leek, thinly sliced	1
1	stalk celery heart with leaves, chopped (see Tips, page 153)	1
2 tbsp	chopped red bell pepper	30 mL
1 cup	sliced mushrooms (about 2 oz/60 g)	250 mL
1/4 tsp	salt (approx.)	1 mL
1/2 cup	shredded Cheddar cheese (2 oz/60 g)	125 mL
1/4 cup	sour cream	60 mL
1	can (6 oz/170 g) tuna in water, drained and broken into chunks	1
	Freshly ground black pepper	
1/2	recipe Uptown Crumb Topping (page 178)	1/2

1. In a large pot of boiling salted water over medium heat, cook beans for 5 to 7 minutes, until tender-crisp. Using a mesh scoop, transfer to a sieve and rinse under cold running water. Drain and set aside.

2. Add noodles to pot and cook over medium heat for 10 to 12 minutes, until tender. Drain and set aside.

3. Meanwhile, in a large measuring cup, whisk together milk, flour, thyme and lemon zest.

4. In a saucepan over medium-low heat, melt butter. Add leek, celery, red pepper, mushrooms and salt. Cook, stirring occasionally, for 5 minutes, until vegetables are softened. Stir in milk mixture. Cook, stirring often, until thickened, about 2 to 3 minutes. Stir in cheese until melted. Stir in sour cream and remove from heat. Add tuna and reserved beans and noodles. Stir to blend and season to taste with pepper and additional salt, if necessary.

5. Scrape mixture into baking dish and scatter topping evenly overtop. Bake in preheated oven for 30 minutes, until sauce is bubbly and topping is golden. Let casserole rest for 10 minutes before serving.

Variations

If you are in a hurry, substitute Quick Crumb Topping (page 178) for the Uptown Crumb Topping.

Substitute an equal quantity of broccoli florets or peas for the green beans.

Substitute an equal quantity of salmon, mackerel, kippers, shrimp, lobster or clams for the tuna.

Lobster in Américaine Sauce

A whole lobster swimming in slippery sauce is the traditional presentation for this dish, making cooking and consuming it a difficult and messy experience. Here I've simplified the technique by using canned lobster in a delightful creamy tomato base. For serving suggestions, see page 155.

Makes 4 small servings

- Guest-worthy

Tips

Instead of an 11.3-ounce (320 g) can of lobster you can use two 6-ounce (170 g) cans, or measure by volume.

Pushing the puréed solids through a sieve makes the sauce silky. You should end up with very little in the way of seeds and other undesirable solids to discard. A sturdy whisk is your best weapon for this task. Use it to stir and press the solids through the sieve. If time is of the essence, you can get the dish on the table even faster by skipping this step.

¼ cup	extra virgin olive oil	60 mL
1	can (11.3 oz/320 g) lobster meat, rinsed, drained and cut in chunks (about 2¼ cups/600 mL)	1
1	onion, diced	1
1	clove garlic, chopped	1
1	carrot, chopped	1
1 tbsp	brandy	15 mL
½ cup	dry white wine	125 mL
½ cup	fish stock	125 mL
4	ripe tomatoes (about 1½ lb/750 g), chopped	4
1 tbsp	tomato paste (see Tips, page 155)	15 mL
1 tbsp	coarsely chopped tarragon leaves	15 mL
1	bay leaf	1
½ tsp	salt (approx.)	2 mL
⅛ tsp	freshly ground black pepper	0.5 mL
2 tbsp	heavy or whipping (35%) cream	30 mL
1 tbsp	chopped parsley leaves	15 mL

1. In a saucepan, heat oil over medium heat until shimmery. Add lobster. Reduce heat to medium-low, cover and simmer for 5 minutes. Using a slotted spoon, transfer lobster to a small bowl. Set aside for 5 minutes to cool, then cover and refrigerate.

2. Increase heat to medium. Add onion, garlic and carrot to pan and cook, stirring often, for 3 to 5 minutes, until softened. Stir in brandy. Add wine, stock, tomatoes, tomato paste, tarragon, bay leaf, salt and pepper. Reduce heat to medium-low and simmer for 30 minutes, until vegetables are very soft. Remove and discard bay leaf.

Tip

Never let leftover tomato paste languish in a can in your fridge. Scoop out the remainder in 1 tbsp (15 mL) portions into an ice cube tray or onto a plate and put it in the freezer. Once the pre-measured dollops are frozen, transfer them to a zip-lock bag.

3. Transfer mixture to a blender and purée. Place a fine-mesh sieve over the pan and pour in purée. Using a firm whisk, press the mixture through the sieve (a small amount of solids such as seeds will be left; discard them). You should have about 2 cups (500 mL) purée. Add lobster to purée in pan and bring to a simmer over medium heat. Reduce heat to medium-low and simmer for 5 to 10 minutes to meld flavors and reduce sauce. Stir in cream. Taste and adjust salt if necessary.

4. Transfer to a warm serving dish and sprinkle with parsley. Serve immediately.

Variations

You can use 8 canned plum tomatoes instead of fresh tomatoes. The sauce will be thicker and more tomatoey, so add about 1/2 cup (125 mL) additional stock to the purée along with the lobster.

Substitute an equal quantity of tuna, salmon, shrimp or crab for the lobster. If using flaky fish such as salmon, stir it in with the cream.

Luxe Lobster

I've adapted a triumvirate of classic lobster dishes in this book: Shortcut Lobster Thermidor and Presto Lobster Newberg as well as Lobster in Américaine Sauce. The originals date back to the days when fine dining involved ornate French restaurants, elaborate, lengthy preparations and sauces as rich as the customers. Originating in France in the mid-1800s, Lobster à l'Américaine is the oldest of the three. Its cousins are Lobster Thermidor and Lobster Newberg. Don't confuse Thermidor and Newberg — the latter is silkier because it is thickened with cream and egg yolks, while Thermidor is made with béchamel sauce, which is thickened with flour. These three luscious lobster dishes make lovely main courses served over rice or noodles. You can also go retro and spoon them into puff pastry shells or over toast, or use them as fabulous crêpe fillings.

Shortcut Lobster Thermidor

This recipe was invented in 1894 at Marie's Restaurant in Paris in honor of the opening of a play called Thermidor. *Preparation involved poaching, making court bouillon and a sauce, and lengthy reductions and oven time, with split lobster shells as the serving vessels. This version is deconstructed but delicious, featuring lobster chunks bathed in a creamy wine sauce and topped with golden Gruyère. For serving suggestions, see page 155.*

Makes 4 small servings

- Fast
- Guest-worthy

Tip

There isn't much choice when it comes to canned lobster. If necessary, substitute two 6-ounce (170 g) cans or measure by volume.

Variation

Substitute an equal quantity of crab for the lobster.

- Preheat broiler
- 4-cup (1 L) heatproof serving dish

3 tbsp	unsalted butter, divided	45 mL
1	can (11.3 oz/320 g) lobster meat, rinsed, drained and cut in chunks (about 2¼ cups/550 mL; see Tip, left)	1
2	shallots, minced	2
2 tbsp	all-purpose flour	30 mL
1 cup	fish stock	250 mL
¼ cup	dry white wine	60 mL
¼ cup	heavy or whipping (35%) cream	60 mL
½ tsp	dry mustard powder	2 mL
3 tbsp	finely chopped parsley leaves, divided	45 mL
½ tsp	salt (approx.)	2 mL
	Freshly ground white pepper	
1 tbsp	freshly squeezed lemon juice	15 mL
1 tbsp	brandy	15 mL
½ cup	shredded Gruyère cheese (2 oz/60 g)	125 mL

1. In a saucepan over medium heat, melt 1 tbsp (15 mL) butter. Add lobster. Reduce heat to medium-low, cover and simmer for 5 minutes. Scrape lobster and pan juices into a small bowl. Cover and set aside.

2. In the same pan over medium heat, melt remaining 2 tbsp (30 mL) butter. Add shallots and cook, stirring, for 1 to 2 minutes, until softened. Stir in flour. Cook, stirring, for 1 minute. Gradually whisk in fish stock, then wine, then cream. Stir in mustard, 2 tbsp (30 mL) parsley, salt and pepper to taste. Stir in lemon juice and brandy. Add lobster, with juices, and simmer for 5 minutes. Add salt to taste if necessary.

3. Scrape mixture into a baking dish and sprinkle cheese overtop. Place under preheated broiler for 2 to 3 minutes, until cheese is golden brown and bubbly. Serve immediately.

Presto Lobster Newberg

The Hotel Fauchère in Milford, Pennsylvania, and Delmonico's Restaurant in New York City both lay claim to Lobster Newberg. As one story goes, Delmonico's dubbed it Lobster à la Wenberg because sea captain Ben Wenberg, a steady customer, described the recipe to the chef. Later it was renamed as an anagram of Wenberg. Instead of wrestling with live lobsters, you can enjoy this Newberg in about half an hour from start to finish. For serving suggestions, see page 155.

Makes 4 small servings

- Fast
- Guest-worthy

Tips

Leeks can be gritty. Here are two ways to clean them: Slice the leek in half lengthwise, fan out the layers, and rinse and rub them under running water. Alternatively, vigorously swish a chopped or thinly sliced leek in a large bowl or sink full of cold water, letting the dirt fall to the bottom, then drain.

You can turn this recipe into a bisque. Simply stir in chicken or vegetable stock to dilute the sauce to the consistency of creamy soup. I sometimes do this to transform leftovers.

Variations

Substitute an equal quantity of tuna, salmon or crab for the lobster. If using flaky fish, add it at the end with the solids.

2 tbsp	unsalted butter	30 mL
1	leek (white and light green parts), thinly sliced (see Tips, left)	1
2 cups	thinly sliced button mushrooms (4 oz/125 g)	500 mL
2 tbsp	dry sherry, divided	30 mL
1 cup	heavy or whipping (35%) cream	250 mL
¼ tsp	salt (approx.)	1 mL
⅛ tsp	freshly ground white pepper	0.5 mL
⅛ tsp	cayenne pepper	0.5 mL
1	can (11.3 oz/320 g) lobster meat, rinsed, drained and cut in chunks (about 2¼ cups/550 mL; see Tip, page 156)	1
2	egg yolks	2
Pinch	ground or freshly grated nutmeg	Pinch
	Sweet paprika	

1. In a saucepan over medium heat, melt butter. Add leek and mushrooms and cook, stirring often, for about 5 minutes or until mushrooms release their liquid and it evaporates. Stir in 1 tbsp (15 mL) sherry. Add cream, salt, pepper and cayenne. Stir in lobster. Reduce heat to low and simmer for 5 minutes.

2. Place a small sieve over a bowl and strain mixture. Set solids aside and return liquid to pan over medium heat. You should have about 1 cup (250 mL); if you have more, simmer until it is reduced. Whisk the yolks in a medium bowl. When liquid returns to a simmer, gradually add a ladleful to the yolks, whisking constantly. While whisking remaining liquid in pan, slowly pour in yolk mixture. Reduce heat to low and cook, whisking constantly, until mixture is hot and thickened, watching carefully to ensure it doesn't boil (which will cause the egg to curdle). Remove from heat. Stir in remaining 1 tbsp (15 mL) sherry, nutmeg and reserved solids. Add salt to taste, if necessary.

3. Sprinkle paprika evenly overtop and serve immediately.

Mediterranean Salmon and Rice Casserole

Mediterranean ingredients invade a retro rice casserole, and the result is tasty indeed. Kids will love the stringy molten cheese. Adults will enjoy it too.

Tips

Wash spinach well in a large bowl or sink full of cold water, swishing the leaves and letting the dirt fall to the bottom.

Toast pine nuts in a dry skillet for 2 to 3 minutes, until fragrant and turning golden. Transfer to a bowl to cool.

• **Preheat oven to 375°F (190°C)**
• **8-inch (20 cm) square baking dish**

1 cup	long-grain white rice, rinsed	250 mL
1 cup	chicken or vegetable stock	250 mL
¾ cup + 2 tbsp	water	200 mL
1	bunch spinach (10 to 12 oz/300 to 375 g), stemmed (see Tips, left)	1
2 tbsp	extra virgin olive oil	30 mL
1	small onion, finely chopped	1
2	cloves garlic, minced	2
2 tbsp	all-purpose flour	30 mL
1½ cups	whole milk	375 mL
1 tbsp	chopped oregano leaves	15 mL
	Salt and freshly ground black pepper	
1	can (7½ oz/213 g) salmon, drained, deboned and broken into chunks (see Tips, page 159)	1
8 oz	smoked mozzarella cheese, cut in ¼-inch (0.5 cm) cubes (see Tips, page 159)	250 g
8	oil-packed sun-dried tomatoes, drained and chopped (about ¼ cup/60 mL)	8
3 tbsp	toasted pine nuts (see Tips, left)	45 mL
1	recipe Uptown Crumb Topping or Quick Crumb Topping (page 178)	1
4 to 6	lemon wedges	4 to 6

1. In a saucepan, bring rice, stock and water to a boil over high heat. Reduce heat to low, cover and cook for 15 minutes, until rice is barely tender and water is absorbed.

2. Meanwhile, in a large pot over medium-high heat, cook rinsed spinach in the water clinging to its leaves for 5 minutes, until wilted. Transfer to a colander and drain. Set aside to cool for 5 minutes. Press lightly with a wooden spoon to extract remaining moisture and drain. Chop into medium clumps.

Many supermarkets sell smoked mozzarella (and other smoked cheeses) at the deli counter.

You can use the milder, less expensive pink salmon in this dish, if desired.

3. In a saucepan, heat oil over medium heat. Add onion and cook, stirring, for 2 to 3 minutes, until softened. Stir in garlic for 20 seconds. Stir in flour and cook for 1 minute. Gradually whisk in milk. Cook for 1 to 2 minutes, until mixture thickens. Stir in oregano and salt and pepper to taste.

4. Place rice, salmon, cheese, spinach, sun-dried tomatoes and pine nuts in a large bowl. Pour the sauce overtop and blend gently with a fork. Adjust salt to taste.

5. Scrape mixture into baking dish and sprinkle topping evenly overtop. Bake in preheated oven for about 15 minutes, until casserole is bubbling at the edges and topping is golden. Let casserole rest for 5 minutes before serving. Serve with lemon wedges alongside.

Variations

Substitute an equal quantity of tuna, mackerel or shrimp for the salmon.

Shrimp Mac and Queso

A riff on queso fundido, *a Mexican dip, is the lively base for this version of macaroni and cheese.* Fundido *means "molten" in Spanish. With its Mexican accents, this dish is a delicious change from the same old mac and cheese. Round out your meal with steamed vegetables such as green beans, broccoli or cauliflower, which all go nicely with cheese.*

Makes 4 to 6 servings

• Guest-worthy

Tips

I prefer to use whole wheat penne in this because it is hearty enough to stand up to the assertive sauce — and better for you.

For a creamier sauce, use whole milk.

Cotija is a firm white cheese sold in some supermarkets and Hispanic grocery stores. It has a salty tang similar to that of feta but is drier. If you can't find any, use feta or simply omit it.

• **Preheat oven to 375°F (190°C)**
• **8-inch (20 cm) square baking dish**

12 oz	penne (see Tips, left)	375 g
12 oz	Monterey Jack cheese, shredded (about 3 cups/750 mL)	500 g
2 tbsp	all-purpose flour	30 mL
1 tbsp	extra virgin olive oil	15 mL
6	green onions, (white and green parts) thinly sliced	6
1 cup	chicken stock	250 mL
1/2 cup	milk (see Tips, left)	125 mL
2 oz	cotija cheese, crumbled (about 1/3 cup/75 mL; see Tips, left)	60 g
1/4 cup	prepared salsa	60 mL
1	can (4 oz/106 g) tiny shrimp, rinsed and drained	1
2 tbsp	chopped cilantro leaves (see Tip, page 161)	30 mL
1 tbsp	chopped parsley leaves	15 mL
	Hot pepper sauce	
	Salt	
1	recipe Uptown Crumb Topping or Quick Crumb Topping (page 178)	1

1. In a large pot of boiling salted water over medium heat, cook penne for 12 to 15 minutes, until barely al dente. Drain.

2. Meanwhile, in a bowl, toss Jack cheese with flour.

3. In a large saucepan, heat oil over medium heat until shimmery. Add green onions and cook, stirring, for 1 minute, until wilted. Add stock, then Jack cheese mixture. Reduce heat to low and cook, stirring often, for 1 to 2 minutes, until cheese melts. Stir in milk, then stir in cotija, salsa and shrimp. Heat for 1 minute. Stir in cilantro, parsley and hot pepper sauce to taste. Remove from heat and season to taste with salt.

Tip

Although we generally call for only the leaves of fresh herbs, you don't have to be obsessively precise when plucking them. For herbs such as parsley and cilantro, it's okay to include some of the tender stems.

4. Stir pasta into the sauce, then scrape mixture into baking dish. Sprinkle topping evenly overtop.

5. Bake in preheated oven for about 30 minutes, until bubbling at the edges and topping is golden. Let casserole rest for 10 minutes before serving.

Variations

Substitute an equal quantity of tuna, salmon, mackerel, lobster or clams for the shrimp.

Macaroni and Cheese

Good old mac and cheese has inspired a lot of creativity in the kitchen. Cheese choices and added attractions vary from cook to cook. Canned fish is a natural enhancement.

If you don't have time to bake, you can turn almost any macaroni and cheese into a creamy stovetop dinner by cooking the pasta a minute or two longer, axing the crumb topping and omitting the oven time. Check out Vintage Tuna Mac and Cheese in the pasta chapter (page 218).

Mack and Cheese with Peas

Fish and pasta shells push macaroni and cheese onto the seafood side of Mom's menus. This version excels because it includes all the food groups. For a great weeknight dinner, add a tomato salad alongside to boost the vegetable content. Steamed cauliflower or broccoli is also good with this cheesy dish.

Makes 4 to 6 servings

- Kid-friendly

Tip

You can use any kind of milk, but 2% will make this creamy enough.

Variations

Substitute an equal quantity of tuna, salmon or kippers for the mackerel.

- **Preheat oven to 375°F (190°C)**
- **8-inch (20 cm) square baking dish**

12 oz	large pasta shells	375 g
2 tbsp	unsalted butter	30 mL
¼ cup	all-purpose flour	60 mL
3 cups	milk	750 mL
6 oz	sharp (old) Cheddar cheese, shredded (about 1½ cups/375 mL)	175 g
6 oz	Gruyère cheese, shredded (about 1½ cups/375 mL)	175 g
2 tsp	Dijon mustard	10 mL
	Hot pepper sauce	
2 tbsp	chopped parsley leaves	30 mL
2	cans (each 4 oz/125 g) mackerel, drained and broken into chunks	2
2 cups	green peas, thawed if frozen	500 mL
	Salt and freshly ground black pepper	
1	recipe Uptown Crumb Topping or Quick Crumb Topping (page 178)	1

1. In a large pot of boiling salted water over medium heat, cook pasta for 12 minutes, until barely al dente. Drain.

2. Meanwhile, in a saucepan over medium heat, melt butter. Add flour and cook, stirring, for 1 minute. Gradually whisk in milk. Cook, whisking often, for 2 to 3 minutes, until the mixture thickens. Reduce heat to medium-low and add cheeses. Cook, stirring, for 1 to 2 minutes, until melted. Stir in mustard, hot pepper sauce to taste, and parsley. Remove from heat.

3. In a large bowl, stir together cooked pasta, mackerel, peas and sauce. Season to taste with salt and pepper. Scrape mixture into baking dish and sprinkle topping evenly over top.

4. Bake in preheated oven for about 30 minutes, until bubbling at the edges and topping is golden. Let casserole rest for 10 minutes before serving.

Deviled Crab

Hot pepper sauce, mustard and crumbs make these little crab casseroles devilishly good. Serve them as an appetizer course or as brunch or luncheon treats with green salad.

Makes 4 small servings

- Guest-worthy

Tips

Keep the sauce suitably creamy by using whole milk.

Use one of the tender inner stalks of celery, known as the heart.

Go upscale with a 1 pound (454 g) container of white lump crabmeat or keep costs down by buying two less expensive 4¼-oz (120 g) shelf-stable cans of claw or flaked crab. If you have leftover crabmeat, check the chart on pages 272 to 278 for more delicious recipe ideas.

Variations

Substitute an equal quantity of tuna, salmon, mackerel, shrimp or lobster for the crab.

- **Preheat oven to 350°F (180°C)**
- **Food processor**
- **Four ¾-cup (175 mL) ramekins**

1	slice stale white bread (about 1¼ oz/35 g)	1
3 tbsp	unsalted butter, divided	45 mL
1 tbsp	chopped parsley leaves	15 mL
1 cup	milk (see Tips, left)	250 mL
2 tbsp	all-purpose flour	30 mL
1 tbsp	dry sherry	15 mL
1 tsp	Dijon mustard	5 mL
¼ tsp	salt (approx.)	1 mL
⅛ tsp	freshly ground white pepper	0.5 mL
¼ cup	chopped white onion	60 mL
¼ cup	chopped green bell pepper	60 mL
¼ cup	chopped celery heart (see Tips, left)	60 mL
1	clove garlic, minced	1
1½ cups	canned crabmeat (8 oz/250 g), rinsed and drained (see Tips, left)	375 mL
1 tbsp	hot pepper sauce	15 mL

1. In food processor fitted with the metal blade, process bread into fine crumbs (you should have about ¾ cup/175 mL). In a medium bowl, melt 1 tbsp (15 mL) butter in a microwave oven on High for 20 to 30 seconds. Stir in bread crumbs and parsley. Set aside.

2. In a large measuring cup, whisk together milk, flour, sherry, mustard, salt and pepper.

3. In a saucepan over medium-low heat, melt remaining 2 tbsp (30 mL) butter. Add onion, green pepper, celery and garlic. Cook, stirring often, for about 5 minutes, until vegetables soften.

4. Gradually add milk mixture, stirring constantly. Cook, stirring often, for 3 to 5 minutes, until mixture thickens. Stir in crab and heat for 1 minute. Add hot pepper sauce. Add salt to taste, if necessary.

5. Divide mixture evenly among ramekins. Sprinkle crumb mixture overtop. Place ramekins on a rimmed baking sheet and bake in preheated oven for 30 minutes, until sauce is bubbly and topping is golden. Serve immediately.

Parmesan Béchamel

The top layer of lasagna can get rubbery or even turn crunchy if it isn't well insulated. I often spread this Parmesan béchamel (another name for white sauce) over my lasagnas to keep the top moist. Covering the baking dish with foil during the first stage of cooking is another preventive measure.

Makes about 2 cups (500 mL)

Tips

To make a suitably thick and creamy béchamel, I use whole milk.

Use a kitchen rasp to grate the Parmesan into fluffy flakes.

This is best made just before using. You can set it aside for a few minutes, but do not cover it to keep it warm — the sauce will get watery.

2 tbsp	unsalted butter	30 mL
2	large cloves garlic, minced	2
2 tbsp	all-purpose flour	30 mL
1½ cups	milk (see Tips, left)	375 mL
4 oz	freshly grated Parmesan cheese (about 2 cups/500 mL)	125 g
2 tbsp	chopped parsley leaves	30 mL
⅛ tsp	freshly ground white pepper	0.5 mL
	Salt	

1. In a saucepan over medium heat, melt butter. Stir in garlic for 10 seconds. Add flour and cook, stirring, for 1 minute. Gradually whisk in milk. Cook, whisking often, for 1 to 2 minutes, until mixture thickens.

2. Stir in Parmesan, parsley and pepper. Reduce heat to medium-low and simmer for 1 to 2 minutes, stirring often, until Parmesan melts and sauce is very thick. Season to taste with salt.

Seafood Lasagnas

Is it lasagna or lasagne? North Americans have got used to the former. Actually, lasagna is the singular form of this wide pasta. The plural, lasagne, is favored in Italy, the U.K. and other parts of Europe. Like the majority of pizzas and pasta dishes, lasagna is usually red (*rosso*), thanks to a tomato-based sauce, but it can be creamy white (*bianco*).

Salmon and Rapini Lasagna

Salmon, rapini, a dash of heat — this is a great combination for pasta lovers. Try this lasagna on a buffet table or at a family get-together. Round out the meal with lightly dressed baby greens.

Makes 12 servings

- Guest-worthy

Tips

Rapini is also known as broccoli rabe. Boiling or blanching reduces its bitterness.

You can buy prepared marinara sauce or, if you have a favorite recipe, make your own.

Variations

Use an equal quantity, by weight, of broccoli florets or broccolini instead of the rapini.

Substitute an equal quantity of tuna, mackerel, kippers or clams for the salmon.

- **Preheat oven to 375°F (190°C)**
- **11- by 15-inch (28 by 38 cm) lasagna pan**

1	bunch rapini (about 1¼ lb/625 g), trimmed (see Tips, left)	1
20	lasagna noodles (about 1 lb/500 g)	20
2½ cups	prepared marinara sauce (22-ounce/650 mL jar; see Tips, left)	625 mL
2	cans (each 7½ oz/213 g) salmon, drained, deboned and broken into chunks	2
1 to 2 tsp	hot pepper flakes	5 to 10 mL
	Salt and freshly ground black pepper	
2 cups	ricotta cheese (1 lb/475 g tub)	500 mL
12 oz	mozzarella cheese, shredded (about 3 cups/750 mL)	375 g
1	recipe Parmesan Béchamel (page 164)	1

1. In a large pot of boiling salted water over medium heat, cook rapini for 8 to 10 minutes, until tender. Transfer to a colander and rinse under cold running water to stop the cooking. Drain well and allow to cool. Chop coarsely.

2. In a separate large pot of boiling salted water, cook noodles over medium heat for 15 to 18 minutes, until tender to the bite (al dente). Transfer to a colander and rinse under cold running water just until cool enough to handle. Drain well. Spread in a single layer on a clean kitchen towel.

3. Spread a thin layer of marinara sauce over bottom of lasagna pan. Place remainder in a bowl. Stir in salmon and season with hot pepper flakes, salt and pepper to taste.

4. Lay 5 noodles evenly over bottom of pan. Cover with half the salmon mixture and dollop half the ricotta evenly overtop. Lay 5 noodles over ricotta and scatter evenly with rapini. Scatter mozzarella over rapini. Lay 5 noodles over rapini and spread with remaining salmon mixture. Dollop remaining ricotta evenly overtop. Cover with remaining 5 noodles. Spread Parmesan Béchamel evenly overtop.

5. Bake in preheated oven for 30 minutes or until bubbly at the edges. Let rest for 10 minutes before serving.

Clam, Bacon and Spinach Lasagna

Shades of spaghetti vongole bianco! *This luscious white lasagna is a twist on spaghetti with clams. It's very rich, so a little goes a long way. For a special meal, serve it with steamed asparagus or a lightly dressed tomato salad on baby greens.*

Makes 12 servings

- Guest-worthy

Tips

Spinach is usually gritty. Wash it well in a large bowl or sink full of cold water, swishing the leaves and letting the dirt fall to the bottom. As a precaution, I even rinse the prewashed kind.

If desired, buy clams that are already chopped.

- Preheat oven to 375°F (190°C)
- 11- by 15-inch (28 by 38 cm) lasagna pan

Lasagna

20	lasagna noodles (about 1 lb/500 g)	20
2	bunches spinach (each 10 to 12 oz/ 300 to 375 g), stems trimmed (see Tips, left)	2
2 cups	ricotta cheese (1 lb/475 g tub)	500 mL
2	large cloves garlic, minced	2
¾ tsp	salt	3 mL
⅛ tsp	freshly ground black pepper	0.5 mL
⅛ tsp	ground or freshly grated nutmeg	0.5 mL

Sauce

4	slices bacon, chopped	4
1 tbsp	extra virgin olive oil (approx.)	15 mL
2	large cloves garlic, minced	2
2 tbsp	all-purpose flour	30 mL
1½ to 2 cups	milk, divided	375 to 500 mL
2 cups	freshly grated Parmesan cheese (4 oz/125 g; see Tip, page 167)	500 mL
2 tbsp	chopped parsley leaves	30 mL
⅛ tsp	freshly ground white pepper	0.5 mL
1	can (5 oz/142 g) surf or meaty clams, rinsed, drained, coarsely chopped and patted dry (see Tips, left)	1
	Salt	

Assembly

1 tbsp	extra virgin olive oil	15 mL
3 cups	shredded fontina cheese (12 oz/375 g)	750 mL

1. *Lasagna:* In a large pot of boiling salted water, cook noodles over medium heat for 15 to 18 minutes, until tender to the bite (al dente). Transfer to a colander and rinse under cold running water just until cool enough to handle. Drain well. Spread in a single layer on a clean kitchen towel.

2. Meanwhile, in a separate saucepan over medium-high heat, cook rinsed spinach in the water clinging to its leaves for 5 minutes, until wilted. Transfer to a colander and drain. Set aside to cool for 5 minutes. Press lightly with a wooden spoon to extract remaining moisture. Chop into medium clumps.

3. In a bowl, stir together spinach, ricotta, garlic, salt, pepper and nutmeg. Set aside.

4. *Sauce:* In a saucepan over medium heat, cook bacon until browned and crisp. Using a slotted spoon, transfer to a plate lined with paper towels.

5. Add enough olive oil to drippings in pan to equal 2 tbsp (30 mL). Heat over medium heat until shimmery. Stir in garlic for 10 seconds. Add flour and cook, stirring, for 1 minute. Gradually whisk in $1\frac{1}{2}$ cups (375 mL) milk, whisking for 1 to 2 minutes, until mixture is thick. Stir in Parmesan, parsley and pepper. Reduce heat to medium-low and simmer for 1 to 2 minutes, stirring often, until cheese melts and sauce is very thick. Stir in clams and bacon. Add some or all of the remaining $\frac{1}{2}$ cup (125 mL) milk to give the sauce the consistency of thick gravy. Remove from heat and season to taste with salt.

6. *Assembly:* Grease lasagna pan with olive oil. Lay 5 noodles evenly over bottom of pan. Cover with half the spinach mixture, spreading evenly. Lay 5 noodles over spinach mixture and spread evenly with clam sauce. Lay 5 noodles over clam sauce and spread evenly with remaining spinach mixture. Cover with remaining 5 noodles and scatter fontina evenly overtop.

7. Bake in preheated oven for 30 minutes or until fontina melts and starts to turn golden. Let casserole rest for 10 minutes before serving.

Variations

Substitute an equal quantity of salmon or lobster for the clams.

Oven Orzo with Shrimp and Feta

Shrimp with tomato and feta, a traditional Greek dish, is easily transformed into a casserole. The result is tasty and tangy. In keeping with the Greek theme, serve this with sautéed greens, grilled zucchini or cold green beans tossed lightly with vinaigrette.

Makes 4 servings

- Healthy

Tips

In Italian, *orzo* means "barley" but it is more commonly described as rice-shaped pasta. I love orzo for its versatility and deliciously slippery texture.

Feta cheeses are produced in many countries and thus vary widely by type and price. Feta is traditionally made from the milk of free-range sheep or goats, but you can get cow's-milk feta cheese. Check the labels. I generally buy imported Greek sheep's-milk feta. Feta is always somewhat crumbly and grainy, but moisture levels range from creamy to dry. For this casserole, I prefer to use a moister feta.

- **Preheat oven to 400°F (200°C)**
- **8-cup (2 L) round casserole dish with lid**

12 oz	orzo (see Tips, left)	375 g
2 tbsp	extra virgin olive oil	30 mL
1 cup	thinly sliced red onion	250 mL
2	cloves garlic, minced	2
½ cup	dry white wine	125 mL
1 cup	puréed canned tomatoes, with juices	250 mL
1 tbsp	chopped oregano leaves	15 mL
½ tsp	salt (approx.)	2 mL
⅛ tsp	freshly ground black pepper	0.5 mL
⅛ tsp	hot pepper flakes	0.5 mL
1	can (4 oz/106 g) tiny shrimp, rinsed and drained	1
½ cup	kalamata olives, pitted and coarsely chopped, divided	125 mL
8 oz	feta cheese, crumbled (about 1¾ cups/425 mL; see Tips, left)	250 g
1 tbsp	chopped mint leaves	15 mL

1. In a large pot of boiling salted water, cook orzo over medium heat for about 7 minutes, until it is just tender to the bite (al dente). Drain.

2. Meanwhile, in a medium saucepan, heat oil over medium heat until shimmery. Add onion and cook, stirring, for 2 minutes, until softened. Stir in garlic for 20 seconds. Stir in wine and cook for 1 minute. Add tomatoes, with juices, oregano, salt, pepper and hot pepper flakes. Bring to a simmer, reduce heat to medium-low and cook for 15 minutes, until mixture thickens and onion is tender. Remove from heat.

3. Add orzo, shrimp and half the olives to pan and stir gently. Add salt to taste, if necessary.

4. Scrape half the orzo mixture into casserole dish. Top with half the feta. Add remaining orzo mixture, then remaining feta. Cover and bake for 15 minutes, until feta looks soft. Uncover and bake for 5 minutes more, until top starts to turn golden.

5. Scatter remaining olives and mint overtop. Let casserole rest for 10 minutes before serving.

Variations

You can double the quantity of shrimp.

If you are in an ultra-Greek mood, substitute octopus for the shrimp. Lobster or squid would also work in this dish.

Jumbo Shells Stuffed with Salmon, Ricotta and Zucchini

Here's a tasty way to get kids to eat some zucchini while also pleasing the grownups at the dinner table. Everyone loves stuffed pasta shells. The salmon and zucchini add oomph to this popular dish.

Makes 4 servings

• Kid-friendly

Tips

Bottled marinara sauce speeds up production, but use your own if you have some at hand.

Zucchini is a very wet vegetable. Thanks to shredding and sautéing, however, you can say goodbye to bland, soggy zucchini. Shred it using a box grater.

• **Preheat oven to 350°F (180°C)**
• **Rimmed baking sheet**
• **13- by 9-inch (33 by 23 cm) baking dish**

1	package (8 oz/250 g) giant pasta shells	1
1 tbsp	extra virgin olive oil	15 mL
3	cloves garlic, minced	3
1	large zucchini (about 8 oz/250 g), trimmed and shredded (see Tips, left)	1
½ tsp	salt (approx.)	2 mL
1	large egg (see Tips, page 171)	1
2 cups	ricotta cheese (1 lb/475 g tub)	500 mL
1	can (7½ oz/213 g) sockeye salmon, drained, deboned and broken into chunks	1
1 cup	freshly grated Parmesan cheese (2 oz/60 g; see Tips, page 171), divided	250 mL
1 tbsp	chopped fresh dill fronds	15 mL
⅛ tsp	freshly ground black pepper	0.5 mL
2½ cups	prepared marinara sauce (22-ounce/ 650 mL jar; see Tips, left), divided	625 mL

1. In a large pot of boiling salted water over medium heat, cook shells for about 15 minutes, until they are tender but still hold their shape. Drain. Rinse under cold running water to stop the cooking and transfer, open side down in a single layer, to baking sheet to drain.

2. Meanwhile, in a skillet, heat oil over medium heat until shimmery. Stir in garlic. Immediately stir in zucchini and sprinkle with salt. Cook, stirring occasionally and scraping up brown bits from bottom of skillet, for about 8 minutes, until zucchini is tender and turning golden and excess moisture has evaporated. Remove from heat and set aside to cool.

Tips

Large eggs are standard in most test kitchens. However, in some recipes, like this one, the size of the egg is not crucial, so you can use whatever kind you have.

If you have a kitchen scale, go by weight when adding grated Parmesan to a dish. Volume measures vary widely, depending on how the Parmesan is grated, how dry it is and how it is packed into the measuring cup.

3. In a bowl, using a fork, mix egg, ricotta, salmon, half the Parmesan, dill and pepper. Add salt to taste.

4. Pour all but 1 cup (250 mL) marinara sauce into baking dish. Working with one shell at a time, stuff with $1\frac{1}{2}$ to 2 tbsp (22 to 30 mL) ricotta mixture and place, open side up, in baking dish (you will have about 5 left over). Pour remaining marinara overtop. Sprinkle remaining Parmesan evenly overtop. Cover with greased foil.

5. Bake in preheated oven for 30 minutes, until sauce is bubbly. Uncover and bake for about 10 minutes more, until cheese is golden. Let casserole rest for 5 to 10 minutes before serving.

Variations

Substitute an equal quantity of tuna, mackerel or kippers for the salmon.

Shrimp Creole

The spicy stew known as shrimp Creole is a New Orleans classic. It starts with the holy trinity of Louisiana cooking — onion, celery and green bell pepper — and finishes with plump shrimp. By using canned seafood and pantry items, you can enjoy a fairly quick shrimp Creole for dinner. This shortcut omits the long simmering but still bursts with traditional flavors. Ladle it over rice.

Makes 4 servings

• Healthy

Tips

Stick to diced tomatoes in this recipe, as they hold their shape better.

Don't skimp on the hot pepper sauce.

If you don't have fish stock, substitute equal amounts of clam juice and water or use twice as much chicken or vegetable stock.

Variations

Substitute an equal quantity of tuna, salmon, crab or lobster for the shrimp.

1 tbsp	unsalted butter	15 mL
1 tbsp	extra virgin olive oil	15 mL
1	onion, chopped	1
1	stalk celery, cut in small dice	1
1	small green bell pepper, cut in small dice	1
3	cloves garlic, minced	3
1	can (14 oz/398 mL) diced tomatoes, with juices	1
¾ cup	tomato sauce	175 mL
½ cup	chicken or vegetable stock	125 mL
½ cup	fish stock	125 mL
1 tbsp	Worcestershire sauce	15 mL
6	large pimiento-stuffed green olives, thinly sliced (about ⅓ cup/75 mL)	6
1 tsp	granulated sugar	5 mL
1	bay leaf	1
1	sprig fresh thyme	1
½ tsp	salt (approx.)	2 mL
¼ tsp	freshly ground black pepper	1 mL
	Hot pepper sauce	
1	can (4 oz/106 g) medium shrimp	1
1 tbsp	chopped parsley leaves	15 mL

1. In a saucepan over medium heat, melt butter with oil. Add onion, celery, green pepper and garlic. Cook, stirring often, for 5 minutes, until vegetables soften.

2. Stir in tomatoes, with juices, tomato sauce, chicken and fish stocks, Worcestershire sauce, olives, sugar, bay leaf, thyme, salt and pepper. Bring to a boil, reduce heat to medium-low and simmer for 20 minutes, stirring occasionally, until sauce is thickened and vegetables are tender but firm.

3. Discard bay leaf and thyme sprig. Season liberally with hot pepper sauce, then stir in shrimp. Add salt to taste, if necessary.

4. Garnish with parsley and serve immediately.

Clam Maque Choux

I love to sink my teeth into maque choux, a Louisiana dish chockfull of corn, peppers, tomato and bacon. It is often served as a side dish, but adding clams (or other seafood) makes it a hearty and colorful meal. Spoon it over a bed of rice.

Makes 6 servings

• Guest-worthy

Tip
If using thawed frozen okra instead of fresh pods, add it to the pan along with the corn.

4	slices bacon, thinly sliced crosswise	4
1 tbsp	unsalted butter	15 mL
4	cloves garlic, minced	4
2	shallots, finely diced	2
1	red bell pepper, cut in small dice	1
1	jalapeño pepper, seeded and cut in small dice	1
½ tsp	salt (approx.)	2 mL
⅛ tsp	freshly ground black pepper	0.5 mL
1 tsp	Cajun seasoning	5 mL
1½ cups	trimmed, thinly sliced okra (6 oz/175 g)	375 mL
2¼ cups	corn kernels (about 12 oz/375 g)	550 mL
1	plum tomato, peeled and diced	1
6	green onions, (white and light green parts), thinly sliced	6
1	can (5 oz/142 g) surf or meaty clams, rinsed, drained and chopped	1

1. In a 12-inch (30 cm) skillet over medium heat, cook bacon for about 5 minutes, until browned and crisp. Using a slotted spoon, transfer to a plate lined with paper towels.

2. Drain all but 1 tbsp (15 mL) drippings from skillet. Over medium heat, stir in butter until it melts. Add garlic, shallots, red pepper, jalapeño, salt, pepper and Cajun seasoning. Cook, stirring occasionally, for about 3 minutes, until vegetables soften. Increase heat to medium-high. Add okra and cook for 2 minutes, stirring occasionally. Add corn and cook for 2 to 3 minutes, until okra is tender-crisp and corn is heated through.

3. Remove skillet from heat. Stir in tomato, onions, clams and bacon. Add salt to taste, if necessary. Serve immediately.

Variations
Substitute an equal quantity of tuna, salmon, mackerel, cod, kippers, shrimp, crab or lobster for the clams.

Crab Étouffé

Here's more Louisiana comfort food. It looks best with large lump crabmeat but you can enjoy it with less expensive claw or small chunk crab. Serve this saucy dish over rice.

Makes 4 small servings

- Fast
- Guest-worthy

Variations

Substitute an equal quantity of tuna, salmon, shrimp, lobster or clams for the crab. If substituting flaky fish such as tuna or salmon, stir it in at the end.

2 tsp	fresh thyme leaves	10 mL
1 tsp	sweet paprika	5 mL
1/2 tsp	freshly ground black pepper	2 mL
1/4 tsp	salt (approx.)	1 mL
2 tbsp	unsalted butter	30 mL
1 1/2 cups	canned crabmeat (8 oz/250 g), rinsed and drained	375 mL
2 tbsp	vegetable oil	30 mL
2 tbsp	all-purpose flour	30 mL
1	small onion, diced	1
1	stalk celery, cut in 1/4-inch (0.5 cm) dice	1
1/2	small green bell pepper, cut in 1/4-inch (0.5 cm) dice	1/2
2	cloves garlic, minced	2
1 cup	chicken or vegetable stock	250 mL
1	bay leaf	1
2 tbsp	heavy or whipping (35%) cream	30 mL
	Hot pepper sauce	
2 tbsp	chopped parsley leaves	30 mL

1. In a small bowl, stir together thyme, paprika, pepper and salt.

2. In a saucepan over medium-low heat, melt butter. Add crab and half the spice mixture. Cook for 2 minutes, stirring gently a couple of times. Transfer to a bowl, cover and set aside.

3. Add oil to pan and place over medium heat until shimmery. Stir in flour. Cook, stirring, for 3 to 5 minutes, until mixture is brown and has a nutty scent. Add onion, celery and green pepper. Cook, stirring, for about 2 minutes, until vegetables soften. Stir in garlic and remaining spice mixture for 1 minute. Stir in stock and add bay leaf. When mixture comes to a simmer, reduce heat to low. Cover and simmer for 10 minutes, until vegetables are tender.

4. Discard bay leaf. Stir in cream and crab mixture and simmer for 2 minutes. Add salt to taste, if necessary. Season liberally with hot pepper sauce.

5. Serve immediately, garnished with parsley.

Salmon Picadillo

Piquant Latin American picadillo, usually made with ground beef, is an economical and enjoyable meal. Although seafood may seem like an odd substitute, the flavor combos work well. The slightly sweet, slightly sour sauce complements salmon. Serve it over rice or couscous.

Makes 4 servings

- Healthy

Tips

I prefer to use the tender inner stalks of celery known as the heart. You can, however, tenderize an outside stalk by peeling it.

Toast almonds in a dry skillet over medium heat, shaking pan often, for about 3 minutes, until golden and fragrant.

1 tbsp	extra virgin olive oil	15 mL
4	large green onions (white and light green parts), sliced	4
2	cloves garlic, minced	2
1	stalk celery heart with leaves, chopped	1
1 cup	prepared tomato sauce	250 mL
¼ cup	water	60 mL
1 tbsp	white vinegar	15 mL
2	plum tomatoes, coarsely chopped	2
1	apple, skin on, cored and chopped	1
¼ cup	raisins	60 mL
¼ cup	sliced pimiento-stuffed green olives (4 large)	60 mL
1 tsp	granulated sugar	5 mL
½ tsp	ground cumin	2 mL
¼ tsp	ground cinnamon	1 mL
¼ tsp	salt (approx.)	1 mL
¼ tsp	freshly ground black pepper	1 mL
1	can (7½ oz/213 g) salmon, drained, deboned and broken into chunks	1
3 tbsp	slivered almonds, toasted (see Tips, left)	45 mL

1. In a skillet, heat oil over medium heat until shimmery. Add green onions, garlic and celery and cook, stirring often, for 1 to 2 minutes, until vegetables start to turn golden. Stir in tomato sauce, water, vinegar, tomatoes, apple, raisins, olives, sugar, cumin, cinnamon, salt and pepper and bring to a simmer.

2. Reduce heat to medium-low, cover and simmer for 15 minutes, stirring occasionally. (If necessary to maintain a simmer, reduce heat to low.) Remove from heat and stir in salmon. Add salt to taste, if necessary.

3. Sprinkle almonds evenly overtop and serve immediately.

Variations

Substitute an equal quantity of tuna or shrimp for the salmon.

Cuban-Style Crab and Plantains with Mojo

Mojo is the signature sauce of Cuba. This delightfully spiced garlicky, tart citrus sauce adds zest to seafood and gives starchy plantains a lift.

Makes 4 servings

• Healthy

Tips

Authentic mojo is made with the juice of dimpled, thick-skinned sour oranges (also known as Seville, bigarade, bitter or marmalade oranges). Out of season, use a mixture of freshly squeezed orange and lime juices. The ideal ratio is $\frac{1}{3}$ cup (75 mL) orange juice to $\frac{1}{4}$ cup (60 mL) lime juice, but you can also go half and half.

Mojo can be either a sauce or a marinade. When using it as a sauce, I put it through the blender.

You will have leftover mojo sauce. You can refrigerate it in a container with a tight lid for up to a week, and it's versatile. Drizzle it over seafood, chicken or starchy vegetables such as sweet potatoes, or employ it as a marinade (particularly for pork).

If you don't have a mortar and pestle, you can squeeze the garlic through a press and stir it together with the cumin and salt in a bowl.

Mojo Sauce

8	cloves garlic	8
1 tsp	salt	5 mL
$\frac{1}{2}$ tsp	ground cumin	2 mL
$\frac{2}{3}$ cup	sour orange juice (see Tips, left)	150 mL
$\frac{1}{3}$ cup	extra virgin olive oil	75 mL

Plantains

3	yellow plantains ($1\frac{3}{4}$ to 2 lb/ 800 g to 1 kg; see Tips, page 177)	3
2 tsp	salt (approx.), divided	10 mL
2 tbsp	extra virgin olive oil	30 mL
1	small onion, diced	1
1	small green bell pepper, cut in small dice (about 1 cup/250 mL)	1
$\frac{1}{2}$ cup	chicken or vegetable stock	250 mL
$\frac{1}{8}$ tsp	freshly ground black pepper	0.5 mL
	Hot pepper sauce, optional	
$1\frac{1}{2}$ cups	canned crabmeat (8 oz/250 g), rinsed and drained (see Tips, page 177)	375 mL

1. *Mojo Sauce:* Mash garlic, salt and cumin into a paste using a mortar and pestle (see Tips, left). Stir in orange juice and set aside for 15 minutes to meld flavors.

2. In a small, deep saucepan, heat oil over medium heat until shimmery. Add juice mixture slowly (it spatters) and simmer for about 5 minutes, until slightly reduced and garlic is soft. Transfer to a blender and purée (makes about $\frac{3}{4}$ cup/175 mL). Set aside.

3. *Plantains:* Fill a large bowl with cold water and add 1 tsp (5 mL) salt. Trim ends off plantains and slit each lengthwise along one seam. Soak in salted water for 5 minutes. Drain. Peel plantains crosswise (not lengthwise, as you would with bananas). Cut into 2-inch (5 cm) segments. Discard soaking water.

Tips

Use small lump or claw crabmeat for this dish. Buy two shelf-stable 4¼ ounce (120 g) cans or a 1 pound (440 g) container. If you have leftover crab, turn to the chart on pages 272 to 278 for other delicious recipe ideas.

Plantains are really three different vegetables, depending on their color. For this recipe, choose plantains that have just turned yellow, with some greenish bits and a few black spots. They have a bit of sweetness at this stage, which complements the tart mojo sauce.

4. In a saucepan, combine plantains with cold water to cover by about 2 inches (5 cm). Add remaining 1 tsp (5 mL) salt. Bring to a boil over high heat. Reduce heat to medium-low, cover and simmer for about 45 minutes, until plantains are very soft.

5. Meanwhile, in a skillet, heat oil over medium heat. Add onion and green pepper and cook, stirring often, for 5 to 7 minutes, until vegetables are soft and golden.

6. When plantains have finished cooking, transfer to a colander, drain and set aside for 1 minute to release steam. Return to saucepan and add stock and pepper. Using a potato masher, mash, leaving some lumps for texture. Stir in onion mixture. Add salt to taste, if necessary. Season to taste with hot pepper sauce, if using.

7. Transfer plantains to a wide serving bowl or individual dishes. In a small, microwave-safe bowl, mix crab and ½ cup (125 mL) mojo sauce (see Tips, page 176). Microwave on High for 30 seconds. Spoon mixture over plantains and serve immediately.

Variations

Substitute an equal quantity of salmon, shrimp or lobster for the crab.

Uptown Crumb Topping

Take a few extra minutes to enhance your casserole experience with this multipurpose topping. Parmesan, garlic and parsley make it extra tasty.

Makes about 1³⁄₄ cups (425 mL)

Tips

The fine texture of dry grated Parmesan works well in both of these recipes. It makes crumb toppings crisper. You can substitute ¼ cup (60 mL) dry grated Parmesan for the freshly grated kind.

This makes enough topping for a 4-to-6-serving casserole in an 8-inch (20 cm) square baking dish. You can halve or double the recipe.

● **Food processor**

1	clove garlic	1
2	slices stale white bread (about 2½ oz/ 70 g), torn in pieces	2
½ cup	freshly grated Parmesan cheese (1 oz/30 g; see Tips, left)	125 mL
1 tbsp	chopped parsley leaves	15 mL
2 tbsp	melted unsalted butter	30 mL

1. In food processor fitted with the metal blade, with the motor running, add garlic through the feed tube to chop.

2. Scrape down the sides of the work bowl. Add bread and process it into coarse crumbs. Add Parmesan, parsley and butter. Pulse a few times until blended. Use immediately.

Quick Crumb Topping

This casserole topping tastes good too. Although its flavor is simpler in comparison to Uptown Crumb Topping (above), it offers the advantage of speedy preparation. No appliances are necessary.

Makes about 1³⁄₄ cups (425 mL)

Tips

Panko is light, crispy Japanese bread crumbs. These have become widely popular in the past decade. Look for panko crumbs in the sushi section or bakery department.

This makes enough topping for a 4-to-6-serving casserole in an 8-inch (20 cm) square baking dish. You can halve or double the recipe.

1½ cups	panko bread crumbs (see Tips, left)	375 mL
½ cup	freshly grated Parmesan cheese (1 oz/30 g; see Tips, above)	125 mL
2 tbsp	melted unsalted butter	30 mL

1. In a bowl, combine panko crumbs, Parmesan and butter. Using a fork, mix until evenly moistened. Use immediately.

Pies and Pizzas

Maritime Quiche

Okay, real men, admit it — who doesn't like quiche? After all, it contains bacon, eggs and cheese. Factoid: classic quiche is a cheese-free pie. But that's not for us. This version is delightfully creamy.

Tips

The egg wash sets on the hot shell and forms a protective layer that combats sogginess. Immediately placing the filled quiche in the oven also helps. Still, make sure any seafood you use is dry; drain it on paper towels or squeeze out the moisture.

This quiche is exceptionally creamy, thanks to the addition of sour cream and the low oven temperature, which prevents the delicate custard from curdling.

Shredded cheese varies quite a bit by volume. When possible, go by weight.

Variations

Bake the filling in mini shells and serve as hors d'oeuvres quiches. You'll have enough for about 48 mini shells, each about 1½ inches (4 cm) wide and holding 1 tbsp (15 mL) filling. Cook the minis on a baking sheet until filling is puffed and pastry is golden, about 30 minutes.

Substitute an equal quantity of tuna, salmon, mackerel, cod, kippers, lobster or clams for the shrimp.

- **Preheat oven to 400°F (200°C)**

2	slices bacon, chopped	2
1	9-inch (23 cm) deep-dish single pie shell	1
3	large eggs, divided	3
1 tsp	cold water	5 mL
1 cup	half-and-half (10%) cream	250 mL
½ cup	full-fat sour cream	125 mL
1 tsp	chopped fresh dill fronds	5 mL
¼ tsp	salt	1 mL
⅛ tsp	freshly ground white pepper	0.5 mL
⅛ tsp	ground or freshly grated nutmeg	0.5 mL
1	can (4 oz/106 g) tiny shrimp, rinsed, drained and patted dry	1
½ cup	shredded Gruyère cheese (2 oz/60 g; see Tips, left)	125 mL

1. In a skillet over medium heat, cook bacon for about 5 minutes, until browned and crisp. Using a slotted spoon, transfer to a plate lined with paper towels to drain.

2. Prick pie shell all over with a fork. Bake in preheated oven for 10 minutes, until dough looks dry.

3. Meanwhile, in a medium bowl, whisk together one egg and water. When pie shell has finished prebaking, remove from oven, place on a baking sheet and brush with a thin layer of the egg wash (you will have some left over). Set aside and reduce oven temperature to 300°F (150°C).

4. To the bowl with the remaining egg wash, add remaining eggs, cream, sour cream, dill, salt, pepper and nutmeg. Whisk to blend.

5. Scatter shrimp evenly across bottom of pie shell. Crumble bacon over shrimp. Ladle cream mixture into shell and scatter cheese evenly overtop.

6. Return to oven for about 1 hour, until crust is golden brown and filling is set at the edges but a bit wobbly in the center. Cool completely on a rack before serving.

Shortcut Tuna Pot Pie

Add a store-bought biscuit topping to creamed tuna and vegetables and presto, you've got a humble but appealing pot pie. My family makes short work of this pie once it hits the table.

Tips

Place the leftover biscuit dough on a greased square of foil and bake it alongside.

I prefer to use the tender inner stalks of celery known as the heart. You can, however, tenderize an outside stalk by peeling it.

Variations

Substitute salmon, mackerel, shrimp or clams for the tuna.

● **Preheat oven to 375°F (190°C)**
● **8-inch (20 cm) square baking dish**

2 tbsp	unsalted butter	30 mL
1	small onion, chopped	1
1/2	red bell pepper, chopped	1/2
1	stalk celery, chopped (see Tips, left)	1
1/4 cup	all-purpose flour	60 mL
1 cup	chicken stock	250 mL
1 cup	whole milk	250 mL
1/2 cup	green peas, thawed if frozen	125 mL
1/2 cup	corn kernels, thawed if frozen	125 mL
2 tbsp	chopped parsley leaves	30 mL
1 tsp	chopped fresh dill fronds	5 mL
1/2 tsp	mustard powder	2 mL
1 tbsp	freshly squeezed lemon juice	15 mL
1	can (6 oz/170 g) tuna in water, drained and broken into chunks	1
1	tube (12 oz/340 g) refrigerated "country biscuit" dough	1

1. In a skillet over medium heat, melt butter. Add onion, red pepper and celery and cook, stirring often, for 5 minutes, until vegetables soften. Stir in flour and cook for 1 minute. Gradually whisk in stock, then milk. When mixture comes to a simmer, stir in peas, corn, parsley, dill and mustard. Reduce heat to medium-low. Simmer, stirring often, for about 10 minutes, until mixture is thickened and vegetables are tender. Stir in lemon juice, then tuna.

2. Scrape mixture into baking dish and lay 9 dough rounds on top (you will have one left over, see Tips, left). Bake in preheated oven for about 15 minutes, until biscuits are golden and filling is bubbling at the edges. Let rest for 5 minutes before serving.

Salmon and Leek Pot Pie

Nostalgia is an ingredient in this old-school pie. The thick, mild-mannered leek and parsley sauce is an appealing partner for flavorful salmon.

Makes 6 servings

- Kid-friendly

Tip

I use whole milk to make the sauce creamier.

Variations

Top the pie with homemade or store-bought biscuit dough instead of pastry (see Shortcut Tuna Pot Pie, page 181.)

Substitute an equal quantity of tuna, mackerel, shrimp, lobster or clams for the salmon.

- **Preheat oven to 375°F (190°C)**
- **Rimmed baking sheet**
- **9-inch (23 cm) pie plate**

1 cup	whole milk (see Tip, left)	250 mL
½ cup	chicken stock	125 mL
¼ cup	all-purpose flour	60 mL
2 tbsp	unsalted butter	30 mL
2	leeks (white and light green parts), thinly sliced	2
½ tsp	salt (approx.)	2 mL
2	cloves garlic, minced	2
¼ cup	dry white wine	60 mL
2	cans (each 7½ oz/213 g) salmon, drained, deboned and broken into chunks	2
1	small roasted red pepper, diced	1
¼ cup	chopped parsley leaves	60 mL
1 tsp	finely grated lemon zest	5 mL
⅛ tsp	freshly ground white pepper	0.5 mL
	Pastry for a single-crust pie	

1. In a bowl, whisk together milk, stock and flour.

2. In a saucepan over medium heat, melt butter. Add leeks and salt. Cook, stirring often, for about 5 minutes, until leeks soften and turn golden. Stir in garlic for 30 seconds. Stir in wine for 30 to 60 seconds, until it has almost evaporated. Stir in milk mixture and bring to a boil. Reduce heat to medium-low and simmer for 3 to 5 minutes, until leeks are tender and sauce is very thick. Remove from heat.

3. Stir in salmon, roasted red pepper, parsley, lemon zest and ground pepper. Add salt to taste, if necessary.

4. Scrape mixture into pie plate. Slash a few vents in the pastry and place it over filling. Press edges onto rim of pie plate. Place pie on sheet.

5. Bake in preheated oven for about 30 minutes, until pastry is golden brown and filling is bubbly. Let pie rest for 10 minutes before serving.

Roasted Vegetable and Salmon Strudel

Bored with the same old same old? This savory strudel is like a surprise package for dinner. It's chockfull of roasted vegetables and chunks of salmon for maximum flavor.

Makes 6 servings

- Guest-worthy

Tip

Roasted vegetables: Preheat oven to 450°F (230°C). Place ½ bunch trimmed asparagus, (about 8 oz/250 g), 1 large portobello mushroom cut in ½-inch (1 cm) slices, 3 slices (each ½-inch/1 cm thick) red onion, and 1 each red and green bell pepper (halved lengthwise, stemmed, seeded and deveined), on a baking sheet in a single layer. Brush with 1 tbsp (15 mL) oil and sprinkle with salt to taste. Roast in preheated oven until tender, removing the vegetables in stages: 10 to 15 minutes for asparagus and mushroom, 20 to 25 minutes for onion and 25 to 30 minutes for peppers. Set aside until cool enough to handle.

Variations

Substitute an equal quantity of tuna, mackerel or cod for the salmon.

- **Preheat oven to 400°F (200°C)**
- **Rimmed baking sheet, lined with parchment**

	Roasted vegetables (see Tip, left)	
1	can (7½ oz/213 g) salmon, drained, deboned and broken into chunks	1
2 tbsp	chopped fresh dill fronds	30 mL
⅛ tsp	freshly ground black pepper	0.5 mL
1 tsp	white wine vinegar or freshly squeezed lemon juice	5 mL
12	sheets phyllo pastry	12
½ cup	unsalted butter, melted	125 mL
2 tsp	sesame seeds	10 mL

1. Coarsely chop roasted asparagus, mushroom and onion and transfer, with juices, to a large bowl. Pull skins off roasted peppers, chop coarsely and transfer to bowl. Gently squeeze salmon to remove excess moisture and add it to the bowl, along with dill, pepper and vinegar. Toss with a fork and season to taste with salt.

2. On a work surface, lay out 1 phyllo sheet horizontally in front of you. Working quickly, brush liberally with butter. Repeat with 5 more sheets, stacking them on top of each other. Spread half the salmon mixture in a strip along the long end closest to you, leaving a 1-inch (2.5 cm) border on each side. Roll the phyllo once over the filling. Tuck in the sides. Finish rolling, jelly-roll fashion, to form a log. Place seam side down on prepared baking sheet. Repeat to make a second strudel. Brush remaining butter over strudels and sprinkle sesame seeds overtop. Make 3 diagonal slashes across the top of each roll.

3. Bake in preheated oven for 20 minutes, until golden. Let cool on baking sheet for 5 minutes. Slice along score marks and serve warm.

Clam Pie

Dr. Atkins would shudder at the classic carbfest known as clam pie. It's like eating clam chowder in pastry, and it's addictively delicious. Like many vintage seafood recipes, clam pie dates back to the 1890s. Culinary historians say it was a thrifty meal enthusiastically and frequently consumed by working-class families, particularly in East Hampton, New York, and among the Acadians. While they used fresh clams, this version is equally appealing but far less work.

Makes 6 servings

- Kid-friendly
- Guest-worthy

Tips

I use yellow-fleshed potatoes in this pie, as they are somewhat creamy but still hold their shape. Try to go by weight, as the amount will affect the consistency of the filling.

Placing the oven rack in the lowest position helps to keep the bottom crust crispy and prevents the top crust from browning too quickly.

Poultry seasoning is a spice blend sold in supermarkets.

- Preheat oven to 400°F (200°C), placing rack in lowest position (see Tips, left)
- 9- or 10-inch (23 or 25 cm) deep-dish pie plate
- Rimmed baking sheet

4	slices bacon, chopped	4
1 lb	potatoes (4), peeled and cut in ¼-inch (0.5 cm) dice (see Tips, left)	500 g
1	carrot (about 2 oz/60 g), cut in ¼-inch (0.5 cm) dice	1
1	onion, diced	1
1	clove garlic, minced	1
½ tsp	salt (approx.)	2 mL
1	bottle (8 oz/240 mL) clam juice (see Tips, page 185)	1
1 tsp	finely grated lemon zest	5 mL
2 tsp	fresh thyme leaves	10 mL
½ tsp	poultry seasoning (see Tips, left)	2 mL
¼ tsp	freshly ground black pepper	1 mL
¾ cup	heavy or whipping (35%) cream	175 mL
2 tbsp	all-purpose flour	30 mL
1	can (5 oz/142 g) surf or meaty clams, drained and coarsely chopped	1
	Pastry for a double-crust pie	

1. In a large saucepan over medium heat, cook bacon for about 5 minutes, until browned and crisp. Using a slotted spoon, transfer to a plate lined with paper towels to drain.

2. Add potatoes, carrot, onion, garlic and salt to the drippings and cook, stirring often, for about 5 minutes, until softened. Add clam juice, lemon zest, thyme, poultry seasoning and pepper. Reduce heat to low, cover and cook for 10 minutes, until vegetables are almost tender.

Tips

Don't substitute the liquid from canned clams for bottled clam juice. The former usually contains additives.

You need meaty clams for this pie. Baby clams are too delicate.

If desired, buy pre-chopped clams.

3. In a measuring cup, whisk together cream and flour. Gradually stir into clam mixture and bring to a simmer. Cook for 1 to 2 minutes, until thickened. Stir in clams and reserved bacon. Remove pan from heat and set aside to cool for 30 minutes, stirring occasionally to disperse the heat. Add salt to taste, if necessary.

4. Press dough for bottom crust into pie plate. Add cooled filling. Place top crust over filling, trimming and crimping the edges. Cut 8 long slits in a spoke pattern on top. Place pie on baking sheet and bake in preheated oven for 30 minutes, until crust is golden. Reduce oven temperature to 350°F (180°C), rotate baking sheet and bake for 30 minutes more, until filling is bubbly and crust is golden brown.

5. Transfer to a wire rack and let cool for 15 to 30 minutes. Serve warm or at room temperature.

Variation

If you don't want to make a double-crust pie, put the filling in a casserole dish, cover the top with pastry dough and reduce the baking time by about 15 minutes, or bake until the filling is bubbly and the crust is golden brown.

Coulibiac

Coulibiac is a fancy name for salmon and rice pie. You don't have to wait for a special occasion to prepare it: coulibiac makes an appealing family meal. Originating in Russia as kulebyaka, *this pie was popularized by French chefs in the 19th century.*

Makes 6 servings

- Kid-friendly

Tips

Puff pastry packages vary in size. If available, use a 14 ounce (400 g) package, which is just the right amount for this recipe.

Many cooks prepare the filling in layers, but I like to mix the salmon with the rice to keep it moist.

- **Preheat oven to 400°F (200°C)**
- **Rimmed baking sheet, lined with parchment**

Filling

⅓ cup	long-grain white rice, rinsed	75 mL
⅔ cup	water	150 mL
¾ tsp	salt (approx.), divided	3 mL
1 tbsp	vegetable oil	15 mL
3 cups	sliced button or cremini mushrooms (8 oz/ 250 g; see Tip, page 187)	750 mL
1 cup	thinly sliced leek (about ½)	250 mL
2	cans (each 7½/213 g) salmon, drained, deboned and broken into chunks	2
3	large eggs, hard-cooked and coarsely chopped	3
¼ cup	chopped parsley leaves	60 mL
1 tbsp	chopped fresh dill fronds	15 mL
¼ tsp	freshly ground black pepper	1 mL

Pastry

1	large egg	1
1 tbsp	cold water	15 mL
1 lb	puff pastry (approx.), thawed, at room temperature (see Tips, left)	500 g
	Flour for dusting	

Sauce (optional)

1 cup	sour cream	250 mL
1 tbsp	vodka	15 mL
1 tbsp	chopped chives	15 mL
	Salt	
1 tbsp	black or red lumpfish caviar (roe)	15 mL

1. *Filling:* In a small saucepan over high heat, bring rice, water and ⅛ tsp (0.5 mL) salt to a boil. Reduce heat to low, cover and simmer for about 15 minutes, until water is absorbed and rice is tender. Fluff with a fork and set aside to cool to room temperature.

Tip

No need to fuss with mushroom brushes. You can rinse dirt off mushrooms; just don't let them soak. They are absorbent, but liquid is released in the hot pan.

2. In a skillet (preferably nonstick), heat oil over medium heat until shimmery. Add mushrooms, leek and $\frac{1}{8}$ tsp (0.5 mL) salt. Cook, stirring often, for about 5 minutes, until liquid from mushrooms is released and evaporates. Set aside and cool to room temperature.

3. Add rice, salmon, eggs, parsley, dill, $\frac{1}{2}$ tsp (2 mL) salt and pepper to mushrooms. Mix gently with a fork. Add salt to taste, if necessary.

4. *Pastry:* In a small bowl, whisk together egg and water.

5. Cut pastry into 2 pieces, one slightly larger. On a lightly floured surface, roll the larger piece into a rectangle 14 by 10 inches (35 by 25 cm). Place on prepared baking sheet and brush with egg wash. Spread filling over pastry, leaving a 1-inch (2.5 cm) border. Roll remaining pastry into a rectangle 12 by 8 inches (30 by 20 cm). Place over filling. Fold edges of bottom pastry up to cover top pastry. Using a fork, press along the border to seal. Brush top with egg wash (you will have some left over).

6. Bake in preheated oven for 25 to 30 minutes, until pie is golden brown. Let rest for 5 minutes before serving.

7. *Sauce (if using):* In a small serving bowl, stir together sour cream, vodka, chives and salt to taste. Just before serving, rinse the caviar and drain well. Scatter over the sour cream. Serve sauce alongside slices of pie.

Variations

If you prefer, serve plain sour cream or hollandaise sauce instead of the vodka sauce.

Instead of making a traditional coulibiac, substitute tuna or mackerel for the salmon.

Shrimp Margherita Pizza

You don't need a fully loaded pizza to hit the spot. Shrimp is the only extra on this Italian tomato and cheese classic.

**Makes one
12-inch (30 cm)
pizza
4 to 6 servings**

- Fast
- Kid-friendly
- Healthy

Tips

Baking the pizza near the bottom of the oven allows the crust to turn golden before the toppings start to overcook.

Don't confuse fresh mozzarella with the firm, more aged yellow mozzarella sold in balls or bricks. You can use fior de latte, a fresh cow's-milk mozzarella, or go upscale and splurge on buffalo mozzarella. Another alternative is to economize with bocconcini balls — use an equal quantity by weight.

Don't put the cheese too close to the edge, as it melts and spreads.

Transfer the loaded pizza to the oven right on the parchment paper.

- **Preheat oven to 500°F (260°C), placing rack in the lowest position (see Tips, left)**
- **Preheated pizza stone or inverted baking sheet**

2 tbsp	extra virgin olive oil	30 mL
2	cloves garlic, minced	2
1/4 tsp	dried oregano	1 mL
3/4 tsp	salt	3 mL
1/8 tsp	freshly ground black pepper	0.5 mL
	Flour for dusting	
1 lb	pizza dough, at room temperature	500 g
1	can (4 oz/106 g) tiny shrimp, rinsed and drained	1
2	balls fresh mozzarella (about 8 oz/250 g), drained and sliced 1/4 inch (0.5 cm) thick, patted dry (see Tips, left)	2
2	plum tomatoes (about 8 oz/250 g), cut in 1/4-inch (0.5 cm) slices	2
10	large basil leaves, coarsely chopped	10

1. In a small bowl, stir together oil, garlic, oregano, salt and pepper.

2. On a lightly floured piece of parchment paper, stretch or roll dough into a 12-inch (30 cm) circle. Brush garlic oil evenly overtop, right to the edges. Scatter shrimp overtop, leaving a 1/2-inch (1 cm) border. Arrange mozzarella overtop, followed by tomato slices.

3. Bake in preheated oven on preheated pizza stone or baking sheet for 15 to 20 minutes or until bottom is golden brown and cheese bubbles.

4. Scatter basil evenly overtop and serve immediately.

Variations

Substitute an equal quantity of lobster or clams for the shrimp, or add anchovies to taste.

Greek Pizza

I love Greek accents on pizza, and what could be more Greek than feta, olives and octopus? Firm, bold octopus isn't easily overpowered by pizza ingredients. In fact, if you're a fan, double the quantity of octopus. Warning: this is a salty pizza.

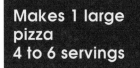

Tips

Baking the pizza with the rack in the lowest position in your oven helps the crust turn golden and ensures that the toppings won't overcook.

You can use lower-fat mozzarella.

Transfer the loaded pizza to the oven right on the parchment paper.

• **Preheat oven to 500°F (260°C), placing rack in the lowest position (see Tips, left)**
• **Preheated pizza stone or inverted baking sheet**

2 tbsp	extra virgin olive oil	30 mL
2	cloves garlic, minced	2
2 tsp	chopped oregano leaves	10 mL
1/8 tsp	freshly ground black pepper	0.5 mL
	Flour for dusting	
1 lb	pizza dough, at room temperature	500 g
1	can (4 oz/120 g) octopus, drained and coarsely chopped	1
1 cup	shredded mozzarella (about 3 oz/90 g; see Tips, left)	250 mL
1/2 cup	sliced red onion	125 mL
1 cup	crumbled feta cheese (about 4 oz/125 g)	250 mL
1/4 cup	kalamata olives, pitted and sliced	60 mL

1. In a small bowl, stir together oil, garlic, oregano and pepper.

2. On a lightly floured piece of parchment, stretch or roll dough into an oval about 16 by 10 inches (40 by 25 cm). Brush oil mixture overtop, right to the edges. Scatter toppings over the dough to within 1/2 inch (1 cm) of the edge, in this order: octopus, mozzarella, onion, feta and olives.

3. Bake in preheated oven on preheated pizza stone or baking sheet for 12 to 15 minutes, until bottom is golden brown and cheese is molten.

> ### Variations
> Substitute an equal quantity of salmon, shrimp or lobster for the octopus.

Personal Pizzas with Lobster and Roasted Garlic

Spoil pizza lovers with these individual lobster pies. Redolent of garlic butter, they smell as tempting as they taste.

Makes 4 servings

- Guest-worthy

Tips

Baking the pizza with the rack in the lowest position in your oven helps the crust turn golden and ensures that the toppings won't overcook.

There's not much choice when it comes to canned lobster. If possible, buy a 6-ounce (170 g) can and use the extra amount on the pizzas. If you end up with a larger can, use the leftovers for other recipes. Check the chart on pages 272 to 278 for more delicious options.

The cheese blend I use includes provolone, mozzarella, Parmesan and Emmenthal.

- **Preheat oven to 400°F (200°C), placing rack in the lowest position (see Tips, left)**
- **Preheated pizza stone or inverted baking sheet**

1	head garlic (see Tip, page 191)	1
1/8 tsp	vegetable oil	0.5 mL
3 tbsp	unsalted butter, softened	45 mL
1/8 tsp	salt	0.5 mL
	Freshly ground black pepper	
1 lb	pizza dough, at room temperature, divided	500 g
	Flour for dusting	
1 cup	canned lobster meat (about 4 oz/125 g), coarsely chopped and patted dry (see Tips, left)	250 mL
1 cup	shredded Italian 4-cheese blend (about 4 oz/125 g)	250 mL
12	small grape tomatoes, halved	12
1/4 cup	coarsely chopped basil leaves	60 mL

1. Cut a thin slice off the top of the garlic. Place it on a square of foil and drizzle oil overtop. Wrap foil over garlic and roast in preheated oven for about 45 minutes, until cloves are tender. Set aside until cool enough to handle. Squeeze cloves out of skins into a small, microwave-safe dish and mash with a fork. Blend in butter, salt and pepper to taste.

2. Cut dough into 4 pieces. Place each on a lightly floured piece of parchment. Stretch and roll out each piece of dough into a 6-inch (15 cm) circle.

3. Microwave garlic-butter mixture on High for a few seconds, until it is easy to spread but not molten. Dividing equally, brush over dough right to the edges. Arrange lobster over dough, dividing equally. Sprinkle cheese evenly overtop each pizza. Arrange tomatoes overtop, cut sides down. Scatter basil evenly overtop.

Two heads are better than one. You are roasting garlic anyway, so why not double the quantity? Refrigerate or freeze the extra to satisfy future cravings.

4. Bake in preheated oven on preheated pizza stone or baking sheet (in batches if necessary, depending on size of stone) for about 12 minutes, until bottom is crispy and golden and cheese is molten. Serve immediately.

Variations

Substitute an equal quantity of shrimp, crab or clams for the lobster.

Seafood Pizzas

Keep pizza simple and more healthful: don't overwhelm it with toppings.

A pizza stone and peel (giant paddle) are handy, but you can substitute an inverted baking sheet for both. A stone should be preheated at your recipe temperature for at least 30 minutes. As for a baking sheet, if you are using it instead of a pizza stone, place it in the oven when you set it to preheat.

You can make your own dough or speed things up by using prepared dough from the supermarket. The recipes here all work with whole wheat as well as regular pizza dough.

Rolling the dough on parchment makes it easier to transfer to the hot oven. Add your toppings, push the pizza peel or a cool inverted baking sheet under the parchment, then slide the pizza, paper and all, onto the preheated stone.

New Haven Clam Pizzas

Thin-crust white clam pie is the signature pizza of New Haven, Connecticut. Purists would flog me for using canned clams instead of fresh-shucked ones, but this shortcut tastes darn good. Adding tomatoes or mozzarella, however, would be considered further sacrilege.

Makes 2 medium pizzas
4 to 6 servings

- Fast
- Guest-worthy

Tips

Baking the pizza near the bottom of your oven helps the crust to turn golden and ensures that the toppings won't overcook.

A pie without tomatoes is called a white pizza.

Use a kitchen rasp to grate the cheese into fluffy flakes.

Avoid using soft baby clams on pizza.

Transfer the loaded pizza to the oven right on the parchment paper.

- **Preheat oven to 500°F (260°C), placing rack in the lowest position (see Tips, left)**
- **Preheated pizza stone or inverted baking sheet**

6 tbsp	extra virgin olive oil	90 mL
3	large cloves garlic, minced	3
1 tsp	thyme leaves	5 mL
¼ tsp	salt	1 mL
⅛ tsp	freshly ground black pepper	0.5 mL
1 lb	pizza dough, at room temperature, divided	500 g
	Flour for dusting	
1	can (5 oz/142 g) surf or meaty clams, rinsed, drained, coarsely chopped and patted dry	1
¾ cup	freshly grated Pecorino Romano cheese (about 1 oz/30 g)	175 mL

1. In a small bowl, stir together oil, garlic, thyme, salt and pepper. Set aside.

2. Divide the dough in half and place each half on a lightly floured piece of parchment. Stretch and roll the dough into thin ovals, each 8 to 10 inches (20 to 25 cm) long. Brush oil mixture overtop, right to the edges. Scatter clams evenly overtop. Sprinkle cheese evenly overtop.

3. With rack in the lowest position, bake in preheated oven on preheated pizza stone or baking sheet (one or both at a time, depending on size of stone) for 10 minutes, until bottom is golden brown and top is bubbly.

Variations

Some people add crumbled bacon, but in my opinion the simpler, the better.

Substitute an equal quantity of shrimp, lobster or octopus for the clams.

Oven Orzo with Octopus and Feta (variation) (page 168)

Clam Maque Choux (page 173)

Personal Pizzas with Crab and
Roasted Garlic (variation) (page 190)

Lemon Pepper Shrimp Pasta (page 204)

Tagliatelle with Tarragon Lobster and Asparagus (page 206)

Easy Ham and Clam Jambalaya (page 236)

Shrimp, Pomegranate and Almond Quinoa (page 245)

Salmon, Spinach and Sweet Potato Frittata (page 255)

Sfincione (Palermo Pizza Bread)

Sicilian-style pizza, also known as sfincione, is more like a pizza bread. The name may be derived from the Latin for "sponge." Unlike the familiar Neapolitan pie, this Palermo-style pizza is rectangular, with a thicker, softer, bread-like crust and scant toppings, which typically include tomatoes, onions, anchovies and caciocavallo cheese. Plain but delicious, sfincione can be eaten straight from the oven while still hot and pillowy, or at room temperature.

Makes 8 slices

- Guest-worthy

Tips

Caciocavallo cheese is a rich Italian melting cheese formed in a teardrop-shaped ball. It is sold in cheese shops and some supermarkets. If you don't have caciocavallo, substitute an equal quantity of provolone, which is drier and more assertive.

I use premium Italian tomatoes called San Marzanos. One can will make twice as much sauce as you need, so freeze the remainder for another sfincione or add it to pasta.

Crushing canned tomatoes by hand is fast and fun to do — just squish each tomato through your fingers.

Italian-style bread crumbs (fine, dry crumbs with Italian seasonings added) are a good shortcut for this recipe. They are sold in most supermarkets. If you don't have any, mix dry bread crumbs with your favorite dried Italian herbs to taste.

- **Preheat oven to 400°F (200°C), placing rack in the lowest position (see Tips, page 192)**
- **13- by 9-inch (33 by 23 cm) baking dish, lightly greased**

1 lb	pizza dough, at room temperature	500 g
2 tbsp	extra virgin olive oil	30 mL
2	onions, diced	2
1/4 tsp	salt (approx.)	1 mL
	Freshly ground black pepper	
1	can (28 oz/796 mL) plum tomatoes, crushed (see Tips, left)	1
1	can (2 oz/50 g) anchovies (about 15), drained and halved lengthwise	1
2 tbsp	Italian-style bread crumbs (see Tips, left)	30 mL
14 oz	caciocavallo cheese, cut in 1/4-inch (0.5 cm) cubes (see Tips, left)	400 g

1. Turn dough in a lightly oiled bowl, cover it and let it rise for about 2 hours at room temperature, until doubled in bulk. Stretch and press dough into prepared baking dish. Cover with a clean tea towel and set aside to rise for 30 minutes.

2. Meanwhile, in a skillet, heat oil over medium heat until shimmery. Add onions, salt and pepper to taste. Cook, stirring often, for 10 minutes, until onions soften and turn golden. Stir in tomatoes and cook, stirring occasionally, for 20 to 30 minutes, until onions are tender and sauce is thick. Remove from heat and set aside to cool to room temperature. Add salt to taste, if necessary.

3. Slightly adjust dough to fit the pan evenly (it may shift as it rises). Spread evenly with half the sauce (store remainder for other uses). Arrange anchovies evenly overtop. Sprinkle breadcrumbs evenly overtop. Scatter with cheese.

4. Bake in preheated oven for about 30 minutes, until crust is golden brown on the bottom and cheese is molten.

Pissaladière

Also known as Provençal pizza, pissaladière is a caramelized onion, anchovy and olive pie. It tastes way better than it sounds and may even convert those with an aversion to anchovies. The French are serious about their pissaladière. A mayor of Nice once declared that the onion topping must be half the thickness of the crust. Pissaladière is traditionally accompanied by pastis, an anise-flavored liqueur — so, cheers!

Makes 1 large pizza
4 to 8 servings

• Guest-worthy

Tip

Placing the rack near the bottom of the oven helps the crust turn golden and ensures that the toppings won't overcook.

• Preheat oven to 400°F (200°C), placing rack positioned second from the bottom position (see Tip, left)
• 13- by 9-inch (33 by 23 cm) baking dish, greased

Onions

1 tbsp	unsalted butter	15 mL
2 tbsp	extra virgin olive oil	30 mL
4	onions (about 1¼ lb/600 g), halved on the vertical and thinly sliced	4
¼ tsp	salt	1 mL
⅛ tsp	freshly ground black pepper	0.5 mL
1	bay leaf	1
1 tsp	fresh thyme leaves	5 mL
1 tsp	fresh rosemary leaves, chopped	5 mL

Pizza

1 tbsp	extra virgin olive oil	15 mL
1	tube (14 oz/391 g) refrigerated pizza dough (see Tip, page 195)	1
16	anchovy fillets, drained and halved lengthwise	16
15	black olives (approx.), pitted and halved	15
2 tsp	fresh thyme leaves	10 mL

1. *Onions:* In a skillet over medium heat, melt butter with oil. Add onions, salt and pepper and cook, stirring often, for 10 minutes, until onions start to brown. Reduce heat to low. Stir in bay leaf, thyme and rosemary. Cover and cook, stirring occasionally, for 20 minutes, until the onions are golden brown and very tender. Uncover and cook, stirring occasionally, for 15 to 20 minutes more, until onions are deep caramel. Remove from heat and set aside until cooled to room temperature.

Tip

A pissaladière crust should be soft and thin, not crispy like pizza crust. The French opt for foccacia-style bread dough or pie pastry. Some cooks make do with puff pastry, but it really is too greasy. Oddly, the pizza dough sold in refrigerated tubes in the supermarket, with its soft, pastry-like texture, is more suitable, so you don't have to make a dough from scratch.

2. *Pizza:* Unroll dough into prepared dish and press evenly into pan. Prick all over with a fork. Bake for 5 minutes in preheated oven.

3. Using a fork, spread onions evenly over dough, right to the edges. Arrange anchovies in a series of crosses overtop. Place olive halves, cut side down, in spaces between the crosses. Scatter thyme overtop.

4. Bake for 15 minutes in preheated oven until crust is golden and topping is hot. Serve immediately.

Salmon Pizza Pinwheels

Add these pinwheels to lunch bags or serve them as easy after-school snacks. They also make fine breakfast buns.

Makes 10 pinwheels

- Fast
- Kid-friendly
- Brown-bag

Tip

Soft cream cheese is sold in tubs in supermarket delis and cheese shops.

- **Preheat oven to 400°F (200°C)**
- **Baking sheet, lined with parchment**

1	can (7½ oz/213 g) salmon, drained, deboned and broken into chunks	1
2 tbsp	soft cream cheese	30 mL
	Flour for dusting	
1	tube (14 oz/391 g) refrigerated pizza dough	1
1 cup	shredded Italian cheese blend (about 4 oz/125 g)	250 mL
4	green onions, thinly sliced	4

1. In a bowl, using a fork, mix salmon and cream cheese.

2. On a lightly floured surface, roll dough into a rectangle about 14 by 10 inches (36 by 25 cm). Spread salmon mixture right to the edges on three sides and about 1 inch (2.5 cm) from the short edge farthest from you (the filling will be pushed to this edge when the dough is rolled up).

3. Scatter cheese, then green onions over the salmon. Beginning with the short end closest to you, roll up the dough as tightly as possible, jelly-roll fashion, to form a log.

4. Pat the ends to flatten slightly and, using a serrated knife, cut the cylinder into 10 slices. Lay, cut side up, on prepared pan.

5. Bake in preheated oven for about 20 minutes, until crust is golden and cheese is molten. Let pinwheels rest for 5 minutes before serving.

Variations

Substitute an equal quantity of tuna or mackerel for the salmon.

Pasta

Caesar Spaghettini

Even professed anchovy haters have a soft spot for Caesar salad. I thought Caesar salad flavors would taste good with pasta, and I was right. This dish is a conversation piece. Score another point for anchovies!

Tips

When preparing pasta, it is always wise to save some of the cooking water as insurance. This starchy water has thickening and/or emulsifying power if you need it, and it can be used to thin a sauce without making it watery or to help toppings stick to the pasta. If your pasta looks dry or clumpy or is difficult to toss with the toppings or sauce, add some of the cooking water in increments until it is suitably moist. Generally you won't need it for creamy dishes or pastas with abundant sauce.

Romaine hearts are the tender inner leaves. They are sold separately in supermarkets.

Fine Parmesan is a cornerstone of this pasta. Keep the dish uptown and use Parmigiano-Reggiano (known as the "king of cheeses"). Use a cheese slicer or a vegetable peeler to shave the Parmesan thinly off the wedge.

12 oz	spaghettini	375 g
¼ cup	extra virgin olive oil	60 mL
4	cloves garlic, minced	4
1	can (2 oz/50 g) anchovies (about 15), drained and mashed with a fork	1
2 tbsp	freshly squeezed lemon juice	30 mL
2 tbsp	heavy or whipping (35%) cream	30 mL
4 cups	finely shredded romaine hearts (about 8 oz/250 g or 1 small head; see Tips, left)	1 L
	Salt	
2 tsp	coarsely ground black pepper	10 mL
2 oz	Parmesan cheese, shaved (see Tips, left)	60 g

1. In a large pot of boiling salted water, cook spaghettini over medium heat for about 10 minutes, until tender to the bite (al dente). Scoop out about ½ cup (125 mL) cooking water and set aside. Drain pasta.

2. Meanwhile, in a 12-inch (30 cm) skillet, heat oil over medium heat until shimmery. Remove from heat, add garlic and anchovies and stir constantly for 1 minute to prevent burning. Stir in lemon juice and cream.

3. Return skillet to medium-low heat and add spaghettini and romaine. Toss with tongs. If pasta seems dry or difficult to toss evenly with romaine, add enough reserved cooking water to moisten and loosen it. Season to taste with salt.

4. Transfer to a serving platter or warmed individual bowls. Top with pepper, then Parmesan. Serve immediately.

Penne with Anchovied Broccolini

For the most lip-smackingly savory pasta, be fearless with your anchovies.
They are fabulous with cruciferous veggies such as broccolini.

Tips

Broccolini is a cross between broccoli and *gai lan*, also known as Chinese kale. It is sometimes called *baby broccoli* because it's more tender than broccoli and not bitter, or *asparation*, because it tastes and looks like a cross between broccoli and asparagus. The British refer to it as *tenderstem broccoli*. The spears are topped with small florets and sometimes yellow flowers. It's all edible — you just have to cut about ¼ inch (0.5 cm) off the base of each spear.

When preparing pasta, save some cooking water. If the pasta seems dry or clumpy, add the cooking water in stages to moisten or loosen it.

12 oz	penne	375 g
2 tbsp	extra virgin olive oil	30 mL
2	cans (each 2 oz/50 g) anchovies in extra virgin olive oil, with oil	2
2	large cloves garlic, minced	2
1 tbsp	finely grated lemon zest	15 mL
¼ tsp	hot pepper flakes	1 mL
2	bunches broccolini (about 12 oz/375 g total), trimmed, stems cut in 1-inch (2.5 cm) lengths and florets left intact (see Tips, left)	2
⅛ tsp	freshly ground black pepper	0.5 mL
1 cup	freshly grated Parmesan cheese (2 oz/60 g)	250 mL

1. In a large pot of boiling salted water, cook penne over medium heat for about 12 minutes or until tender to the bite (al dente). Scoop out about ½ cup (125 mL) cooking water and set aside. Drain pasta.

2. Meanwhile, in a large skillet, heat oil over medium heat until shimmery. Add anchovies, with their oil, and cook, stirring, for 1 minute, until they start to dissolve. Stir in garlic, lemon zest and hot pepper flakes for 30 seconds. Add broccolini, cover and cook, stirring occasionally, for about 10 minutes, until softened. Uncover and cook, stirring often, for about 2 minutes, until tender-crisp. Sprinkle pepper overtop and remove from heat.

3. Add penne and Parmesan and toss well. If pasta seems dry or difficult to toss evenly, add enough reserved cooking water to moisten and loosen it. Serve immediately.

Variation

If you are watching your wallet, substitute an equal quantity of broccoli florets (by weight) instead of using broccolini.

Citrusy Linguine with Smoked Mussels and Baby Spinach

Linguine is fit for a special occasion when tossed with a smoky, citrusy dressing, piled on a bed of spinach and topped with mussels.

Tip

When preparing pasta, save the starchy cooking water. It has thickening and emulsifying power in case you need it. If your pasta looks dry or clumpy or is difficult to toss with the toppings or sauce, add some cooking water in stages.

1 lb	linguine	500 g
2	cans (each 3 oz/85 g) smoked mussels	2
2 tbsp	extra virgin olive oil (approx.)	30 mL
¼ cup	freshly squeezed orange juice	60 mL
2 tbsp	freshly squeezed lemon juice	30 mL
1	clove garlic, minced	1
½ tsp	Dijon mustard	2 mL
1 tsp	salt (approx.)	5 mL
¼ tsp	freshly ground black pepper	1 mL
6 cups	baby spinach leaves (about 3 oz/90 g)	1.5 L
6	green onions (white and light green parts), thinly sliced, divided	6

1. In a large pot of boiling salted water, cook linguine over medium heat for about 12 minutes, until tender to the bite (al dente). Scoop out about ½ cup (125 mL) cooking water and set aside. Drain pasta.

2. Meanwhile, drain mussels, pouring their oil into a measuring cup. Add enough olive oil to make ¼ cup (60 mL). Whisk in orange and lemon juices, garlic, mustard, salt and pepper.

3. Place spinach leaves on a serving platter or in warmed individual bowls.

4. In a large bowl, toss hot linguine with oil mixture and half the green onions. If pasta seems dry or difficult to toss evenly, add enough reserved cooking water to moisten and loosen it. Add salt to taste, if necessary.

5. Pile pasta mixture on top of spinach. Scatter mussels evenly overtop. Sprinkle remaining green onions evenly overtop.

Variations

Substitute an equal quantity of smoked oysters or sprats for the mussels.

Clam Carbonara

Carbonara is basically spaghetti with bacon and eggs. No wonder it tastes so good! The addition of clams puts this luscious dish right over the top.

Makes 4 to 6 servings

• Fast

Tips

You can use larger, meatier clams instead of the baby ones.

Pancetta is Italian bacon, sold in most supermarkets. You can buy it already diced. You may substitute bacon, but drain all but 1 tbsp (15 mL) of the grease after browning.

If you have concerns about your egg supply, be aware that the eggs in this recipe will coagulate in the hot skillet, which means they have reached the "safe zone" (160°F/71°C) where any salmonella, if present, will be killed.

For a smoother result, toss the pasta and sauce with tongs for about 1 minute in the hot skillet.

1 lb	spaghetti	500 g
8 oz	pancetta, cut in ¼-inch (0.5 cm) dice	250 g
2	cloves garlic, minced	2
½ cup	diced (⅛ inch/3 mm) green bell pepper	125 mL
8 oz	cremini mushrooms, sliced (3 cups/ 750 mL)	250 g
¼ cup	dry white wine	60 mL
1	can (5 oz/142 g) baby clams, rinsed and drained (see Tips, left)	1
4	large eggs	4
½ cup	half-and-half (10%) cream	125 mL
1 cup	freshly grated Parmesan cheese (2 oz/60 g)	250 mL
	Salt and freshly ground black pepper	
1 tbsp	finely chopped parsley leaves	15 mL

1. In a large pot of boiling salted water, cook spaghetti over medium heat until tender to the bite (al dente), 12 to 15 minutes. Drain pasta.

2. Meanwhile, in a 12-inch (30 cm) skillet over medium heat, cook pancetta, stirring, until it starts to brown, about 5 minutes. Stir in garlic. Add bell pepper and mushrooms. Cook, stirring, until mushrooms release their liquid and start to brown, about 5 minutes. Stir in wine, scraping up brown bits from bottom of skillet. Add pasta and toss briefly until coated and hot. Add clams. Remove from heat.

3. In a bowl, whisk eggs. In a small pan over medium heat (or in a measuring cup on High in the microwave), heat cream for about 1 minute, until scalded (do not allow it to boil). Whisking constantly, gradually add cream to eggs. Whisk in Parmesan.

4. Add egg mixture to hot spaghetti and toss to coat evenly and thoroughly. Season to taste with salt and pepper.

5. Transfer to warm serving bowls. Sprinkle parsley overtop and serve immediately.

Variations

Substitute tuna, salmon, mackerel, shrimp or lobster for the clams.

Farfalle with Cajun Shrimp and Broccoli Pesto

Farfalle are little pasta bows, although the name is actually translated as "butterflies." The shape originated in Italy's Emilia-Romagna region. Farfalle look cute in a pasta bowl, especially when tinted with broccoli pesto.

Tips

The pesto recipe on its own is a bonus. It makes about 2¼ cups (550 mL). Spoon a dollop on fish, stir some into rice to doll it up or use it to garnish soup. Don't try to use the broccoli stalks, because they are too tough for pesto.

Grate Parmesan into fluffy flakes by using a kitchen rasp. Volume amounts can vary wildly, depending upon the kind of grater used, so go by weight when possible. If you prefer a firmer pesto, use ½ cup (125 mL) dry grated Parmesan instead.

• **Food processor**

Pesto

4 cups	broccoli florets (8 oz/250 g)	1 L
3	cloves garlic	3
½ cup	pine nuts	125 mL
¼ cup	coarsely chopped basil leaves	60 mL
¼ cup	extra virgin olive oil	60 mL
1 tbsp	freshly squeezed lime juice	15 mL
¼ tsp	freshly ground black pepper	1 mL
1 cup	freshly grated Parmesan cheese (2 oz/60 g; see Tips, left)	250 mL

Pasta

1 lb	farfalle	500 g
2 tbsp	extra virgin olive oil	30 mL
1 to 2 tbsp	Cajun seasoning (see Tips, page 203)	15 to 30 mL
1	can (4 oz/106 g) medium shrimp, rinsed and drained	1
	Salt	

1. *Pesto:* In a large pot of boiling salted water over medium heat, cook broccoli for 4 to 5 minutes, until tender-crisp. Drain and set aside to cool.

2. In a food processor fitted with the metal blade, with the motor running, add garlic through the feed tube to chop. Stop machine and add broccoli, pine nuts, basil, oil, lime juice and pepper to the work bowl. Pulse until ingredients are coarsely chopped. Scrape down sides. Add Parmesan and pulse until mixture is blended but still has some texture (see Tips, left).

3. *Pasta:* In a large pot of boiling salted water, cook farfalle over high heat for about 12 minutes, until tender to the bite (al dente). Scoop out about ½ cup (125 mL) cooking water and set aside. Drain pasta.

Tips

When preparing pasta, save some cooking water as insurance. If your pasta or sauce looks dry or clumpy or it is difficult to toss together, add cooking water in stages.

Cajun seasoning is a salt, spice, herb and vegetable blend. Mixtures vary by brand. It may include black pepper, cayenne, thyme and oregano, as well as dried garlic and brown sugar. Buy the kind that specifies no MSG is added.

4. Meanwhile, in a microwave-safe bowl, stir together oil and Cajun seasoning. Heat in microwave for 30 seconds on High or until hot. (Alternatively, heat oil and Cajun seasoning in a very small pan over medium heat for 1 to 2 minutes.) Stir in shrimp.

5. Scrape pesto into a large bowl and add enough reserved cooking water to make it loose enough to stir and toss easily with pasta. Add farfalle and toss to coat. Season to taste with salt.

6. Transfer pasta to a large, shallow serving platter or warmed individual bowls. Spoon shrimp mixture overtop.

Variations

Substitute an equal quantity of salmon, large lump crabmeat or lobster for the shrimp.

Cooking Pasta

Traditional wisdom suggests that pasta should be cooked at a rolling boil, which some cooks translate to mean constant high heat. However, medium heat is fine. The water will still maintain a lively boil and the cook will save a bit on energy costs. Medium heat is also better for pots — if you read the fine print in some stainless steel cookware brochures, high heat is not recommended for longest life.

Interestingly, you don't actually need to boil pasta at all. Not to be too scientific, but this is related to the fact that starches start to absorb water at well below the boiling point. You can bring water to a boil, toss in the pasta, cover the pot, turn off the heat and let it sit. The timing is tricky, however, and the texture of the cooked pasta seems to end up a bit uneven. So I'll stick to my old-fashioned method of boiling on medium heat.

Lemon Pepper Shrimp Pasta

This lemon pepper sauce is luscious. It stands up to all kinds of seafood, with or without pasta (see Variations, below).

Makes 4 servings

- Fast
- Guest-worthy

Tips

When preparing pasta, it is wise to save some cooking water as insurance. Add the water in stages to loosen your pasta or sauce.

Tricolor rotini is a mixture of white, spinach and tomato pastas. If you prefer, use plain or whole wheat rotini.

If you prefer, strip the leaves from the thyme sprigs and sprinkle them over the pasta rather than garnishing with the whole sprig.

Variations

Bonus: Serve this lemon pepper sauce with grilled or steamed seafood and rice instead of over pasta.

Substitute an equal quantity of tuna, salmon, crab or lobster for the shrimp.

12 oz	tricolor rotini (see Tips, left)	375 g
1 tbsp	unsalted butter	15 mL
2 tbsp	extra virgin olive oil	30 mL
6	slender green onions (white and green parts), cut diagonally into 1-inch (2.5 cm) segments	6
1	clove garlic, minced	1
2 tsp	finely grated lemon zest	10 mL
2 to 3 tbsp	freshly squeezed lemon juice, divided	30 to 45 mL
½ tsp	salt (approx.)	2 mL
½ tsp	freshly ground black pepper	2 mL
⅓ cup	heavy or whipping (35%) cream	75 mL
1	can (4 oz/106 g) small shrimp, rinsed and drained	1
¼ cup	freshly grated Parmesan cheese	60 mL
4	small sprigs thyme	4

1. In a large pot of boiling salted water, cook rotini over high heat for about 12 minutes, until tender to the bite (al dente). Scoop out about ½ cup (125 mL) cooking water and set aside. Drain pasta.

2. Meanwhile, in a 12-inch (30 cm) skillet over medium heat, melt butter with oil. Add green onions and cook, stirring, for 1 minute, until softened. Remove from heat. Stir in garlic for 20 seconds. Stir in lemon zest, 2 tbsp (30 mL) lemon juice, salt and pepper. Stir in cream, then shrimp. Return skillet to medium-low heat and bring just to a simmer.

3. Add rotini and toss to coat. If pasta seems dry or difficult to toss evenly with sauce, add enough reserved cooking water to loosen it. Taste and, if desired, add remaining 1 tbsp (15 mL) lemon juice and more salt to taste, if necessary.

4. Transfer the pasta to warmed serving bowls. Sprinkle Parmesan overtop and garnish with thyme sprigs.

Lobster and Shells in Ginger Tomato Sauce

Tomato sauce with ginger may seem like an odd combination but it is absolutely delicious. This is my favorite tomato sauce. It goes exceedingly well with seafood, as well as pasta.

Makes 4 to 6 servings

- Fast
- Guest-worthy

Tip

Transfer juices from the drained tomatoes to a zip-lock bag and freeze for other uses.

Variations

Shells suit the theme, but you can use any kind of pasta in this recipe.

Substitute an equal quantity of tuna, salmon, shrimp or crab for the lobster.

- **Blender**

1 lb	large pasta shells	500 g
¼ cup	unsalted butter	60 mL
4	shallots, diced	4
2 tbsp	chopped gingerroot	30 mL
2	cloves garlic, chopped	2
1	can (28 oz/796 mL) plum tomatoes, drained (about 2 cups/500 mL)	1
1 tsp	granulated sugar	5 mL
½ tsp	salt (approx.)	2 mL
1	can (11.3 oz/320 g) lobster meat, rinsed, drained and sliced or diced	1
5 tbsp	chopped parsley leaves, divided	75 mL
	Freshly ground black pepper	

1. In a large pot of boiling salted water, cook shells over medium heat for about 12 minutes, until tender to the bite (al dente). Drain and transfer to a large warmed bowl.

2. Meanwhile, in a large skillet, melt butter over medium-low heat. Add shallots, ginger and garlic. Cook for 5 minutes, stirring often, until shallots soften and turn golden. Stir in tomatoes, sugar and salt. Simmer for 15 minutes, stirring occasionally and breaking up tomatoes with a wooden spoon.

3. Transfer to blender, in batches if necessary, and purée. Return to pan. Stir in lobster, 3 tbsp (45 mL) parsley and pepper to taste. Add salt to taste, if necessary. Pour over shells and toss well.

4. Spoon pasta into warmed individual serving bowls. Sprinkle remaining 2 tbsp (30 mL) parsley overtop, dividing equally.

Tagliatelle with Tarragon Lobster and Asparagus

This is a pretty spring dish with a popular flavor profile. You can prepare it with ease and serve it with pride.

Makes 4 servings

- Fast
- Guest-worthy

Tips

When preparing pasta, it is wise to save some of the starchy cooking water. If necessary, add it in stages to moisten or loosen your pasta.

To maintain more control over the final result, I always use unsalted butter in recipes. The amount of salt in salted butter varies by brand, and it contains more moisture, which may affect some recipes. Salt also masks rancidity, which means you can be more confident that you're using a fresh product when your butter isn't salted.

1	bunch asparagus (about 1 lb/500 g), trimmed	1
12 oz	tagliatelle	375 g
2 tbsp	unsalted butter	30 mL
1/4 cup	extra virgin olive oil	60 mL
2	shallots, chopped	2
1 tbsp	vodka	15 mL
2 tbsp	heavy or whipping (35%) cream	30 mL
1 tbsp	chopped tarragon leaves	15 mL
1/4 tsp	salt (approx.)	1 mL
1/4 tsp	freshly ground white pepper	1 mL
1	can (11.3 oz/320 g) lobster meat, rinsed, drained and chopped into chunks	1
	Freshly grated Parmesan cheese	

1. In a pot large enough to accommodate the pasta, bring salted water to a boil over high heat.

2. Meanwhile, cut off asparagus tips. Slice remaining asparagus on the diagonal into 1/2-inch (1 cm) segments. Add asparagus (tips and stems) to pot and cook until tender-crisp, about 3 minutes. Using a mesh scoop, transfer to a sieve and rinse under cold running water to stop the cooking. Set tips and stems aside separately.

3. Add pasta to boiling water and cook over medium heat until tender to the bite (al dente), about 12 minutes. Scoop out about 1/2 cup (125 mL) cooking water and set aside. Drain pasta.

4. Meanwhile, in a large skillet over medium heat, melt butter with oil. Add shallots. Cook, stirring, for 2 to 3 minutes, until they turn golden brown. Stir in vodka and boil for 30 seconds. Stir in cream, tarragon, salt, pepper and lobster. Reduce heat to medium-low, cover and simmer for 2 minutes, until the lobster warms up and releases excess liquid. Remove from heat and set aside, covered.

5. Add pasta and asparagus stem segments (not the tips) to skillet and toss to coat evenly. If pasta seems dry or difficult to toss, add enough reserved cooking water to moisten and loosen it. Taste and add salt, if desired.

6. Transfer to a warmed serving platter or individual bowls. Sprinkle with Parmesan and scatter asparagus tips overtop. Serve immediately.

Variations

Substitute an equal quantity of tuna, salmon, mackerel, shrimp, oysters or mussels for the lobster. If using delicate or flaky seafood, don't simmer it; just toss it gently with the pasta. Smoked oysters or mussels would be an interesting choice — scatter them over the pasta before serving.

Orzo with Salmon, Asparagus and Smoked Mozzarella

Here's a tasty one-pan family dinner that you can whip up quickly. For a flavor boost, rice-shaped orzo can be cooked in stock, like rice. The molten cheese is an added attraction.

Makes 4 servings

- Fast
- Kid-friendly
- Healthy

Variations

Substitute Israeli couscous, a pearl-shaped pasta, for the orzo. You may have to increase the cooking time.

Substitute an equal quantity of tuna, mackerel, cod, shrimp or lobster for the salmon.

2 tbsp	extra virgin olive oil	30 mL
2	shallots, chopped	2
3	cloves garlic, chopped	3
12 oz	orzo	375 g
1½ cups	chicken stock	375 mL
1½ cups	water	375 mL
¼ tsp	salt (approx.)	1 mL
1	bunch asparagus (about 1 lb/500 g), trimmed and cut diagonally into 1-inch (2.5 cm) lengths	1
1½ tsp	fresh thyme leaves, divided	7 mL
2 tbsp	freshly squeezed lemon juice	30 mL
	Freshly ground black pepper	
4 oz	smoked mozzarella, cut in small dice	125 g
1	can (7½ oz/213 g) salmon, drained, deboned and broken into chunks	1

1. In a large saucepan, heat oil over medium heat until shimmery. Add shallots and garlic and cook, stirring often, for 1 to 2 minutes, until softened. Add orzo and cook, stirring often, for 2 minutes. Add stock, water and salt. Bring to a simmer, then reduce heat to medium-low. Cover and cook for 5 minutes. Add asparagus and 1 tsp (5 mL) thyme. Cover and cook for 5 minutes. Stir and cook, uncovered, for 2 minutes more or until liquid is absorbed, orzo is tender to the bite (al dente) and asparagus is tender-crisp.

2. Stir in lemon juice and pepper to taste. Stir in mozzarella until melted. Add salt to taste, if necessary.

3. Transfer to warmed serving plates. Scatter salmon evenly overtop, dividing equally. Sprinkle with remaining thyme, dividing equally.

Pasta with Spicy Salmon and Rapini

Rapini is also known as broccoli rabe. Its slight bitterness is a fabulous asset in spicy and hearty pastas.

Tips

Mezzi rigatoni are short, wide tubes. You can use any large, short pasta.

Blanching or cooking rapini in boiling water takes the edge off its bitterness.

Variations

Add a couple of chopped anchovy fillets with the garlic, and reduce the salt.

If you are not a fan of rapini, use broccoli or broccolini (also known as asparation or baby broccoli).

Substitute an equal quantity of tuna, mackerel, cod, shrimp, lobster or clams for the salmon, or add anchovies to taste, instead.

1 lb	mezzi rigatoni (see Tips, left)	500 g
1	bunch rapini (about 1 1/4 lb/625 g)	1
1/3 cup	extra virgin olive oil	75 mL
4	cloves garlic, minced	4
1 tsp	hot pepper flakes	5 mL
1	can (7 1/2 oz/213 g) sockeye salmon, drained, deboned and broken into chunks	1
1 1/4 tsp	salt (approx.), divided	6 mL
1/4 tsp	freshly ground black pepper	1 mL
1/2 cup	freshly grated Parmesan cheese (1 oz/30 g)	125 mL

1. In a large pot of boiling salted water, cook rigatoni over medium heat for 12 to 15 minutes, until tender to the bite (al dente). Drain and set aside.

2. Meanwhile, bring a saucepan of salted water to a boil over high heat. Trim off dry bases of rapini stalks and discard. Cut stalks into 1-inch (2.5 cm) lengths. Coarsely chop leaves and florets. Add rapini to boiling water and reduce heat to medium. Cook for about 5 minutes, until stalks are tender-crisp. Drain and rinse under cold running water to stop the cooking. Set aside.

3. In a skillet, heat oil over medium heat. Stir in garlic and hot pepper flakes for 20 seconds. Remove from heat. Stir in salmon, 1/4 tsp (1 mL) salt and pepper.

4. In a large warmed serving bowl, toss together rigatoni, rapini and remaining 1 tsp (5 mL) salt. Add salmon mixture and toss gently. Add salt to taste, if necessary. Sprinkle Parmesan evenly overtop and serve immediately.

Salmon Herb Agnolotti

Don't have a pasta machine? You can make stuffed pasta by using dumpling wrappers from the supermarket. Be traditional and top agnolotti with tomato sauce and Parmesan, or simply toss them with browned butter or olive oil and grated cheese. You can add them to soup too.

Makes 4 servings

- Kid-friendly

Tips

For the finest minced garlic, push it through a press.

When making this recipe, it's important to drain the ricotta; otherwise, the filling will be too wet.

You can make the filling the day before you want to use it. Refrigerate it in a small storage tub with a tight lid.

Don't bother trying to make stuffed pasta, such as agnolotti, using fresh lasagna sheets from the supermarket; they are not thin or soft enough.

You can use these agnolotti warm or at room temperature, so don't worry if they cool down a bit while you prepare a sauce. Alternatively they can be refrigerated, but they are not at their best once chilled — they tend to toughen and stick together.

Variations

Make giant ravioli with square wonton wrappers. Scoop filling into the center of one square, moisten edges, top with another square and press to seal.

Substitute an equal quantity of mackerel or finely chopped shrimp for the salmon.

- **2 rimmed baking sheets, lightly greased**

2 cups	ricotta cheese (1 lb/475 g tub)	500 mL
1	large egg	1
1	can (7½ oz/213 g) salmon, drained, deboned and broken into chunks	1
1	clove garlic, minced (see Tips, left)	1
¼ cup	chopped parsley leaves	60 mL
1 tbsp	chopped basil leaves	15 mL
½ tsp	salt	2 mL
¼ tsp	freshly ground black pepper	1 mL
45	round 3¼-inch (8 cm) dumpling wrappers (approx.) (about 1⅓ lb/600 g)	45

1. Place a fine-mesh sieve over a bowl. Add ricotta and drain for 10 to 15 minutes. Set aside.

2. In a bowl, using a fork, lightly whisk egg. Gently squeeze excess moisture from salmon and add it to bowl. Add garlic, parsley, basil, salt, pepper and drained ricotta. Mix with a fork until well blended, but do not overmix so that it becomes a paste.

3. Bring a large pot of salted water to a boil over high heat.

4. Meanwhile, working in batches, place wrappers on a work surface. Place a small bowl of cold water alongside. Scoop about 2 tsp (10 mL) filling onto center of each wrapper. One at a time, dip your finger in water, moisten edges and fold wrapper over filling to create a half-moon. Pat gently to get rid of any air pockets and press edges together to seal. Place on prepared baking sheet. Repeat until all the filling is used up.

5. When the water boils, reduce heat to medium or medium-low to maintain a gentle boil. Cook agnolotti in batches of 10 to 12. After adding to pot, use a wooden spoon to nudge sticky ones off the bottom. Simmer for about 5 minutes, until they rise to the surface and dough is cooked through. Using a slotted spoon, transfer to prepared baking sheets in a single layer. Serve immediately (see Tips, left).

Spinach Linguine with Salmon and Caviar

Simple enough for a family dinner yet luxurious enough for company, this pasta is a people-pleaser. The rich, luscious sauce with its shot of vodka stands up to almost any kind of canned fish.

Makes 4 to 6 servings

- Guest-worthy

Variations

Substitute an equal quantity of tuna, mackerel, shrimp, crab, lobster or clams for the salmon.

1 lb	spinach linguine	500 g
3 tbsp	unsalted butter	45 mL
1	shallot, chopped	1
1	clove garlic, minced	1
2	small plum tomatoes, peeled and chopped	2
1 tsp	salt	5 mL
	Freshly ground black pepper	
2 tbsp	vodka	30 mL
1 cup	heavy or whipping (35%) cream	250 mL
1/3 cup	milk	75 mL
1	can (7 1/2 oz/213 g) salmon, drained, deboned and broken into chunks	1
1/2 cup	chopped parsley leaves, divided	125 mL
1 cup	freshly grated Parmesan cheese (1 oz/30 g)	250 mL
1 1/2 tbsp	black lumpfish caviar (roe), rinsed and drained	22 mL

1. In a large pot of boiling salted water, cook linguine over high heat for about 12 minutes, until tender to the bite (al dente). Drain.

2. Meanwhile, in a skillet over medium heat, melt butter. Add shallot and garlic and cook, stirring, for 2 to 3 minutes, until golden. Add tomatoes, salt and pepper to taste. Increase heat to medium-high and cook, stirring, for 2 minutes. Add vodka. Reduce heat to medium-low and simmer for 5 minutes, until thickened. Add cream and milk and increase heat to medium. Bring to a simmer and cook for 5 minutes, until reduced to 1 1/2 cups (375 mL). Stir in salmon and remove from heat.

3. In a warmed serving bowl, toss linguine with salmon mixture and all but 2 tbsp (30 mL) parsley. Sprinkle Parmesan overtop. Scatter remaining parsley overtop, then caviar. Serve immediately.

Farfalle with Smoky Tuna, Mushrooms and Green Peppercorns

This exotic pasta is made with easy-to-find ingredients. I love the way the green peppercorns pop in your mouth, treating your taste buds to a burst of heat and spice.

Makes 4 servings

- Fast
- Guest-worthy

Tips

When preparing pasta, save some of the starchy cooking water to make adjustments. Add it gradually, and only if necessary.

Liquid smoke is produced by passing smoke (often from hickory wood) through water. It is sold in supermarkets alongside the condiments. Instead of liquid smoke, you can use smoked salt or buy smoked tuna at a fine food shop.

Variations

Substitute an equal quantity of salmon or kippers for the tuna.

12 oz	farfalle	375 g
1 tbsp	extra virgin olive oil	15 mL
1	small onion, diced	1
3 cups	sliced cremini mushrooms (8 oz/250 g)	750 mL
¼ cup	dry white wine	60 mL
1 cup	heavy or whipping (35%) cream	250 mL
2 tbsp	green peppercorns, drained	30 mL
1 tsp	rosemary leaves, chopped	5 mL
¼ tsp	salt (approx.)	1 mL
1	can (6 oz/170 g) tuna in water, drained and broken into chunks	1
	Liquid smoke (see Tips, left)	
4	small sprigs rosemary	4

1. In a large pot of boiling salted water, cook farfalle over high heat for about 12 minutes, until tender to the bite (al dente). Scoop out about ½ cup (125 mL) cooking water and set aside. Drain pasta and set aside.

2. Meanwhile, in a large skillet, heat oil over medium heat until shimmery. Add onion and cook, stirring often, for 2 to 3 minutes, until softened. Add mushrooms and cook, stirring often, for about 5 minutes, until they release their liquid and start to turn golden. Add wine, scraping up brown bits from bottom of pan. Stir in cream, peppercorns, rosemary and salt. Reduce heat to medium-low and simmer, stirring occasionally, for about 10 minutes, until slightly thickened. Stir in tuna. Add liquid smoke in dashes, to taste. Add salt to taste, if necessary.

3. Stir in farfalle. If sauce seems too thick and/or pasta is difficult to toss, add enough reserved cooking water to loosen it.

4. Transfer pasta to warmed individual serving bowls. Garnish each with a rosemary sprig and serve immediately.

Pasta with Tuna, Beans, Sage and Olives

I get cravings for this hearty pasta, which is packed with wholesome nourishment.

Tips

Cavatappi looks like penne twisted into a spiral. It is sometimes labeled "scoobi doo." You can substitute whole wheat macaroni, penne or rotini.

I prefer to use the 19 ounce (540 mL) can of beans.

12 oz	whole wheat cavatappi (see Tips, left)	375 g
½ cup	lightly packed sage leaves, divided	125 mL
2 tbsp	extra virgin olive oil	30 mL
2	cloves garlic, minced	2
1	can (14 to 19 oz/398 to 540 mL) cannellini (white kidney) beans, rinsed and drained (see Tips, left)	1
2 cups	cherry tomatoes, quartered	500 mL
1 cup	black olives, pitted and coarsely chopped	250 mL
1	can (6 oz/170 g) tuna in water, drained and broken into chunks	1
¼ tsp	salt (approx.)	1 mL
¼ tsp	freshly ground black pepper	1 mL

1. In a large pot of boiling salted water, cook pasta over medium heat for about 10 minutes, until tender to the bite (al dente). Scoop out about ½ cup (125 mL) cooking water and set aside. Drain pasta.

2. Meanwhile, finely chop 2 of the sage leaves and set aside. Cut remainder into thin slivers. Set aside separately.

3. In a skillet, heat oil over medium heat until shimmery. Stir in garlic for 20 seconds. Stir in slivered sage and beans. Heat for 1 minute. Remove from heat and add tomatoes and olives.

4. In a large warmed bowl, toss together pasta, tuna, bean mixture, salt and pepper. If pasta seems dry or difficult to toss evenly, add enough reserved cooking water to moisten and loosen it. Add salt to taste, if necessary. Sprinkle with chopped sage and serve immediately.

Variations

Use any type of beans in your cupboard.

Substitute an equal quantity of salmon or mackerel for the tuna.

Tortellini Toss-Up

This easy pasta is halfway between homemade and store-bought, and all-the-way delicious.

- Brown-bag

Tip

If you have access to a microwave, brown-bagging leftover pasta is a tasty alternative to packing sandwiches. This sturdy pasta is a good candidate for lunch.

Using a serrated vegetable peeler is a fuss-free way to peel tomatoes.

2	cans (each 3 oz/85 g) tuna in olive oil, drained (oil reserved) and broken into chunks	2
1	onion, diced	1
½ cup	chopped parsley leaves	125 mL
½ tsp	hot pepper flakes	2 mL
4	ripe tomatoes (about 2 lb/1 kg), peeled, seeded and coarsely chopped (see Tips, left)	4
½ tsp	salt (approx.)	2 mL
¼ tsp	freshly ground black pepper	1 mL
2	jars (each 6 oz/375 g) marinated artichoke hearts	2
12 oz	cheese tortellini	375 g

1. In a wide saucepan, heat 2 tbsp (30 mL) oil from the tuna over medium heat until shimmery. Add onion and cook, stirring often, for about 3 minutes, until softened. Stir in parsley and hot pepper flakes. Stir in tomatoes, salt and pepper. Bring to a simmer, reduce heat to medium-low and simmer, stirring occasionally, for 10 minutes.

2. Drain artichokes and set marinade aside. Coarsely chop artichokes and add to pan along with marinade. Bring to a simmer and cook for 20 minutes, until sauce is thickened.

3. Meanwhile, in a large pot of boiling salted water, cook tortellini over high heat for about 7 minutes, until tender. Drain.

4. Add tortellini and tuna to artichoke mixture. Add salt to taste, if necessary. Let pasta rest for 5 minutes before serving.

Variations

Substitute an equal quantity of salmon, mackerel or kippers for the tuna.

Tuna Fettuccine Alfredo

My simple Alfredo sauce adapts to all kinds of pasta and seafood. It's easy to make and kids like it. But it's very creamy, so be careful not to overindulge.

Makes 4 servings

- Fast
- Kid-friendly

Tips

You can use lower-priced flaked tuna — the rich sauce compensates.

I use a kitchen rasp to grate the Parmesan into fluffy flakes. Volume amounts for Parmesan can vary wildly, depending upon how it is packed into the measuring cup and how long it sits, dries out and settles. When possible, go by weight.

12 oz	whole wheat fettuccine	375 g
¼ cup	unsalted butter	60 mL
2	cloves garlic, minced	2
1 cup	heavy or whipping (35%) cream	250 mL
2 cups	freshly grated Parmesan cheese (4 oz/125 g; see Tips, left)	500 mL
1	can (6 oz/170 g) tuna in water, drained and broken into chunks	1
¼ cup	chopped parsley leaves, divided	60 mL

1. In a large pot of boiling salted water, cook fettuccine over high heat for about 12 minutes, until tender to the bite (al dente). Drain.

2. Meanwhile, in a saucepan over medium-low heat, melt butter. Stir in garlic for 20 seconds, then stir in cream. When mixture returns to a simmer, cook for 5 minutes, stirring occasionally. Stir in Parmesan until melted. Stir in tuna and 3 tbsp (45 mL) parsley. Remove from heat.

3. Place fettuccine in warmed individual serving bowls. Ladle sauce overtop and sprinkle with remaining parsley.

> ### Variations
> Substitute an equal quantity of salmon, mackerel, shrimp, lobster or clams for the tuna.

Tuna and Olive Rotini

A bit of tuna can go a long way in pasta. This rotini is both tasty and pretty.

Tip

Save some of the starchy cooking water in case your pasta seems dry or difficult to toss evenly. Add the water in stages.

12 oz	rotini	375 g
2	cans (each 3 oz/85 g) tuna in olive oil, with oil	2
1 cup	sliced pitted green olives (20 large)	250 mL
1	small red bell pepper, slivered	1
1	large clove garlic, minced	1
2 tbsp	extra virgin olive oil	30 mL
1/2 tsp	salt (approx.)	2 mL
1/4 tsp	freshly ground black pepper	1 mL
1/2 cup	parsley leaves, coarsely chopped	125 mL

1. In a large pot of boiling salted water, cook rotini over medium heat for about 12 minutes, until tender to the bite (al dente). Scoop out about 1/2 cup (125 mL) cooking water and set aside. Drain pasta.

2. Meanwhile, in a large warmed serving bowl, stir together tuna, with oil, olives, red pepper, garlic, extra virgin olive oil, salt and pepper. Add rotini. If the pasta seems dry or clumpy, add enough reserved cooking water to moisten and loosen it. Add salt to taste, if necessary.

3. Scatter parsley overtop and serve immediately.

Variations

Substitute an equal quantity of salmon, sardines, sprats or shrimp for the tuna.

If the seafood you are using is not packed in olive oil, add an extra 2 tbsp (30 mL) extra virgin olive oil to this dish.

Whole Wheat Penne with Tuna, Arugula and Roasted Tomatoes

Roasted tomatoes make this healthy, fiber-filled pasta taste so bright. Nutritious and delicious — who can resist that combination?

Tip

When preparing pasta, it is wise to save some of the cooking water. Add it in stages if your pasta seems dry or clumpy.

Variations

Substitute an equal quantity of salmon or mackerel for the tuna and add about 2 tbsp (30 mL) extra virgin olive oil, or use chopped anchovies, to taste, instead.

- **Preheat oven to 300°F (150°C)**
- **Rimmed baking sheet**

1 lb	large cherry tomatoes, halved	500 g
2 tbsp	extra virgin olive oil	30 mL
1 tsp	salt (approx.), divided	5 mL
1/2 tsp	granulated sugar	2 mL
12 oz	whole wheat penne	375 g
2	cans (each 3 oz/85 g) tuna in olive oil, with oil	2
2	cloves garlic, minced	2
1/8 tsp	freshly ground black pepper	0.5 mL
1	small bunch arugula, stemmed and coarsely chopped (2 to 2 1/2 cups/ 500 to 625 mL)	1
1/4 cup	freshly grated Parmesan cheese (1/2 oz/15 g)	60 mL

1. In a bowl, gently toss together tomatoes, extra virgin olive oil, 1/2 tsp (2 mL) salt and sugar. Transfer to baking sheet, spreading evenly. Arrange tomatoes, cut side down, in a single layer. Roast in preheated oven for about 1 hour, until tomatoes are caramelized at the edges but still juicy, rather than leathery.

2. In a large pot of boiling salted water, cook penne over medium heat for about 15 minutes, until tender to the bite (al dente). Scoop out about 1/2 cup (125 mL) cooking water and set aside. Drain pasta.

3. Scrape tomatoes and their juices into a large serving bowl. Add tuna, with its oil, breaking fish into small chunks with a fork. Add garlic, 1/2 tsp (2 mL) salt and pepper. Stir together gently. Scatter arugula overtop.

4. Add penne and toss gently. Add salt to taste, if necessary. If pasta seems dry or difficult to toss evenly, add enough reserved cooking water to moisten and loosen it. Sprinkle Parmesan overtop and serve immediately.

Vintage Tuna Mac and Cheese

This simple vintage comfort food dish, its source forgotten in the mists of time, makes me feel like a kid when I eat it. It is quickly prepared on the stovetop and, yes, it calls for a can of condensed soup.

Makes 4 to 6 servings

- Fast
- Kid-friendly

Tip

I use whole milk to make the sauce creamy.

12 oz	elbow macaroni (about 3 cups/750 mL)	375 g
2 tbsp	unsalted butter	30 mL
1	small onion, chopped	1
1	stalk celery, chopped	1
1	can (10 oz/284 mL) condensed cream of mushroom soup	1
1 cup	milk (see Tip, left)	250 mL
3 cups	shredded sharp (old) Cheddar cheese (12 oz/375 g)	750 mL
1	can (6 oz/170 g) tuna in water, drained and broken into chunks	1
4	canned plum tomatoes, drained and coarsely chopped	4
	Salt and freshly ground black pepper	

1. In a large pot of boiling salted water, cook macaroni over medium heat for about 12 minutes, until tender to the bite (al dente). Drain.

2. Meanwhile, in a large saucepan, melt butter over medium-low heat. Add onion and celery and cook, stirring often, for 5 minutes, until vegetables soften. Add soup and milk and stir well to smooth out lumps. After mixture comes to a simmer, cook, stirring often, for 5 minutes. Stir in cheese until melted. Stir in tuna and tomatoes. Remove from heat.

3. Stir in macaroni and season to taste with salt and pepper. Serve immediately.

> **Variations**
>
> Substitute an equal quantity of salmon or mackerel for the tuna.

The Ziti Caper

Pasta meets tuna, anchovies, beans and caperberries. It's a delectable combination of lively, bold flavors.

Makes 4 servings

• Healthy

Tips

When preparing pasta, save some of the cooking water. Use it to moisten or loosen the pasta dish if necessary.

Cranberry beans are also known as romano or borlotti beans. I prefer the 19 ounce (540 mL) can.

Capers are the buds and caperberries the olive-shaped fruit of the caper plant. Caperberries are now sold in many supermarkets, as well as in specialty shops. Leave the stems intact when serving them so diners can pick them up.

12 oz	ziti	375 g
1 tbsp	extra virgin olive oil	15 mL
2	cloves garlic, chopped	2
2 cups	grape tomatoes, halved	500 mL
1	can (2 oz/50 g) anchovies, drained (oil reserved) and chopped	1
2	cans (each 3 oz/85 g) tuna in olive oil	2
1	can (14 to 19 oz/398 to 540 mL) cranberry beans, rinsed and drained (see Tips, left)	1
3 tbsp	capers, drained	45 mL
	Salt and freshly ground black pepper	
12	caperberries with stems (see Tips, left)	12

1. In a large pot of boiling salted water, cook ziti over high heat for about 15 minutes, until tender to the bite (al dente). Scoop out $\frac{1}{2}$ cup (125 mL) cooking water and set aside. Drain ziti.

2. Meanwhile, in a large skillet, heat extra virgin olive oil over medium-high heat until shimmery. Stir in garlic for 20 seconds. Add tomatoes and anchovies, with their oil, and cook, stirring, for 1 to 2 minutes, until tomatoes soften. Remove from heat.

3. Stir in tuna, with oil, and beans. Add ziti and capers. Season to taste with salt and pepper. Toss. If pasta seems difficult to toss evenly, add enough reserved cooking water to loosen it.

4. Transfer to warmed individual serving bowls. Garnish with caperberries, dividing equally. Serve immediately.

Variations
Substitute an equal quantity of salmon or mackerel for the tuna and add about 2 tbsp (30 mL) extra virgin olive oil.

Sicilian-Style Sardine Pasta

This dish may sound strange but it tastes good. Pasta con le sarde is a Sicilian classic starring sardines, fennel and bucatini. Although many cooks will disagree, I go by the nothing-is-sacred philosophy of cooking. So my knock-off calls for canned sardines, omits the Arab-influenced raisins and pine nuts, and gussies up the crumb topping.

Makes 4 small servings

Tips

When making bread crumbs for this recipe, I like to use whole wheat and/or rye bread for full flavor.

If you prefer, toast the crumbs in your toaster oven rather than in the oven (Step 2). Place them on the miniature baking sheet that comes with the oven.

When preparing pasta, save some of the cooking water in case you need to moisten or loosen the dish.

- **Preheat oven or toaster oven to 300°F (150°C) (see Tips, left)**
- **Food processor**
- **Rimmed baking sheet**

1	bulb fennel	1
2	slices stale white bread (about 2½ oz/70 g)	2
	Salt	
½ cup + 1 tbsp	extra virgin olive oil, divided	140 mL
1	large clove garlic, minced	1
1	onion, diced	1
½ tsp	salt (approx.)	2 mL
½ cup	dry white wine	125 mL
¼ tsp	saffron threads, crumbled, optional	1 mL
12 oz	bucatini (see Tip, page 221)	375 g
2	cans (each 4 oz/120 g) boneless, skinless sardines in oil, drained	2

1. Slice off the top of the fennel with the tough stalks. Remove the tender leafy fronds, chop and set aside (you should have 2 to 4 tbsp/30 to 60 mL). Discard stalks. Cut a thin slice off the base of the bulb and discard. Cut bulb in half lengthwise. Cut out and discard the triangular core from each half. Discard any browned outer layers. Cut each half into thin slivers, then crosswise to obtain a ⅛- to ¼-inch (3 to 5 mm) dice (you should have about 2½ cups/625 mL).

2. In food processor fitted with the metal blade, process bread into fine crumbs (you should have about 1½ cups/375 mL). Transfer to baking sheet and toast in preheated oven for 5 to 10 minutes, stirring twice, until golden brown. Remove from oven and let cool to room temperature. When cool, drizzle with 1 tbsp (15 mL) olive oil. Sprinkle garlic, fennel fronds and salt to taste overtop. Blend with a fork and set aside.

Bucatini are long pasta straws. They are sometimes called perciatelli.

3. Bring a large pot of salted water to a boil over high heat.

4. Meanwhile, in a skillet, heat remaining $\frac{1}{2}$ cup (125 mL) oil over medium heat until shimmery. Add diced fennel, onion and salt. Cook, stirring occasionally, for 10 minutes, until fennel is tender and golden brown. Add wine and saffron, if using. Simmer for 1 minute. Remove from heat and set aside.

5. Add bucatini to the boiling water and cook over medium heat for about 15 minutes, until tender to the bite (al dente). Scoop out about $\frac{1}{2}$ cup (125 mL) cooking water and set aside. Drain pasta.

6. In a large warmed serving bowl, toss bucatini with fennel mixture. If pasta seems dry or difficult to toss evenly, add enough reserved cooking water to moisten and loosen it. Add the sardines and toss gently.

7. Sprinkle crumb mixture overtop. Serve immediately.

Variations

You can use regular sardines, but they are more tender and likelier to fall apart than the boneless, skinless fillets.

Substitute an equal quantity of sprats or mackerel for the sardines.

Triple-S Pearl Couscous

The S stands for shrimp, shallots and sun-dried tomatoes, the tasty triumvirate in this quick meal.

Tip

"Pearl couscous" is the better but lesser-known name for Israeli couscous, a pearl-shaped pasta. It is versatile, and I love the silky texture.

8 oz	pearl couscous (see Tip, left)	250 g
2 tbsp	extra virgin olive oil	30 mL
8 oz	shallots (8 to 10), thinly sliced	250 g
¼ tsp	salt (approx.)	1 mL
⅛ tsp	freshly ground black pepper	0.5 mL
¼ cup	slivered sun-dried tomatoes	60 mL
1	can (4 oz/106 g) tiny shrimp, rinsed and drained	1
¼ cup	coarsely chopped parsley leaves	60 mL
1 tbsp	freshly squeezed lime juice	15 mL

1. In a medium pan of boiling salted water, cook couscous over medium heat for about 8 minutes, until tender but firm. Drain.

2. Meanwhile, in a skillet, heat oil over medium-high heat until shimmery. Add shallots, salt and pepper and cook, stirring often, for about 5 minutes, until browned. Stir in sun-dried tomatoes and shrimp for 30 to 60 seconds.

3. In a warmed serving bowl, stir together couscous, shallot mixture, parsley and lime juice. Add salt to taste, if necessary.

Variations

Substitute an equal quantity of tuna, salmon, mackerel, cod, sardines, sprats, lobster or octopus for the shrimp.

Spanish Noodles

This love-child of paella and risotto won't win any awards for good looks, but it sure tastes good. I've put it on my comfort-food list.

Tips

Freeze the liquid from the tomatoes and stir it into your next soup.

If you can find them, use the short, thin Spanish noodles called fideos, which are sold in specialty shops in some regions.

Variations

If you don't like spicy food, use smoked sweet paprika.

If you prefer, substitute baby clams for the meaty ones. Stir them in at the end.

Substitute an equal quantity of cod, shrimp, lobster or octopus for the clams.

3 tbsp	extra virgin olive oil, divided	45 mL
12 oz	vermicelli pasta, broken into 2- to 3-inch (5 to 7.5 cm) segments (see Tips, left)	375 g
2	shallots, finely chopped	2
2	cloves garlic, minced	2
1	can (14 oz/398 mL) diced tomatoes, drained	1
4 cups	chicken stock	1 L
2 cups	water	500 mL
1 tsp	smoked hot paprika	5 mL
1/4 tsp	saffron, crumbled	1 mL
1	can (5 oz/142 g) surf clams, coarsely chopped	1
	Salt	
1 cup	sliced pitted green olives (about 15 large)	250 mL
1	small roasted red pepper, cut in thin strips	1

1. In a 12-inch (30 cm) skillet, heat 2 tbsp (30 mL) oil over medium heat until shimmery. Add vermicelli and cook, tossing often with tongs, for about 5 minutes, until coated in oil and lightly toasted. Transfer to a bowl.

2. Add remaining 1 tbsp (15 mL) oil to skillet and heat over medium heat until shimmery. Add shallots and cook, stirring often, for about 3 minutes, until softened. Stir in garlic for 20 seconds. Stir in tomatoes. Add stock, water, paprika, saffron and toasted vermicelli. After mixture comes to a boil, cook for about 10 minutes, stirring often, until noodles are just tender and sauce is only slightly soupy.

3. Add clams and reduce heat to low. Cover and cook for about 5 minutes, until noodles have absorbed remaining liquid (the noodles will be moist and sticky, similar to risotto). Stir, scraping up brown bits from bottom of pan. Season to taste with salt.

4. Transfer noodles to a serving dish or individual bowls. Top with olives and roasted pepper strips. Serve immediately.

Express Chinese Noodle Dinner

A quick trip to the produce section will net you the main ingredients for this tasty weeknight dinner. Pick up some vacuum-packed precooked yellow wheat noodles and a bag of coleslaw mixture (red and green cabbage and carrot slivers). Dinner will be on the table quickly and your family will applaud you.

Makes 4 servings

- Fast
- Kid-friendly

Tip

In supermarkets, look for Chinese wheat noodles (precooked, vacuum-packed and often tinted yellow) in refrigerated cases near the produce.

¼ cup	hoisin sauce	60 mL
¼ cup	water	60 mL
3 tbsp	vegetable oil	45 mL
1	onion, thinly sliced	1
3	cloves garlic, minced	3
½ tsp	hot pepper flakes (approx.)	2 mL
1	package (about 1 lb/500 g) coleslaw mixture	1
1 tsp	salt (approx.)	5 mL
1	can (4 oz/106 g) small shrimp, rinsed and drained	1
1	package (14 oz/400 g) fresh Chinese wheat noodles (see Tip, left) Chopped cilantro leaves	1

1. Bring a large pot of salted water to a boil over high heat.

2. Meanwhile, in a measuring cup, stir together hoisin sauce and water. Set aside.

3. In a large skillet, heat oil over medium-high heat until shimmery. Add onion and stir-fry for 2 minutes, until it starts to turn golden. Stir in garlic and hot pepper flakes for 20 seconds. Add coleslaw mixture and salt and stir-fry for 5 minutes, until cabbage is tender but still crunchy. Remove from heat. Scatter shrimp evenly overtop. Cover skillet and set aside.

4. Add noodles to the boiling water and cook for 1 to 2 minutes, until heated through. Drain. Add to skillet and pour hoisin mixture over top. Using tongs, toss until well combined. Serve immediately, garnished with cilantro.

Variations

Substitute an equal quantity of tuna, salmon or lobster for the shrimp.

Rice and Grains

Sushi Rice

The Japanese say rice is the heart of sushi. I marvel at how good sushi rice tastes, considering its simplicity. Leftover sushi rice is delicious. Enjoy it as a side dish, use it to experiment with other types of sushi rolls or make informal hand rolls or sushi salad.

Makes about 6 cups (1.5 L) Enough to cover 6 sheets of nori

Tips

Sushi rice is sold in supermarkets as well as in Asian grocery stores. It is sticky but not mushy and may be short- or medium-grain. White sushi rice is most commonly used, but brown sushi rice is also available. Sushi rice may be labeled "Japanese rice" or "sticky rice." A popular type of sushi rice developed in California is Calrose.

You need plenty of cold water to efficiently rinse the starchy sushi rice. It helps to tilt the handle of the pan against the rim of the sink, then let water run into the pan in a slow stream on one side and spill out the other.

Fanning dissipates steam and helps the individual rice grains maintain their shape. I usually just grab a magazine to fan the rice. However, you can use a bamboo fan or even set up an electric fan to blow on the rice. After mixing and fanning, the rice should be moist and shiny, not mushy or broken.

● **Rimmed baking sheet**

2 cups	white sushi rice (see Tips, left)	500 mL
2½ cups	cold water, plus additional for rinsing rice	625 mL
1 tbsp	salt, divided	15 mL
⅓ cup	unseasoned rice vinegar	75 mL
3 tbsp	granulated sugar	45 mL

1. Place rice in a saucepan (preferably nonstick). Rinse and swish with cold running water until the water runs clear (see Tips, left). Drain rice in a sieve and return to saucepan. Add 2½ cups (625 mL) cold water. Set aside for 1 hour.

2. Add 1 tsp (5 mL) salt to saucepan and bring to a boil over high heat. Stir well, reduce heat to low and cover. Simmer for about 15 minutes, until rice is tender and water has been absorbed. Remove from heat. Lift off lid and place a clean tea towel over top of saucepan. Replace lid and set aside for 10 minutes.

3. Meanwhile, in a very small saucepan, combine vinegar, sugar and remaining 2 tsp (10 mL) salt. Cook, stirring, over medium heat for 1 to 2 minutes, until sugar dissolves and mixture is warm (be careful not to boil). Remove from heat and set aside.

4. Transfer rice to baking sheet and, using the tip of a fork, quickly spread it across the sheet (it doesn't have to be tidy). Drizzle vinegar mixture evenly overtop. With one hand, use a short-handled spatula to gently mix, using scooping and flipping motions. With the other hand, fan the rice (see Tips, left). (Better still, enlist a helper to fan.) Mix the rice gently; do not mash. Mix and fan for 5 minutes, until vinegar is absorbed and rice has cooled.

Uses for Sushi Rice

For a quick hand roll, spread a handful of rice at one end of a sheet of nori (it doesn't have to be tidy), lay any filling you like diagonally across the rice, then roll up the nori in a cone shape.

To make simple sushi salad, put sushi rice in a bowl, top with cut vegetables such as cucumber, carrot or avocado and drizzle with a bit of soy sauce.

Wasabi Mayonnaise

Wasabi mayonnaise is trendy, tasty and versatile. It is a great finishing touch for sushi and so much more.

• Fast

Tip

You can spread wasabi mayonnaise on wraps, party sandwiches or lobster rolls; use it to give tuna salad a contemporary twist; add it to deviled egg filling; smear it on fish burgers or croquettes; or simply dollop it alongside fresh sliced tomatoes and canned seafood such as crab, tuna and salmon.

1/2 cup	mayonnaise	125 mL
1 tsp	wasabi powder	5 mL
1	green onion, finely chopped	1
1 tbsp	finely chopped parsley leaves	15 mL

1. In a small measuring cup, stir together mayonnaise and wasabi powder. Stir in green onion and parsley.

2. Serve immediately or transfer to a small airtight storage tub and refrigerate for up to 3 days.

Seafood Sushi Rolls

Don't shy away from making your own sushi rolls. They are complicated to explain but simple to make. The only problem is, they do require preparation time.

Supplies, including bamboo rolling mats, sushi rice, nori (toasted seaweed sheets) and toasted sesame seeds (I like the mixed black and beige ones) are available in supermarkets. Japanese grocery stores sell tobiko (flying fish roe) but you can substitute other kinds of roe, such as lumpfish.

Sushi fish are traditionally, but not always, raw. Thus sushi-making lends itself well to experimentation with canned seafood.

The recipes on pages 228 to 232 will get you started, but remember, sushi-making is an endless adventure.

Tuna and Cucumber Sushi Rolls

Makes 32 pieces

- Kid-friendly
- Healthy
- Brown-bag
- Guest-worthy

Tips

Nori sheets are almost square. Luckily, you can use the perforations on them as a placement guide. They should be perpendicular to the slats of the sushi mat.

When spreading the rice over the nori, be aware that it will be very sticky, so moisten your fingers as needed. Don't compact the rice onto the nori too enthusiastically. Sushi chefs say you should still be able to see the individual grains of rice.

To prepare the cucumber for this recipe, peel it, cut it lengthwise into $\frac{1}{2}$-inch (1 cm) strips, then cut each strip lengthwise into $\frac{1}{4}$-inch (0.5 cm) strips.

4	sheets nori	4
4 cups	Sushi Rice (page 226)	1 L
4 tsp	toasted sesame seeds	20 mL
1	can (6 oz/170 g) tuna in water, drained and broken into flakes	1
4	strips cucumber (each 8 by $\frac{1}{2}$ by $\frac{1}{4}$ inch/20 by 1 by 0.5 cm)	4
$\frac{1}{3}$ cup	carrot cut into matchsticks	75 mL
$\frac{1}{4}$ cup	Wasabi Mayonnaise (page 227)	60 mL
1 tbsp	tobiko roe, optional	15 mL

1. Place sushi mat on top of a large cutting board with bamboo strips running crosswise. Place a bowl of cold water next to the board.

2. Lay 1 sheet of nori, shiny side down, with the longer side facing you and the perforations perpendicular to the bamboo strips on the mat (see Tips, left). Place about 1 cup (250 mL) rice on top. Using the tip of a fork, break up large clumps and push rice loosely across nori. With moistened fingers, spread rice evenly over nori, gently patting it down (see Tips, left). Spread right to the edges but leave a $\frac{1}{2}$- to 1-inch (1 to 2.5 cm) border at the top.

3. Sprinkle 1 tsp (5 mL) sesame seeds evenly over rice. Lay one-quarter of the tuna, 1 strip cucumber and one-quarter of the carrot matchsticks horizontally and evenly across the rice, almost at the center (about 3 inches/7.5 cm from the bottom).

4. Lift mat and bottom edge of nori and fold it over filling. Pulling back on the mat, run your fingers from the center to the ends to tuck in nori and create an even cylinder. Roll nori up to border at top (you can either let go of the mat and finish rolling by hand or push the mat over the cylinder). When you get to the border, use the mat to pull back on the roll to tighten it a bit, then roll to the end. From the top, roll the sushi mat completely around the cylinder and press and squeeze along its length to create a firm, even roll. Pat the ends of the cylinder to push in any protruding rice or fillings. Set the roll aside, seam side down. Repeat with remaining ingredients. Let rolls rest for 5 minutes before slicing (see Tips, page 229).

Tips

For sushi rolls, use top-quality tuna. I chose chunk white albacore in water because the Wasabi Mayonnaise is creamy. Alternatively, you can buy rich, silky belly tuna or tuna fillets in olive oil, sold in specialty food stores. Drain before using and omit the Wasabi Mayonnaise if desired.

For neater cuts, I let the rolls sit briefly before slicing. It also helps to wipe the knife on a wet towel before each cut.

5. Place a roll on cutting board. If ends are ragged, slice them off neatly, using a small, sharp knife. Cut roll in half, then cut each half into 4 pieces. Repeat with remaining rolls.

6. Place sushi slices, rice side up, on a serving platter. Garnish each with a dab of Wasabi Mayonnaise and a sprinkling of tobiko, if using, dividing equally. Serve immediately.

Variations

Substitute an equal quantity of salmon or mackerel for the tuna.

Spicy Salmon and Asparagus Sushi Rolls

Spicy salmon is a popular Japanese roll for good reason. I love the bold, creamy filling.

	Makes 40 pieces	

Makes 40 pieces

- Brown-bag
- Guest-worthy

Tips

Nori sheets are almost square. Luckily, you can use the perforations on them as a placement guide. They should be perpendicular to the slats of the sushi mat.

When spreading the rice over the nori, be aware that it will be very sticky, so moisten your fingers as needed. Don't compact the rice onto the nori too enthusiastically. Sushi chefs say you should still be able to see the individual grains of rice.

You can eat delicious leftover sushi rice as a side dish, use it to experiment with other types of sushi rolls or make informal hand rolls or sushi salad. For a quick hand roll, spread a handful of rice at one end of a sheet of nori (it doesn't have to be tidy), lay any filling you like diagonally across the rice, then roll up the nori in a cone shape. To make informal hand rolls or a simple sushi salad see page 226.

10	slender stalks asparagus, trimmed and cut into 4-inch (10 cm) lengths	10
1/3 cup	mayonnaise	75 mL
1 tsp	Asian chili sauce (such as sriracha)	5 mL
1	can (7 1/2 oz/213 g) salmon, drained, deboned and broken into chunks	1
5	sheets nori	5
5 cups	Sushi Rice (page 226)	1.25 L
1 tbsp	toasted sesame seeds, optional	15 mL

1. Fill a skillet with water to a depth of 1/4 inch (0.5 cm) and bring to a boil over high heat. Add asparagus and cook for 2 to 4 minutes or until tender. Drain and rinse under cold running water to stop the cooking. Drain and pat dry. Set aside.

2. In a medium measuring cup, stir together mayonnaise and chili sauce. Using a fork, blend in salmon (the mixture should be a bit chunky, not paste-like). Set aside.

3. Follow instructions for spreading sushi rice over nori on page 228, Steps 1 and 2.

4. Spread about 3 tbsp (45 mL) salmon mixture in a strip horizontally and evenly across rice, almost at the centre (about 3 inches/7.5 cm from bottom). Top with 2 asparagus stalks, ends facing out. Follow instructions for rolling and cutting sushi, pages 228 and 229, Steps 4 and 5.

5. Place sushi slices, rice side up, on a serving platter. Garnish each with sesame seeds (if using), dividing equally. Serve immediately.

Variations

Substitute watercress for the asparagus, using about 1/4 cup (60 mL) per nori sheet.

You can use other types of chili sauce or a Japanese dried chile blend.

Substitute an equal quantity of tuna, mackerel, shrimp, crab or lobster for the salmon.

Mackerel and Green Onion Sushi Rolls

Mackerel sushi, known as saba*, is enjoyed in Japan. North Americans don't care much for the fishy taste, but canned mackerel is more subdued. Here a combination of lemony mackerel, green onions and sesame makes for tasty rolls.*

Makes 40 pieces

- Healthy
- Brown-bag
- Guest-worthy

Tips

When spreading the rice over the nori, be aware that it will be very sticky, so moisten your fingers as needed. Don't compact the rice onto the nori too enthusiastically. Sushi chefs say you should still be able to see the individual grains of rice.

For neater cuts, I let the rolls sit briefly before slicing. It also helps to wipe the knife on a wet towel before each cut.

5	sheets nori (see Tips, page 230)	5
5 cups	Sushi Rice (page 226)	1.25 L
5 tsp	toasted sesame seeds	25 mL
2	cans (each 4 oz/125 g) mackerel, drained and broken into chunks	2
2	lemon wedges	2
5	slim green onions, trimmed and cut into 8-inch (20 cm) lengths	5
¼ cup	Wasabi Mayonnaise (page 227)	60 mL

1. Follow the instructions for spreading sushi rice over nori on page 228, Steps 1 and 2.

2. Sprinkle 1 tsp (5 mL) sesame seeds evenly over rice. Lay one-fifth of the mackerel horizontally and evenly across the rice, almost at the center (about 3 inches/7.5 cm from the bottom). Squeeze lemon juice evenly over mackerel. Top with 1 green onion. Complete Steps 4 and 5 for rolling and cutting sushi (pages 228 and 229).

3. Place sushi slices, rice side up, on a serving platter. Garnish each with a dab of Wasabi Mayonnaise.

> ### Variations
> Substitute an equal quantity of tuna, salmon, roe, shrimp or lobster for the mackerel.

Caviar and Avocado Sushi Rolls

If you spring for salmon caviar — large, creamy, pink and pricy — this will make Cadillac sushi, a rich roll in more ways than one. But you can get away with delightfully crunchy tobiko or lumpfish caviar instead.

Tips

Nori sheets are almost square. Luckily, you can use the perforations on them as a placement guide. They should be perpendicular to the slats of the sushi mat.

When spreading the rice over the nori, be aware that it will be very sticky, so moisten your fingers as needed. Don't compact the rice onto the nori too enthusiastically. Sushi chefs say you should still be able to see the individual grains of rice.

Avocados turn brown quickly. Do not cut the avocado until you are ready to roll the sushi.

For neater cuts, I let the rolls sit briefly before slicing. It also helps to wipe the knife on a wet towel before each cut.

Variations

Instead of using roe, pair tuna, salmon, crab or lobster with the avocado for completely different rolls.

3	sheets nori	3
½	recipe Sushi Rice (page 226)	½
½	ripe avocado, thinly sliced (see Tips, left)	½
1	jar (3½ oz/100 g) salmon caviar	1
1 tbsp	toasted sesame seeds, optional	15 mL

1. Place sushi mat on top of a large cutting board with bamboo strips running crosswise. Place a bowl of cold water next to the board.

2. Lay 1 sheet of nori, shiny side down, with the longer side facing you and the perforations perpendicular to the bamboo strips on the mat (see Tips, left). Place about 1 cup (250 mL) rice on top. Using the tip of a fork, break up large clumps and push rice loosely across nori. With moistened fingers, spread rice evenly over nori, gently patting it down (see Tips, left). Spread right to the edges but leave a ½- to 1-inch (1 to 2.5 cm) border at the top.

3. Lay one-third of the avocado horizontally and evenly across the rice, almost at the center (about 3 inches/7.5 cm from the bottom). Top with one-third of the caviar.

4. Lift mat and bottom edge of nori and fold it over filling. Pulling back on the mat, run your fingers from the center to the ends to tuck in nori and create an even cylinder. Roll nori up to border at top (you can either let go of the mat and finish rolling by hand or push the mat over the cylinder). When you get to the border, use the mat to pull back on the roll to tighten it a bit, then roll to the end. From the top, roll the sushi mat completely around the cylinder and press and squeeze along its length to create a firm, even roll. Pat the ends of the cylinder to push in any protruding rice or fillings. Set the roll aside, seam side down. Repeat with remaining ingredients. Let rolls rest for 5 minutes before slicing (see Tips, left).

5. Place a roll on cutting board. If ends are ragged, slice them off neatly, using a small, sharp knife. Cut roll in half, then cut each half into 4 pieces. Repeat with remaining rolls.

6. Place sushi slices, rice side up, on a serving platter. Garnish each with sesame seeds, if using, dividing equally.

Tuna and Spinach Risotto

Risotto is a popular dish for both everyday suppers and dinner parties. You can make good risotto with canned seafood. Here is one simple idea.

Makes 4 to 6 servings

- Kid-friendly
- Guest-worthy

Tips

Risotto is traditionally made with hot stock. However, you don't have to keep the stock simmering. Even room-temperature stock will work.

I find store-bought stock (particularly vegetable stock) too aggressive, so I water it down.

Risotto rice is short-grained, creamy and starchy. Arborio (used here) is most popular, while Carnaroli and Vialone Nano are pricier.

The speed at which risotto cooks depends on the width of the pan, the heat level and the temperature of the stock.

If you've purchased a package containing three small cans of tuna, feel free to add the third can.

5 cups	chicken or vegetable stock	1.25 L
1 cup	water	250 mL
2	cans (each 3 oz/85 g) tuna in olive oil, drained (oil reserved) and broken into chunks (see Tips, left)	2
1½ cups	Arborio rice (see Tips, left)	375 mL
2	cloves garlic, minced	2
¼ cup	dry white wine	60 mL
1 tbsp	unsalted butter	15 mL
2½ cups	thinly sliced spinach leaves (2 oz/60 g)	625 mL
1 tsp	finely grated lemon zest	5 mL
	Freshly ground black pepper	
½ cup	freshly grated Parmesan cheese (1 oz/30 g)	125 mL

1. In a saucepan over medium-high heat, bring stock and water to a boil. Remove from heat and place on a back burner.

2. Pour 2 tbsp (30 mL) of the oil drained from the tuna into another saucepan and heat over medium heat until shimmery. Add rice and cook, stirring often, for 3 to 5 minutes, until rice is toasted and turning golden. Stir in garlic for 10 seconds. Stir in wine until it evaporates. Reduce heat to medium-low. Add stock mixture 1 cup (250 mL) at a time, stirring often. Do not add liquid until previous addition is almost absorbed. Repeat until all the liquid has been used and rice is creamy and tender but firm. This should take 20 to 30 minutes (see Tips, left).

3. Remove from heat. Stir in butter, spinach, lemon zest and pepper. Stir in tuna and Parmesan cheese. Serve immediately.

> **Variations**
> Substitute an equal quantity of salmon, mackerel, shrimp or lobster for the tuna.

Lemony Salmon and Asparagus Risotto

Risotto comes in many glorious guises. This variation pairs salmon, asparagus and fresh herbs for a springtime meal.

Tips

Risotto is traditionally made with hot stock. However, you don't have to keep the stock simmering. Even room-temperature stock will work.

I find store-bought stock (particularly vegetable stock) too aggressive, so I water it down.

The speed at which risotto cooks depends on the width of the pan, the heat level and the temperature of the stock.

Risotto is traditionally finished with butter, but heavy cream is a smooth, satiny alternative.

Variations

Substitute an equal quantity of tuna, shrimp, lobster, clams or octopus for the salmon.

5 cups	chicken or vegetable stock	1.25 L
1 cup	water	250 mL
8 oz	asparagus, trimmed and cut into 1-inch (2.5 cm) segments	250 g
1 tbsp	unsalted butter	15 mL
1 tbsp	extra virgin olive oil	15 mL
1	onion, diced	1
1½ cups	Arborio rice (see Tips, page 235)	375 mL
2 tsp	finely grated lemon zest	10 mL
2 tbsp	freshly squeezed lemon juice	30 mL
	Freshly ground white pepper	
2 tbsp	coarsely chopped parsley, divided	30 mL
1 tbsp	chopped fresh dill fronds	15 mL
2 tbsp	heavy or whipping (35%) cream	30 mL
½ cup	freshly grated Parmesan cheese (1 oz/30 g)	125 mL
	Salt	
1	can (7½ oz/213 g) salmon, drained, deboned and broken into chunks	1

1. In a saucepan over medium-high heat, bring stock and water to a boil. Add asparagus. Reduce heat to medium-low and simmer for 5 to 7 minutes, until tender-crisp. Using a mesh scoop, transfer asparagus to a small bowl. Remove pan from heat and place on a back burner.

2. In another saucepan, melt butter with oil over medium heat. Add onion and cook, stirring often, for about 5 minutes, until it starts to turn golden. Add rice and stir for 1 minute, until coated.

3. Reduce heat to medium-low. Add stock mixture 1 cup (250 mL) at a time, stirring often. Do not add liquid until previous addition is almost absorbed. Repeat until all the liquid has been used and rice is creamy and tender but firm. This should take 20 to 30 minutes (see Tips, left).

4. Remove pan from heat. Stir in asparagus, lemon zest and juice, pepper to taste, 1 tbsp (15 mL) parsley and dill. Stir in cream and Parmesan. Add salt to taste. Scatter salmon overtop. Cover pan and let risotto rest for 5 minutes, then mix gently. Sprinkle remaining 1 tbsp (15 mL) parsley overtop. Serve immediately.

Shrimp and Shiitake Risotto

In this bold variation, earthy mushrooms and cilantro nudge risotto away from its Italian roots.

Makes 4 to 6 servings

- Kid-friendly
- Guest-worthy

Tip

Risotto rice is short-grained, creamy and starchy. Arborio (used here) is most popular, while Carnaroli and Vialone Nano are pricier.

Variations

Substitute an equal quantity of salmon or lobster for the shrimp.

5 cups	chicken or vegetable stock	1.25 L
1 cup	water	250 mL
2 tbsp	unsalted butter, divided	30 mL
1 tbsp	extra virgin olive oil	15 mL
8 oz	shiitake mushrooms, stems removed, sliced	250 g
2	shallots, chopped	2
2	cloves garlic, chopped	2
1½ cups	Arborio rice (see Tips, left)	375 mL
2 tbsp	coarsely chopped cilantro leaves	30 mL
½ cup	freshly grated Parmesan cheese (1 oz/30 g)	125 mL
	Salt	
1	can (4 oz/106 g) medium shrimp, rinsed and drained	1

1. In a saucepan, bring stock and water to a boil over medium-high heat. Remove from heat and place on a back burner.

2. In another saucepan over medium heat, melt 1 tbsp (15 mL) butter with the oil. Stir in mushrooms, shallots and garlic. Cook, stirring often, for 2 to 3 minutes, until mixture softens. Add rice and stir for 1 minute, until coated.

3. Reduce heat to medium-low. Add hot stock mixture 1 cup (250 mL) at a time, stirring often. Do not add liquid until previous addition is almost absorbed. Repeat until all the liquid has been used and rice is creamy and tender but firm. This should take 20 to 30 minutes (see Tips, left).

4. Remove from heat. Stir in remaining 1 tbsp (15 mL) butter, half the cilantro and the Parmesan. Season to taste with salt. Scatter shrimp evenly overtop. Cover pan and let risotto rest for 5 minutes, then mix gently.

5. Sprinkle remaining cilantro overtop and serve immediately.

Easy Ham and Clam Jambalaya

This plain one-pot dinner won't win any haute cuisine awards, but it's mighty good on the family dinner table.

Tips

Stick to diced tomatoes in this recipe — they will hold their shape better, so the dish looks neater. Drain them well.

I like to use basmati rice because it doesn't get as sticky or clumpy as generic white rice, but you can substitute.

1 tbsp	extra virgin olive oil	15 mL
1	small onion, diced	1
2	cloves garlic, minced	2
1	stalk celery, chopped	1
½	green bell pepper, chopped	½
1 cup	basmati rice, rinsed (see Tips, left)	250 mL
8 oz	chunk smoked ham, cut in ½-inch (1 cm) cubes	250 g
1 cup	okra cut in ½-inch (1 cm) segments (about 4 oz/125 g)	250 mL
1 cup	chicken or vegetable stock	250 mL
1	bottle (8 oz/240 mL) clam juice	1
2 tsp	Cajun seasoning	10 mL
1	can (5 oz/142 g) surf or meaty clams, coarsely chopped	1
1	can (14 oz/398 mL) diced tomatoes, drained	1
	Salt and freshly ground black pepper	
	Cayenne pepper	
1 tbsp	chopped parsley leaves	15 mL

1. In a saucepan, heat oil over medium heat until shimmery. Add onion, garlic, celery and green pepper and cook, stirring often, for about 3 minutes, until vegetables soften. Add rice and stir for 1 minute, until coated. Add ham, okra, stock, clam juice and Cajun seasoning and stir well. Bring to a simmer, reduce heat to low, cover and simmer for about 18 minutes, until rice is just tender and liquid has been absorbed.

2. Arrange clams and tomatoes evenly overtop. Set pan aside, uncovered, for 5 minutes. Season to taste with salt and pepper and mix gently. Before serving, sprinkle with cayenne to taste and parsley.

Variations

Switch to andouille sausage instead of ham.

You can use baby clams for this recipe.

Substitute an equal quantity of shrimp or lobster for the clams.

Quick Mock Paella

This is the lazy man's paella — or the working mom's, depending on your perspective. You can pick up all the ingredients in the supermarket and it's ready in a jiffy. If you have unexpected guests, you can dress up the recipe with lobster instead of shrimp and sprinkle fresh herbs overtop.

Makes 4 servings

- Fast

Tip

I've called for Arborio rice because Spanish paella rice, such as bomba, is sold mainly in specialty stores. However, if you have access to it, substitute it for the Arborio. It is not as sticky.

Variations

Substitute thawed frozen lima beans for the canned ones, or use an equal quantity of green peas.

Substitute an equal quantity of lobster, clams or octopus for the shrimp. This is good with meaty clams. If you are substituting surf clams for the shrimp, chop them coarsely.

1 cup	Arborio rice, rinsed (see Tip, left)	250 mL
2 cups	chicken stock	500 mL
½ cup	water	125 mL
¼ tsp	saffron, crumbled	1 mL
2 tbsp	extra virgin olive oil	30 mL
1	small green bell pepper, cut in small dice	1
½	Spanish onion, diced	½
2	cloves garlic, minced	2
1 cup	canned diced tomatoes, with juices	250 mL
½ tsp	salt (approx.)	2 mL
½ tsp	smoked sweet paprika	2 mL
1	can (14 oz/398 mL) lima beans, drained and rinsed	1
1	can (4 oz/106 g) medium shrimp, rinsed and drained	1
4	lemon wedges	4

1. In a saucepan, bring rice, stock, water and saffron to a boil over high heat. Reduce heat to low, cover and simmer for 20 minutes, until rice is tender and liquid has been absorbed. Remove from heat. Fluff rice with a fork and let rest, uncovered, for 5 minutes.

2. Meanwhile, in a skillet, heat oil over medium heat until shimmery. Stir in green pepper, onion and garlic. Cook, stirring often, for 5 minutes, until vegetables soften and onion starts to turn golden. Stir in tomatoes and salt. Cook, stirring often, for 2 minutes, until mixture is very thick. Stir in paprika and beans.

3. Pour tomato mixture and shrimp over rice. Mix with a fork.

4. Transfer to warmed serving plates. Serve lemon wedges alongside to squeeze overtop.

Curried Shrimp Pilaf

Well-toasted rice gives this quick pilaf an extra-nutty flavor, and the cranberries, almonds and cilantro make it look pretty.

Makes 4 servings

- Fast
- Guest-worthy

Tip

Indian curry paste is sold in supermarkets. There are many kinds. Use your favorite.

1 tbsp	unsalted butter	15 mL
1 cup	basmati rice, rinsed	250 mL
1 tbsp	extra virgin olive oil	15 mL
1	onion, diced	1
1	stalk celery, thinly sliced diagonally	1
1 tbsp	prepared Indian curry paste (see Tip, left)	15 mL
2 cups	chicken stock	500 mL
¼ tsp	salt (approx.)	1 mL
⅛ tsp	freshly ground black pepper	0.5 mL
1	can (4 oz/106 g) tiny shrimp, rinsed and drained	1
½ cup	slivered almonds	125 mL
¼ cup	dried cranberries	60 mL
2 tbsp	cilantro leaves	30 mL

1. In a saucepan, melt butter over medium heat. Add rice and cook, stirring often, for 3 to 5 minutes, until toasted and golden. Scrape into a small bowl and set aside.

2. In the same pan, heat oil over medium heat. Add onion, celery and curry paste. Cook, stirring often, for 5 minutes, until vegetables soften. Stir in stock, rice, salt and pepper. When mixture comes to a boil, reduce heat to low. Cover and simmer for 18 minutes, until rice is tender and liquid has been absorbed. Remove from heat. Fluff with a fork and let rest, uncovered, for 5 minutes.

3. Using a fork, gently stir in shrimp, almonds and cranberries. Add salt to taste, if necessary. Transfer to a serving bowl and garnish with cilantro. Serve immediately.

Variations

Substitute an equal quantity of salmon, crab or lobster for the shrimp.

Crab and Sesame-Lime Rice

This simple one-pot rice dish smells irresistible. So why resist? Indulge yourself. You can add some Asian flare by serving shelled edamame alongside.

Tip

I prefer to use the bolder-tasting, firmer claw crabmeat in this dish. You can increase the amount in this recipe to taste. If you end up with leftovers from a 1 pound (454 g) container, check the chart on pages 272 to 278 for more delicious recipe ideas.

1 cup	basmati rice, rinsed	250 mL
2 cups	water	500 mL
1/2 tsp	salt (approx.)	2 mL
2 tbsp	unsalted butter	30 mL
1/4 cup	sesame seeds	60 mL
1 tsp	finely grated lime zest	5 mL
2 tbsp	freshly squeezed lime juice	30 mL
	Freshly ground black pepper	
1 1/4 cups	crabmeat (6 oz/175 g), rinsed and drained (see Tip, left)	300 mL
1 tbsp	chopped chives	15 mL

1. In a saucepan over high heat, bring rice, water and salt to a boil. Reduce heat to low. Cover and simmer for 18 minutes, until rice is tender and water has been absorbed. Remove from heat. Fluff rice with a fork and let rest, uncovered, for 5 minutes.

2. Meanwhile, in a small skillet, melt butter over medium-low heat. Stir in sesame seeds and cook, stirring, for about 4 minutes, until they turn golden brown. Add to rice, along with lime zest and juice, pepper to taste and crabmeat. Stir with a fork. Add salt to taste, if necessary.

3. Garnish with chives and serve immediately.

Variations

Substitute an equal quantity of tuna, salmon, shrimp or lobster for the crab.

Chipotle Salmon on Rice

Trendy chipotle chiles in adobo sauce propel creamed salmon into the 21st century. The smoky tomato flavor is yummy.

Tip

Mincing a saucy chipotle can be messy. Instead, mash it with a fork.

1 cup	long-grain white rice, rinsed	250 mL
2 cups	water	500 mL
	Salt	
1 tbsp	extra virgin olive oil	15 mL
1	shallot	1
2	cloves garlic, chopped	2
1/4 cup	chopped green bell pepper	60 mL
2 tbsp	tomato paste	30 mL
1	chipotle chile in adobo sauce, with sauce, mashed (see Tip, left)	1
1/2 cup	heavy or whipping (35%) cream	125 mL
1/2 cup	chicken or vegetable stock	125 mL
2 tsp	freshly squeezed lime juice	10 mL
2	cans (each 7 1/2 oz/213 g) salmon, drained, deboned and broken into chunks	2
2 tbsp	chopped cilantro leaves	30 mL

1. In a saucepan over high heat, bring rice, water and salt, to taste, to a boil. Reduce heat to low. Cover and simmer for about 18 minutes, until rice is tender and water has been absorbed. Remove from heat. Fluff rice with a fork and let rest, uncovered, for 5 minutes.

2. Meanwhile, in a skillet, heat oil over medium heat until shimmery. Stir in shallot, garlic and green pepper and cook, stirring, for 2 to 3 minutes, until vegetables soften. Stir in tomato paste and chipotle chile, with sauce. Stir in cream and stock. Simmer for 5 minutes, until thickened. Stir in lime juice, then salmon.

3. Fluff rice with a fork. Spoon onto warmed serving plates, dividing equally. Top with salmon mixture, dividing equally. Sprinkle cilantro overtop.

Variations

If the spicing is too much for you, halve the quantity of chipotle.

This dish will work over pasta too.

Substitute an equal quantity of tuna for the salmon.

Portuguese Rice with Clams

My kind Portuguese neighbors taught me the secrets to making this zesty rice. Although it is usually served as a side dish, it's worth adding seafood to make this a meal. Add a green salad as accompaniment.

Tips

Make sure the vegetables are minced very finely. The red pepper should be almost puréed.

Piri piri is Portuguese hot pepper sauce.

The olives are usually tossed on the rice whole, but you can pit them if you wish.

Variations

Portuguese sausages come in mild and spicy versions. I start with the mild kind and add heat with piri piri sauce. However, you can start with spicy sausage instead.

The rice should be firm, not sticky. You can use converted (parboiled) rice if you prefer.

Substitute an equal quantity of shrimp, squid or octopus for the clams.

2 cups	water	500 mL
	Salt	
1 cup	long-grain white rice, rinsed	250 mL
1/4 cup	extra virgin olive oil	60 mL
1/2 cup	minced red bell pepper	125 mL
1	shallot, minced	1
1/4 cup	skinned, finely chopped chouriço or linguiça sausage	60 mL
1	clove garlic, minced	1
2 tbsp	tomato paste	30 mL
1	can (5 oz/142 g) surf or meaty clams, rinsed, drained and coarsely chopped	1
	Piri piri sauce, optional (see Tips, left)	
	Freshly ground black pepper	
2 tbsp	chopped parsley leaves	30 mL
16 to 20	black olives (see Tips, left)	16 to 20

1. In a saucepan over high heat, bring rice, water and salt, to taste, to a boil. Reduce heat to low. Cover and simmer for about 18 minutes, until rice is tender and water has been absorbed. Remove from heat. Fluff rice with a fork and let rest, uncovered, for 5 minutes.

2. Meanwhile, in a small saucepan, heat oil over medium-low heat until shimmery. Add red pepper and shallot and cook, stirring often, for about 10 minutes, until vegetables are very soft. (Do not brown the vegetables. Lower the heat if necessary — the mixture should poach rather than fry.) Add sausage and garlic and cook, stirring often, for 5 minutes. Stir in tomato paste.

3. Add clams and vegetable mixture to rice and mix gently with a fork. Add piri piri sauce (if using), salt and pepper to taste. Garnish with parsley and scatter olives overtop. Serve immediately.

Shrimp Fried Rice

If you've tried to make fried rice and it turned to mush, you probably forgot to dry out the cooked rice before frying it. Some people refrigerate leftover cooked rice overnight to get that restaurant-style texture. I am too impatient to do this when I crave fried rice, so mine turns out a bit softer and fresher-tasting than the stuff that is served in eateries. This Chinese-restaurant staple is not as simple as you might suppose. It is easy to make but has many steps, so don't try to multitask.

Makes 6 to 8 main-course servings

- Kid-friendly

Tips

When you're making Chinese food, prep everything in advance. Otherwise the logistics will give you a headache.

Be sure to start this recipe well ahead of time to ensure the rice dries out properly (Step 2).

Rinsing the rice removes some of the starch that makes it sticky. For the driest rice, transfer cooked rice to a storage tub and refrigerate overnight. You can also use 8 cups (2 L) leftover rice.

This works well with basmati rice, which is less sticky than generic white rice.

- Wok (see Tips, page 243)
- Rimmed baking sheet

2 cups	long-grain white rice, rinsed	500 mL
4 cups	water	1 L
	Salt	
3 tbsp	soy sauce	45 mL
2 tbsp	chicken stock	30 mL
2 tbsp	toasted sesame oil, divided (see Tips, page 243)	30 mL
1 tbsp	rice vinegar	15 mL
1/8 tsp	freshly ground black pepper	0.5 mL
2	large eggs, lightly beaten	2
6 tbsp	peanut or vegetable oil, divided	90 mL
4 oz	snow peas, trimmed and cut in thirds lengthwise (about 1¾ cups/425 mL)	125 g
½ cup	corn kernels	125 mL
½ cup	shredded carrot	125 mL
6	green onions, (white and green parts), thinly sliced	6
2	cloves garlic, minced	2
1	can (4 oz/106 g) small shrimp, rinsed and drained	1
1 cup	thinly sliced oyster or stemmed shiitake mushrooms (about 1 oz/30 g)	250 mL
1 tbsp	chopped cilantro leaves	15 mL

1. In a saucepan over high heat, bring rice, water and salt, to taste, to a boil. Reduce heat to low. Cover and simmer for about 18 minutes, until rice is tender and water has been absorbed. Remove from heat and let rest, uncovered, for 5 minutes.

2. Transfer rice to baking sheet and, using a spatula, spread it out to dry for at least 2 hours, stirring and flipping occasionally. You should have about 8 cups (2 L).

Tips

Toasted sesame oil, also known as Asian sesame oil, is made from toasted or roasted seeds. Dark and aromatic, it is sold in small bottles as a flavoring agent. Do not confuse toasted sesame oil with yellow sesame oil, which is pressed from raw seeds.

Don't try to double this recipe. Make two separate batches instead.

If you don't have a wok, use a 12-inch (30 cm) skillet and decrease the cooking times.

3. In a small bowl, stir together soy sauce, stock, 1 tbsp (15 mL) sesame oil, vinegar and pepper. Set aside.

4. In a small nonstick skillet, heat $\frac{1}{2}$ tbsp (7 mL) of the remaining sesame oil over medium heat. Add eggs. Sprinkle with salt to taste. Cook for 1 to 2 minutes, until set, lifting edges occasionally with a spatula to allow liquid to run underneath. Remove from heat. Using a spatula, break egg into chunks. Set aside.

5. In a wok, heat 2 tbsp (30 mL) peanut oil over medium-high heat. Stir in snow peas, corn, carrot, green onions and garlic. Stir-fry for 2 to 3 minutes, until vegetables are glossy and softened but still tender-crisp. Scrape into a bowl. Add shrimp to bowl.

6. Return wok to heat and add remaining $\frac{1}{2}$ tbsp (7 mL) sesame oil. Add mushrooms and stir-fry for about 2 minutes, until softened. Using a slotted spoon, transfer to a separate bowl.

7. Add remaining 4 tbsp (60 mL) peanut oil to pan and heat over high heat until shimmery. Add rice and cook for 5 to 7 minutes, until glossy and hot, stirring and flipping with a small spatula and scraping up the crust as it forms on the bottom of wok.

8. Stir in reserved soy sauce mixture, then vegetables with shrimp. Remove wok from heat. Add salt to taste. Gently fold in eggs. Scrape onto a large serving platter. Scatter mushrooms evenly overtop and garnish with cilantro. Serve immediately.

Variations

Substitute an equal quantity of salmon, mackerel, lobster, clams, squid or octopus for the shrimp.

Couscous with Tuna, Feta and Lemon Mint Dressing

Couscous is a quick-cooking, wholesome carb. Made from granular semolina, couscous is akin to pasta but is used like a grain. It is good warm, cold or at room temperature. This is a dinner salad, with couscous, vegetables and seafood packed into one delicious bowl.

Makes 4 servings

- Fast
- Healthy
- Brown-bag

Tip

North America supermarkets sell instant couscous. Authentic Moroccan couscous (not instant) is steamed and dried several times. It is cooked in a double pot called a couscoussière over a simmering stew or salted water.

Variations

Substitute an equal quantity of salmon or shrimp for the tuna.

2	cans (each 3 oz/85 g) tuna in olive oil, drained (oil reserved) and broken into chunks	2
2 tbsp	extra virgin olive oil (approx.)	30 mL
1 tbsp	freshly squeezed lemon juice	15 mL
1 tsp	salt	5 mL
1/8 tsp	freshly ground black pepper	0.5 mL
1 tbsp	finely chopped mint leaves	15 mL
1 1/4 cups	chicken or vegetable stock	300 mL
1 cup	instant couscous (see Tip, left)	250 mL
1	large tomato, cut in 1/4-inch (0.5 cm) dice	1
1/2	English cucumber, peeled and cut in 1/4-inch (0.5 cm) dice	1/2
1/2	red bell pepper, cut in 1/4-inch (0.5 cm) dice	1/2
1/2 cup	thinly sliced red onion	125 mL
4 oz	feta cheese, broken into small chunks (about 1 cup/250 mL)	125 g
2 tbsp	slivered mint leaves	30 mL

1. Pour oil from tuna into a small measuring cup and set tuna aside. Add enough extra virgin olive oil to make 1/4 cup (60 mL). Whisk in lemon juice, salt, pepper and finely chopped mint. Set aside.

2. In a saucepan over medium-high heat, bring stock to a boil. Add couscous in a steady stream, stirring constantly. When mixture returns to a simmer, immediately cover and remove from heat. Set aside for 5 minutes, until liquid has been absorbed.

3. Transfer couscous to a large serving bowl and let cool for 5 minutes. Add tomato, cucumber, red pepper, onion and reserved tuna. Drizzle tuna oil dressing overtop. Toss gently. Scatter feta overtop.

4. Garnish with slivered mint leaves. Serve at room temperature.

Shrimp, Pomegranate and Almond Quinoa

This looks so pretty and tastes so good, who would think you were treating your body to a healthy whole grain?

Makes 4 servings

- Healthy
- Brown-bag
- Guest-worthy

Tips

Quinoa is coated with saponin, a natural detergent found in many plants that has a bitter taste. Although it has usually been removed by the time you purchase it, it's always a good idea to rinse quinoa well. Count on 1 cup (250 mL) dry quinoa making about 3¾ cups (925 mL) cooked quinoa.

Pomegranate arils are the fruit's ruby-red seeds. You should get more than enough from one pomegranate for this recipe. But you may not have to mess with whole pomegranates; fresh arils are now available in specialty stores and some supermarkets. Avoid using the frozen ones for this dish — they are too soft and soggy when thawed.

1 cup	quinoa, rinsed and drained (see Tips, left)	250 mL
1 cup	vegetable stock	250 mL
1 cup	water	250 mL
2 tbsp	freshly squeezed lemon juice	30 mL
2 tbsp	extra virgin olive oil	30 mL
½ tsp	salt (approx.)	2 mL
⅛ tsp	freshly ground black pepper	0.5 mL
1	can (4 oz/106 g) tiny shrimp, rinsed and drained	1
1 cup	pomegranate arils (see Tips, left)	250 mL
¾ cup	sliced almonds	175 mL
½ cup	sliced green onions (white and light green parts)	125 mL
½ cup	chopped parsley leaves	125 mL

1. In a dry saucepan over medium heat, toast quinoa, stirring, for 5 minutes, until it smells nutty and no longer steams. Carefully add stock and water (the mixture will sputter). Once mixture comes to a full boil, reduce heat to medium-low, cover and simmer for 15 minutes, until quinoa is tender-firm and liquid has been absorbed. Remove from heat, fluff with a fork and set aside, uncovered, for 5 minutes. Transfer to a large serving bowl and set aside to cool to room temperature.

2. Meanwhile, in a small bowl, whisk together lemon juice, oil, salt and pepper. Add to cooled quinoa. Add shrimp, pomegranate, almonds, green onions and parsley and mix gently. Add salt to taste, if necessary.

3. Serve immediately or cover and refrigerate for up to 3 days.

Variations

Substitute an equal quantity of tuna, salmon or lobster for the shrimp.

Citrus Quinoa with Crab and Cress

Seafood and citrus have had a long and happy relationship. This uptown quinoa dish smells fragrant and tastes sublime. It is quick to prepare if you multitask by prepping the remaining ingredients while the quinoa cooks.

Makes about 2 to 4 servings

- Fast
- Healthy
- Guest-worthy

Tips

Small-chunk shelf-stable crab is fine in this, but avoid ultra-flaky "salad" crab; it will get lost in the mixture. Alternatively, dress up this dish with part of a 1 pound (454 g) container of premium lump crabmeat. To use up the leftovers, check the chart on pages 272 to 278 for more delicious recipes.

You can also serve this cold. Cover and refrigerate the dressed quinoa for up to 2 hours, then stir in the crab and watercress before serving.

Variations

You can use almost any kind of seafood in this tasteful mixture. Substitute an equal quantity of tuna, salmon, shrimp or lobster for the crab.

1 cup	quinoa, rinsed and drained	250 mL
1¼ cups	chicken or vegetable stock	300 mL
¾ cup	freshly squeezed orange juice (2 oranges)	175 mL
1 tsp	finely grated lemon zest	5 mL
1 tsp	finely grated lime zest	5 mL
2 tbsp	extra virgin olive oil	30 mL
1 to 2 tbsp	freshly squeezed lime juice, divided	15 to 30 mL
1 tsp	liquid honey	5 mL
½ tsp	salt (approx.)	2 mL
⅛ tsp	freshly ground black pepper	0.5 mL
¼ tsp	ground cumin	1 mL
1	clove garlic, minced	1
1	can (4.25 oz/120 g) crabmeat, rinsed and drained (see Tips, left)	1
2 cups	watercress leaves	500 mL

1. In a dry skillet over medium heat, toast quinoa, stirring, for 5 minutes, until it smells nutty and no longer steams. Carefully add stock (the mixture will sputter), then orange juice and lemon and lime zest. Once mixture comes to a full boil, reduce heat to medium-low, cover and simmer for 15 minutes, until quinoa is tender-firm and liquid has been absorbed. Remove from heat, fluff with a fork and set aside, uncovered, for 5 minutes. Transfer to a large serving bowl.

2. Meanwhile, in a small bowl, whisk together oil, 1 tbsp (15 mL) lime juice, honey, salt, pepper, cumin and garlic. Pour over quinoa and mix with a fork. Add crab and watercress and mix gently. Add salt to taste, if necessary, and some or all of the remaining 1 tbsp (15 mL) lime juice, to taste.

3. Serve warm or at room temperature.

Moroccan-Style Salmon Quinoa

Make an exotic quinoa pilaf with just a can of fish and supermarket ingredients. This is delish.

Makes 4 servings

- Healthy
- Brown-bag
- Guest-worthy

Tip

Toast pine nuts in a dry skillet on medium heat for 2 to 3 minutes, until fragrant and golden.

1 cup	quinoa, rinsed and drained	250 mL
1 cup	chicken or vegetable stock	250 mL
1 cup	water	250 mL
2 tbsp	extra virgin olive oil	30 mL
1 tbsp	freshly squeezed lemon juice	15 mL
1	clove garlic, minced	1
1/2 tsp	salt (approx.)	2 mL
1/4 tsp	ground cumin	1 mL
1/8 tsp	freshly ground black pepper	0.5 mL
1/8 tsp	ground cinnamon	0.5 mL
1	can (7 1/2 oz/213 g) salmon, drained, deboned and broken into chunks	1
1/2 cup	dried apricots (12), coarsely chopped	125 mL
1/2 cup	diced red onion	125 mL
1/4 cup	chopped parsley leaves	60 mL
1/4 cup	chopped cilantro leaves	60 mL
2 tbsp	chopped mint leaves	30 mL
1/4 cup	pine nuts, toasted (see Tip, left)	60 mL

1. In a dry skillet over medium heat, toast quinoa, stirring, for 5 minutes, until it smells nutty and no longer steams. Carefully add stock (the mixture will sputter) and water. Once mixture comes to a full boil, reduce heat to medium-low, cover and simmer for 15 minutes, until quinoa is tender-firm and liquid has been absorbed. Remove from heat, fluff with a fork and set aside, uncovered, for 5 minutes. Transfer to a large serving bowl.

2. Meanwhile, in a small bowl, whisk together oil, lemon juice, garlic, salt, cumin, pepper and cinnamon. Pour over quinoa and mix with a fork. Add salmon, apricots, onion, parsley, cilantro and mint. Mix gently. Add salt to taste, if necessary. Sprinkle with pine nuts.

3. Serve warm or at room temperature, or cover and refrigerate overnight.

Variations

Substitute an equal quantity of tuna, shrimp, crab or lobster for the salmon.

Shrimp and Grits with Tomato Gravy

Grits, a Southern staple made from ground dried corn, are often mistakenly pegged as a breakfast food. You can have your way with them any time of day and they go very well with seafood. In this dish I matched up two of the hungry South's great culinary inventions: tomato gravy and grits with shrimp.

Makes 4 servings

• Guest-worthy

Tip

Grits run the gamut from instant to quick to traditional or old-fashioned to stone-ground, and they take anywhere from 5 minutes to many hours to cook. They are difficult to obtain in some regions. Follow the package directions for the type you have. If you can't find grits, try coarse or stone-ground cornmeal.

Tomato Gravy

4	slices bacon, chopped	4
2 to 3 tbsp	extra virgin olive oil	30 to 45 mL
1	small onion, finely chopped	1
1	clove garlic, minced	1
1/3 cup	all-purpose flour	75 mL
1	can (28 oz/796 mL) tomatoes, with juices, puréed (see Tips, page 249)	1
1/4 cup	heavy or whipping (35%) cream	60 mL
2 tsp	fresh thyme leaves	10 mL
1/2 tsp	salt (approx.)	2 mL
1/2 tsp	freshly ground black pepper	2 mL

Grits

2 cups	water	500 mL
2 cups	vegetable stock	500 mL
1 cup	quick-cooking grits (see Tip, left)	250 mL
2 tbsp	unsalted butter	30 mL
1/4 cup	freshly grated Parmesan cheese (1/2 oz/15 g)	60 mL
2	cans (each 4 oz/106 g) small shrimp, rinsed and drained	2

Garnish

4	dill sprigs	4

1. *Tomato Gravy:* In a saucepan over medium heat, cook bacon for about 5 minutes, until browned and crisp. Using a slotted spoon, transfer to a plate lined with paper towels to drain.

Briefly purée the tomatoes in a food processor.

Bonus: The tomato gravy is luscious. You can enjoy leftover tomato gravy on everything from fried chicken to biscuits.

2. Pour drippings into a small measuring cup and add enough oil to equal $\frac{1}{4}$ cup (60 mL). Pour into the same pan and heat over medium heat until shimmery. Add onion and garlic. Reduce heat to medium-low and cook, stirring occasionally, for 5 minutes, until onion turns golden. Stir in flour for 1 minute. Gradually whisk in tomatoes. Stir in cream. Add thyme, salt and pepper. Simmer, stirring often, for 10 minutes, until mixture is thick. Stir in bacon. You should have about 4 cups (1 L) of gravy.

3. *Grits:* In a deep medium pan, bring water and stock to a boil over high heat. While stirring constantly, slowly add grits. Reduce heat to medium-low and simmer for 15 minutes, stirring often, or until tender. (Alternatively, follow package directions.)

4. Stir in butter and Parmesan. Remove from heat and stir in shrimp.

5. To serve, ladle grits into warmed serving bowls and pour tomato gravy overtop (you will have some gravy left over). Garnish with dill sprigs.

Variations
Substitute an equal quantity of lobster or clams for the shrimp. Use meaty surf clams — baby clams are too delicate for this dish.

Shrimp Pad Thai

Feel like having pad thai for dinner? Take a shortcut with canned seafood. Pad Thai success is all in the timing: you want your noodles silky but your sprouts still crunchy. Ketchup is authentic in this dish, believe it or not. Just don't overdo it.

Makes 4 servings

- Kid-friendly

Tips

Tamarind paste gives pad thai a distinctive sweet-and-sour taste. It is sold in Asian grocery stores. Be sure to buy tamarind paste (sometimes labeled "concentrate"), which comes in a jar. Dried tamarind comes compressed in a block, seeds and all; it has to reconstituted, then pressed through a sieve to extract the pulp.

Instead of tamarind paste you can substitute freshly squeezed lemon juice mixed with an equal amount of chopped dates, prunes or dried apricots.

Rice noodles may be labeled "rice sticks."

- **Wok (see Tips, page 251)**

Sauce

2 tbsp	granulated sugar	30 mL
2 tbsp	tamarind paste (see Tips, left)	30 mL
2 tbsp	ketchup	30 mL
2 tbsp	fish sauce	30 mL
2 tbsp	freshly squeezed lime juice	30 mL
1 tbsp	soy sauce	15 mL
2 tsp	Asian chili sauce (such as sambal oelek)	10 mL

Noodles

8 oz	rice noodles, (1/8 or 1/4 inch/3 or 5 mm) wide	250 g
2	large eggs, lightly whisked	2
1/2 tsp	salt (approx.)	2 mL
3 tbsp	oil	45 mL
3	cloves garlic, minced	3
3 cups	bean sprouts	750 mL
1/2 cup	unsalted roasted peanuts, coarsely chopped, divided	125 mL
1	can (4 oz/106 g) medium shrimp, drained and rinsed	1
3	green onions (white and light green parts), thinly sliced	3
2 tbsp	chopped cilantro	30 mL

1. *Sauce:* In a small bowl, stir together sugar, tamarind paste, ketchup, fish sauce, lime juice, soy sauce and chili sauce.

2. *Noodles:* In a large pan of boiling salted water, cook noodles over medium heat for about 5 minutes, until just tender. Drain and rinse briefly with cold water to stop the cooking. Drain.

3. Meanwhile, pour eggs into a dry medium nonstick pan over medium heat. Sprinkle lightly with salt and stir briefly. Cook eggs, undisturbed, for 1 to 2 minutes, until set. Remove pan from heat. Using a wooden spoon, break eggs into large pieces.

Tips

Do not try to double this recipe, because it won't fit or cook properly in the wok. If you want more you'll have to make separate batches.

If you don't have a wok, use a large skillet and reduce the cooking times.

4. In a wok over medium-high heat, heat oil until shimmery. Stir in garlic for 20 seconds. Add sprouts, all but 2 tbsp (30 mL) of the peanuts, noodles and $\frac{1}{2}$ tsp (2 mL) salt. Distribute sauce overtop. Turn heat to high. Gently toss mixture with tongs for 2 minutes or until it is heated through. Remove wok from heat. Gently stir in shrimp and eggs. Adjust salt to taste.

5. Transfer pad thai to a large platter. Sprinkle green onions, cilantro and remaining 2 tbsp (30 mL) peanuts overtop.

Variations

Substitute an equal quantity of salmon, crab, lobster or clams for the shrimp. If you are using salmon, keep it in large chunks.

Tuna, Tomato and Herb Spelt

Here's a satisfying spin on spelt, a nutritious and delicious ancient form of wheat. It is nutty-tasting, chewy and hearty.

Tips

Spelt is sold in natural foods stores and many supermarkets. Buy spelt berries, not the flakes, for this recipe. Spelt berries may also be called "spelt kernels."

Some cooks like to soak spelt berries overnight, but this is not crucial. If soaked, the spelt will still be chewy but will have a more even texture. To soak the spelt, combine with 4 cups (1 L) cold water, cover and set aside for 8 hours or overnight. Drain and rinse before using.

White balsamic vinegar is milder than its assertive darker sibling. Some supermarkets sell it, or you can substitute an equal quantity of white wine vinegar.

Because of the tomatoes, this dish doesn't hold up well in the fridge. That's okay — you won't be able to resist eating it all up quickly.

1 cup	spelt berries (about 6 oz/175 g), rinsed or soaked (see Tips, left)	250 mL
4 cups	water (approx.)	1 L
1½ tsp	salt (approx.), divided	7 mL
1 tbsp	extra virgin olive oil	15 mL
1 tbsp	white balsamic vinegar	15 mL
1	clove garlic, minced	1
⅛ tsp	freshly ground black pepper	0.5 mL
2	cans (each 3 oz/80 g) tuna in olive oil, with oil	2
2 cups	grape tomatoes, halved	500 mL
¼ cup	chopped parsley leaves	60 mL
¼ cup	chopped chives	60 mL
2 tbsp	chopped oregano leaves	30 mL

1. In a saucepan, combine spelt berries with water. Add 1 tsp (5 mL) salt and bring to a boil. Reduce heat to low, cover and simmer for 45 minutes to 1 hour, until tender but chewy. Drain. Transfer to a serving bowl and set aside to cool for at least 10 minutes.

2. In a large bowl, whisk together olive oil, vinegar, garlic, remaining ½ tsp (2 mL) salt and pepper. Stir in spelt, tuna, with oil, tomatoes, parsley, chives and oregano. Toss well. Add salt to taste, if necessary. Serve warm or at room temperature.

Variations

Substitute an equal quantity of salmon, mackerel, sardines or sprats for the tuna.

Breakfast, Brunch and Lunch

Curried Scrambled Eggs and Crab

No more ho-hum scrambled eggs, please. Try this delicious mishmash instead.

Tips

Use good-quality curry powder. The "brand X" ones contain too much turmeric, which gives them a bitter edge.

You can dress this dish up or down. Use either pasteurized lump/claw crabmeat or shelf-stable small-chunk/leg crabmeat.

8	large eggs	8
1/4 tsp	salt (approx.)	1 mL
1/8 tsp	freshly ground black pepper	0.5 mL
1 tbsp	oil	15 mL
2	large green onions (white and light green parts), cut diagonally into 1/2-inch (1 cm) segments	2
1	jalapeño pepper, seeded and cut in 1/8-inch (3 mm) dice	1
2 tsp	curry powder (see Tips, left)	10 mL
1	plum tomato, cut in 1/4-inch (0.5 cm) dice	1
1/4 cup	chopped cilantro leaves, divided	60 mL
1	can (4.25 oz/120 g) crabmeat, rinsed and drained (see Tips, left)	1
	Cayenne pepper	

1. In a bowl, lightly whisk eggs, salt and pepper.

2. In a nonstick skillet, heat oil over medium-high heat until shimmery. Add green onions and jalapeño and cook, stirring often, for 2 to 3 minutes, until they turn golden. Stir in curry powder. Add tomato and 3 tbsp (45 mL) cilantro. Cook for 1 minute, stirring constantly, until liquid evaporates.

3. Reduce heat to medium-low. Add eggs and cook, stirring occasionally, for 2 minutes, until they start to set but are still slightly moist. Fold in crab. Cook, stirring occasionally, for 1 minute, until eggs are just set. Add salt to taste, if necessary.

4. Sprinkle cayenne and remaining 1 tbsp (15 mL) cilantro overtop. Serve immediately.

Variations

Substitute an equal quantity of tuna, salmon, mackerel, kippers, shrimp, lobster or mussels for the crab.

Salmon, Spinach and Sweet Potato Frittata

A frittata is an easy choice for brunch or a family dinner. It's basically an open-faced omelet, so you don't have to fuss with folding, flipping or rolling. It's finished under the broiler — the heat causes the eggs to puff attractively.

Makes 4 to 6 servings

- Fast
- Healthy
- Guest-worthy

Tip

If you don't have a cast-iron skillet, use a nonstick skillet and wrap the handle in foil to protect it from the heat of the broiler.

Variations

For an unusual twist, substitute an equal quantity of smoked oysters or mussels for the salmon.

You can also substitute tuna, mackerel, kippers, shrimp, crab, lobster, clams or plain oysters or mussels.

- **Preheat broiler, placing oven rack one level down from top position**

1	small sweet potato (about 8 oz/250 g), peeled and cut in ¼-inch (0.5 cm) dice	1
1½ cups	stemmed, torn spinach leaves (1 oz/30 g)	375 mL
8	large eggs	8
¾ tsp	salt	3 mL
⅛ tsp	freshly ground black pepper	0.5 mL
1 tbsp	extra virgin olive oil	15 mL
1	onion, diced	1
1	small green bell pepper, cut in tiny dice	1
1	clove garlic, minced	1
1	can (6 oz/170 g) boneless, skinless salmon, drained	1

1. In a pot of boiling salted water over medium heat, cook sweet potato for 3 to 4 minutes, until tender but firm. Using a mesh scoop, transfer to a sieve. Drain and set aside.

2. Return water to a boil. Add spinach and blanch for 30 seconds. Drain. When cool enough to handle, squeeze dry and chop coarsely. Set aside.

3. In a bowl, whisk together eggs, salt and pepper.

4. In a 12-inch (30 cm) cast-iron skillet (see Tip, left), heat oil over medium-high heat until shimmery. Add onion, green pepper and garlic and cook, stirring often, for about 5 minutes, until vegetables soften. Add spinach and sweet potato and cook, stirring, for 1 minute. Add eggs and stir gently to distribute ingredients. Squeeze salmon to remove excess moisture and scatter it over the eggs. Cook for about 2 minutes, occasionally lifting edges and tilting pan to let uncooked egg run underneath, until bottom has set and browned but top is a bit runny.

5. Place skillet under preheated broiler for 1 to 2 minutes to set top. Serve immediately.

Shiitake Frittata with Garlicky Shrimp Sauce

Here's another take on the tasty dinner frittata, this time enhanced with a savory Asian-style sauce.

Tips

If you don't have a cast-iron skillet, use a nonstick skillet and wrap the handle in foil to protect it from the heat of the broiler.

Mirin is a sweet Japanese rice wine sold in Asian grocery stores and some supermarkets.

For the finest minced garlic, push it through a press.

● **Preheat broiler, placing oven rack one level down from top position**

Sauce

⅔ cup	chicken stock (approx.), divided	150 mL
2 tbsp	soy sauce	30 mL
2 tbsp	mirin or dry sherry (see Tips, left)	30 mL
½ to 1 tsp	Asian chili sauce (such as sambal oelek or sriracha)	2 to 5 mL
1 tbsp	cornstarch	15 mL
1 tbsp	vegetable oil	15 mL
1	green onion (white and light green parts), thinly sliced	1
3	cloves garlic, minced (see Tips, left)	3
1 tsp	finely grated gingerroot	5 mL
1	can (4 oz/106 g) small shrimp, rinsed and drained	1

Frittata

8	large eggs	8
¼ tsp	salt (approx.)	1 mL
⅛ tsp	freshly ground black pepper	0.5 mL
1 tbsp	unsalted butter	15 mL
1 tbsp	vegetable oil	15 mL
1½ cups	sliced shiitake mushroom caps (about 4 oz/125 g; see Tip, page 257)	375 mL
1 tbsp	chopped cilantro leaves	15 mL

1. *Sauce:* In a small measuring cup, stir together ½ cup (125 mL) stock, soy sauce, mirin, chili sauce to taste, and cornstarch. Set aside.

2. In a small saucepan, heat oil over medium heat until shimmery. Add green onion, garlic and ginger and cook, stirring, for 30 to 60 seconds, until softened. Give the soy sauce mixture a stir and add to pan. Simmer, stirring, for about 1 minute, until sauce thickens. Remove from heat and stir in shrimp. Add 1 to 2 tbsp (15 to 30 mL) stock to adjust consistency of sauce; it should be no thicker than gravy.

Tip

Shiitake mushroom stems are too fibrous to eat. To remove them, just twist, pinch and pull them gently off the cap. If "waste not" is your mantra, use the stems to flavor stock before discarding them.

3. *Frittata:* In a bowl, whisk together eggs, salt and pepper.

4. In a 12-inch (30 cm) cast-iron skillet (see Tips, page 256), melt butter with oil over medium heat. Add mushrooms and sprinkle with salt to taste. Cook for about 3 minutes, until mushrooms release their liquid and soften. Add egg mixture and cook for 2 to 3 minutes, occasionally lifting edges and tilting pan to let uncooked egg run underneath, until bottom is golden brown but top is a bit runny.

5. Place skillet under preheated broiler for about 2 minutes to set top.

6. Spoon shrimp sauce overtop and garnish with cilantro. Serve immediately.

Variations

Substitute an equal quantity of salmon, crab, lobster or clams for the shrimp.

Scrambled Eggs with Caviar on Crumpets

Coddle yourself — add luscious, salty caviar to your scrambled eggs.

Tip

The eggs will finish cooking in their own heat, so it's safe to take them off the burner while slightly wet. Don't overcook them or they will get rubbery.

4	large eggs	4
1 tbsp	half-and-half (10%) cream	15 mL
1/8 tsp	salt	0.5 mL
4	crumpets	4
2 tbsp	unsalted butter	30 mL
2 tsp	extra virgin olive oil	10 mL
2 tbsp	red lumpfish caviar (roe), rinsed and drained	30 mL
	Freshly ground black pepper	
1 tbsp	chopped chives	15 mL

1. In a bowl, whisk together eggs, cream and salt.

2. Toast crumpets until golden and slather with butter. Transfer to individual serving plates.

3. Meanwhile, in a 10-inch (25 cm) nonstick skillet, heat oil over medium heat until shimmery. Add eggs and stir for 30 seconds, breaking up slightly as they start to set. Sprinkle caviar evenly overtop. Cook for 1 minute, stirring once or twice, until eggs have set in large clumps but are still slightly wet.

4. Spoon eggs over crumpets, dividing equally. Season to taste with pepper and sprinkle chives evenly overtop. Serve immediately.

Variation

Use any kind of roe. You can go upscale with big pink salmon caviar.

Salmon and Egg Smørrebrød

Danish open-faced sandwiches on dark rye are eaten with a knife and fork. In this delicious translation, canned salmon replaces the traditional (and pricier) smoked salmon.

Makes 4 servings

- Fast
- Kid-friendly

Tip

Capers come bottled in brine or dry-salted. The latter are less common but superior in pungency and firmness. You can use either type in this recipe.

4 oz	block cream cheese, softened (½ cup/125 mL)	125 g
1	can (7½ oz/213 g) salmon, drained, deboned and broken into flakes	1
4	large eggs	4
	Salt and freshly ground black pepper	
1 tbsp	unsalted butter	15 mL
4	slices dark rye	4
20	thin slices peeled English cucumber (about ½ cup/125 mL), patted dry	20
¼ cup	chopped red bell pepper	60 mL
4 tsp	capers, rinsed, drained and chopped (see Tip, left)	20 mL

1. In a bowl, using a fork, mix together cream cheese and salmon.

2. In a small bowl, whisk together eggs and salt and pepper to taste.

3. In a 10-inch (25 cm) nonstick skillet, melt butter over medium heat. Add eggs and cook for about 2 minutes, until firm, stirring at first to incorporate uncooked egg, then leaving the mixture to set. Remove from heat.

4. Spread salmon mixture over bread, dividing equally. Transfer to individual serving plates. Arrange cucumber slices overtop, dividing equally. Divide eggs into 4 portions and arrange on top. Sprinkle red pepper and capers evenly over eggs. Serve immediately.

Variations

Substitute canned smoked salmon or tuna or smoked oysters or mussels. You can also try mackerel, sprats, kippers, shrimp or lobster.

Hard-Cooked Eggs with Anchovy Vinaigrette

Anchovies and eggs were made for each other. Here's another simple, savory way to combine them. The anchovy vinaigrette gives the humble eggs extra appeal. These eggs are great for a breakfast or brunch buffet, or simply as a snack.

Makes 4 to 8 servings

- Fast
- Guest-worthy

Tip

For the tidiest eggs, with no pockmarks in the whites and no ugly dark ring around the yolk, as soon as they have finished cooking, run cold water over the eggs until they are cool enough to handle. Peel immediately. Remove the shells by starting at the wide end, where the air pocket is. If the shells start to stick, peel under cold running water.

- **Blender**

8	large eggs	8
1	clove garlic	1
3 to 4	anchovy fillets	3 to 4
1 tbsp	white wine vinegar	15 mL
½ tsp	Dijon mustard	2 mL
¼ tsp	granulated sugar	1 mL
⅛ tsp	freshly ground black pepper	0.5 mL
¼ cup	extra virgin olive oil	60 mL
2 tbsp	chopped parsley leaves	30 mL

1. Place eggs in a small pan and add enough water to cover them by about ½ inch (1 cm). Bring to a boil over high heat. Immediately cover pan and turn off heat. Set aside for 10 minutes.

2. Meanwhile, with the motor running, add garlic to blender through hole in lid to chop. Stop the motor and add anchovies to taste, vinegar, mustard, sugar and pepper to blender. Blend briefly at high speed. Scrape down the sides. With the machine running, drizzle oil through hole in lid and blend thoroughly. You will have about ¼ cup (60 mL) vinaigrette.

3. Run eggs under cold running water. Crack and peel off shells. Using a wet knife, cut each egg in half or, better still, use an egg slicer to slice each egg, then fan it out. Place on a serving plate.

4. Drizzle about 1½ tsp (7 mL) vinaigrette over each egg. Sprinkle parsley evenly overtop and serve immediately.

> ## Variation
> You can enhance this dish by cooking some fresh asparagus and adding it to the plate.

Deviled Eggs with Tuna

You can embellish deviled eggs with all kinds of seafood, herbs and spices. Here's one idea to get you started.

Makes 24

- Fast
- Guest-worthy

Tips

Extremists press the yolks through a sieve for a smoother filling. Don't bother — you will just drive yourself crazy.

You can use a food processor fitted with the metal blade to mix the filling.

If you don't have a piping bag, use a zip-lock bag with a little hole cut in one corner.

To keep deviled eggs from sliding around, line the serving plate with a doily or paper towel. If you are obsessive you can cut a thin slice off the base of each egg, but it will look strange. If you make these a lot, spring for a deviled egg platter and/or storage tub.

12	large eggs	12
1	can (3 oz/85 g) tuna in olive oil, with oil	1
1/4 cup	mayonnaise	60 mL
1 tsp	freshly squeezed lemon juice	5 mL
1 tsp	honey mustard	5 mL
1 tsp	capers, rinsed, drained, patted dry and chopped	5 mL
	Salt and freshly ground black pepper	

1. Place eggs in a pan and add enough water to cover by about $1/2$ inch (1 cm). Bring to a boil over high heat. Immediately cover pan and turn off heat. Set aside for 10 minutes.

2. Run eggs under cold running water. Crack and peel off shells. Using a wet knife, cut each egg in half lengthwise.

3. Using a small spoon, scoop out yolks and transfer to a bowl. Add tuna, with oil, mayonnaise, lemon juice, mustard and capers. Mash with a fork. Season to taste with salt.

4. Pipe or spoon mixture into cavities of egg whites (see Tips, left). Grind pepper overtop to taste.

Variations

Try mashing the yolks with smoked oysters or mussels.

Substitute roe for the tuna and sprinkle it over the yolks rather than blending it in.

You can also use salmon, anchovies or crab in the filling.

Frisée with Salmon and Poached Eggs

Salade Lyonnaise, with bitter greens, smoky bacon and poached eggs, is a fixture on bistro menus in Paris. The bacon and shallot dressing is poured hot over the frisée, wilting it slightly and tempering its bitterness. The French serve this salad as a first course, lunch or even a light dinner. Adding salmon makes it a more substantial meal.

Makes 4 servings

- Fast
- Guest-worthy

Tips

Homemade croutons are preferable because they are softer than store-bought varieties.

To make croutons: Cut stale bread into ¾-inch (2 cm) cubes. Toss with oil, salt, pepper and dried herbs to taste. Spread out on a rimmed baking sheet and bake in a preheated 375°F (190°C) oven until golden brown, about 10 to 15 minutes, stirring once. Alternatively, sauté bread cubes in olive oil and/or butter until golden brown. Spread out to cool.

Dressing

4	slices bacon, chopped	4
2 to 3 tbsp	extra virgin olive oil	30 to 45 mL
1	shallot, finely chopped	1
2 tbsp	sherry vinegar	30 mL
½ tsp	Dijon mustard	2 mL
½ tsp	granulated sugar	2 mL
⅛ tsp	salt (approx.)	0.5 mL
¼ tsp	freshly ground black pepper	1 mL

Salad

	Salt	
1 tbsp	white vinegar	15 mL
4	large eggs	4
6 cups	inner frisée leaves torn into bite-sized pieces (about 6 oz/175 g), (see Tip, page 263)	1.5 L
1	can (7½ oz/213 g) salmon, drained, deboned and broken into chunks	1
1 cup	croutons (see Tips, left)	250 mL

1. *Dressing:* In a skillet over medium heat, cook bacon for about 5 minutes, until browned and crisp. Using a slotted spoon, transfer to a plate lined with paper towels to drain.

2. Pour drippings into a measuring cup. Add enough olive oil to make ¼ cup (60 mL). Add oil mixture to skillet and return to medium heat. Add shallot and cook, stirring, for 1 minute, until softened. Stir in vinegar for 5 seconds. Remove from heat and shake pan for a few seconds until sputtering dies down. Whisk in mustard, sugar, salt and pepper. Set aside. You will have about ¼ cup (60 mL) dressing.

Tip

Identifying frisée can be confusing. It's also called chicory or curly endive, although the latter may be more bitter and mature and coarser. Don't confuse it with football-shaped Belgian endive. Complicating matters, the British call Belgian endive chicory and the French call it endive. Frisée is hardier than lettuce and less likely to wilt under the hot dressing. The green outer leaves are tough, so use the yellowish or pale inner leaves for this salad.

3. *Salad:* Fill a 10-inch (25 cm) sauté pan with water to a depth of 1 inch (2.5 cm). Add salt, to taste, and vinegar. Bring to a boil over high heat, then reduce heat to medium-low to maintain a simmer. Crack each egg into a small, heatproof bowl and gently slip into the water. Poach until whites are firm but yolks are still runny, about 5 minutes.

4. Meanwhile, divide frisée among 4 wide, shallow serving bowls. Reheat dressing over high heat until on the verge of boiling. Spoon about 1 tbsp (15 mL) over each portion of frisée, then lift and toss greens quickly with tongs. Scatter salmon overtop.

5. One at a time, using a slotted spoon, remove eggs from pan, dab bottoms on paper towels and place in center of serving bowls. Scatter croutons around perimeter. Crumble bacon overtop and serve immediately.

Variations

Use about 4 oz (125 g) diced slab bacon instead of slices.

For convenience, substitute 4 sliced hard-cooked eggs for the poached ones.

Substitute an equal quantity of tuna, sardines, sprats, kippers, shrimp or lobster for the salmon.

Crab Louis

You can't go wrong with this simple idea: crabmeat topped with spicy mayo and accompanied by tomato and egg. It's called Crab Louis or the King of Salads. The salad started appearing on tony West Coast menus at the beginning of the 20th century, but its origins are murky. Eateries in both San Francisco and Seattle lay claim to inventing it.

Makes 4 servings

- Fast
- Guest-worthy

Tips

For the best presentation, use larger lump crabmeat.

Bonus: This chili mayonnaise perks up all kinds of seafood.

Campari tomatoes are generically known as cocktail tomatoes and are sold in supermarkets. You can substitute 8 halved cherry tomatoes for the Camparis.

Louis Sauce

½ cup	mayonnaise	125 mL
2 tbsp	prepared tomato-based chili sauce	30 mL
2	small green onions (white and light green parts), minced	2
1 tbsp	finely chopped green bell pepper	15 mL
	Salt and freshly ground black pepper	

Salad

6 cups	shredded iceberg lettuce	1.5 L
1½ cups	lump crabmeat (8 oz/250 g; see Tips, left)	375 mL
4	large eggs, hard-cooked and quartered	4
4	cocktail tomatoes, quartered (see Tips, left)	4
1 tbsp	capers, rinsed, drained and finely chopped	15 mL
4	small lemon wedges	4

1. *Louis Sauce:* In a measuring cup, stir together mayonnaise, chili sauce, green onions and bell pepper. Season to taste with salt and pepper. Set aside.

2. *Salad:* Line shallow serving bowls with lettuce. Place crabmeat in the center and dollop Louis Sauce overtop. Arrange eggs and tomatoes around crab. Scatter capers overtop and place a lemon wedge in each bowl.

Variations

Add steamed asparagus spears.

Substitute an equal quantity of tuna, salmon, shrimp or lobster for the crab.

Tuna with Artichoke Heart Relish

This is lip-smacking good with toast or crusty bread. It can serve as a snack, a lunch or even a light dinner.

Makes 2 servings

- Fast
- Healthy
- Brown-bag

Tip

Dry Italian seasoning is sold in supermarkets. You can make your own by combining equal parts dried basil, oregano and marjoram with a pinch of sage, or use an equal quantity of dried oregano or marjoram.

3 tbsp	extra virgin olive oil, divided	45 mL
4	cloves garlic, slivered	4
1	can (14 oz/398 mL) artichoke hearts, rinsed, drained and coarsely chopped	1
¼ cup	diced red onion	60 mL
2 tbsp	chopped oil-packed sun-dried tomatoes	30 mL
1 tsp	dry Italian seasoning (see Tip, left)	5 mL
¼ tsp	salt (approx.)	1 mL
⅛ tsp	freshly ground black pepper	0.5 mL
1	can (6 oz/170 g) tuna in water, drained and broken into chunks	1
1 tsp	freshly squeezed lemon juice, optional	5 mL
4	leaves Boston lettuce, optional	4

1. In a skillet, heat 1 tbsp (15 mL) oil over medium heat. Stir in garlic for 30 seconds, until it turns golden. Add artichokes, onion and sun-dried tomatoes. Cook, stirring often, for about 2 minutes, until heated through. Remove from heat. Stir in remaining 2 tbsp (30 mL) oil, Italian seasoning, salt and pepper. Stir in tuna. Add salt to taste, if necessary. Stir in lemon juice, if using.

2. Line serving plates with lettuce, if using. Scoop tuna mixture onto plates. Serve warm or at room temperature.

Variations

Substitute an equal quantity of salmon, mackerel, sardines or sprats for the tuna.

Crab and Corn Griddle Cakes

These delicious morsels start as polenta and morph into griddle cakes. They seem to get snapped up the second they leave the griddle, so you'll want to make this big batch for brunch, a buffet or luncheon guests. However, you can halve the recipe for a weekend family meal. As a finishing touch, serve vinaigrette-drizzled tomatoes alongside.

Makes about 22 griddle cakes 8 to 10 servings

- Kid-friendly
- Guest-worthy

Tips

Use small lump or claw crabmeat. Avoid the flaked kind, as it will disappear in the batter.

Corn griddle cakes aren't leaden or gritty when you precook the cornmeal.

If you don't have a griddle, use a large nonstick pan.

Variations

Substitute an equal quantity of salmon, mackerel, kippers, shrimp or lobster for the crab. You can also substitute clams, but use baby clams, not the meaty ones.

- **Nonstick griddle (see Tips, left)**

2 cups	all-purpose flour	500 mL
1 tsp	salt	5 mL
1 tsp	baking powder	5 mL
½ tsp	baking soda	2 mL
1½ cups	buttermilk	375 mL
1	large egg	1
2 tbsp	extra virgin olive oil, divided	30 mL
1½ cups	water	375 mL
½ cup	fine cornmeal	125 mL
1¼ cups	canned crabmeat (6 oz/175 g), rinsed and drained (see Tips, left)	300 mL
1 cup	corn kernels, patted dry	250 mL
¼ cup	chopped basil	60 mL
	Lumpfish caviar (roe), rinsed and drained, optional	

1. Sift flour, salt, baking powder and baking soda into a bowl.

2. In a large measuring cup, lightly whisk together buttermilk, egg and 1 tbsp (15 mL) oil.

3. In a small saucepan, whisk together water and cornmeal. Bring to a simmer over high heat, whisking often. Reduce heat to medium-low and simmer for 5 minutes, whisking often.

4. Scrape cornmeal mixture into a large bowl. Whisking constantly, add buttermilk mixture. Stir in flour mixture just until moistened (do not overmix). Gently squeeze crab to remove excess moisture. Add to bowl along with corn and basil.

5. Heat griddle over medium heat. Before cooking each batch, brush griddle lightly with some of the remaining oil. Ladle ¼ cup (60 mL) batter per cake onto hot griddle. Cook for about 2 minutes, until bubbles form on the tops and bottoms are golden. Flip and cook for 1 to 2 minutes more, until bottoms are golden and cakes are cooked through. Keep warm and continue with remaining batter.

6. Before serving, sprinkle caviar, if using, over each griddle cake.

Blini with Caviar

Blini are the signature pancakes of Russia, traditionally served before Lent. Classic blini are light yet substantial and are made with buckwheat flour. Often they are accompanied by shots of vodka, so if you're in a Russian mood, go for it.

Makes about 20 blini

- Guest-worthy

Tips

Don't overheat the milk or it will kill the yeast.

The singular of *blini* is *blin*.

Add the batter to the griddle slowly, letting it drip from the spoon. This keeps the blini rounder.

Blini can be made ahead, wrapped in foil and refrigerated. If you want to freeze them, wrap in foil, then plastic. Reheat in foil in a 350°F (180°C) oven for 10 to 20 minutes.

Variations

Go upscale and try salmon caviar rather than lumpfish roe.

Make the topping with canned smoked salmon instead of caviar.

● **Preheat oven to 200°F (100°C)**

Blini

½ cup	all-purpose flour	125 mL
½ cup	buckwheat flour	125 mL
1 tbsp	granulated sugar	15 mL
½ tsp	salt	2 mL
1 tsp	active dry yeast	5 mL
1 cup	lukewarm whole milk (see Tips, left)	250 mL
1	large egg, separated	1
2 to 3 tbsp	melted butter, cooled, divided	30 to 45 mL

Topping

1 cup	sour cream	250 mL
2	large eggs, hard-cooked and finely chopped	2
¼ cup	finely chopped red onion	60 mL
	Salt and freshly ground white pepper	
1	jar (2 oz/50 g) black or red lumpfish caviar (roe), rinsed, drained and patted dry	1

1. *Blini:* In a bowl, whisk together all-purpose and buckwheat flours, sugar and salt. Whisk in yeast. Make a well in the centre, add lukewarm milk and stir well. Cover and set aside in a warm place for 1 to 2 hours, until batter looks bubbly and doubles in size.

2. Stir in egg yolk and 1 tbsp (15 mL) melted butter.

3. In a bowl, beat egg white until stiff peaks form. Fold into batter.

4. Heat a griddle or large, nonstick skillet over medium heat. Brush lightly with some of the remaining butter. Spoon in about 2 tbsp (30 mL) batter per blin to make 3-inch (7.5 cm) rounds. Cook until bubbles form on the top and underside is brown, about 30 seconds. Transfer to a baking sheet as completed, cover loosely with foil, and keep warm in preheated oven. Grease skillet and adjust heat between batches as necessary.

5. *Topping:* In a measuring cup, stir together sour cream, chopped eggs, onion and salt and pepper to taste. Dollop about 1 tbsp (15 mL) onto each warm blin, then top each with about ½ tsp (2 mL) caviar. Serve immediately.

Whole Wheat Crêpes with Curried Creamed Salmon

You can put virtually anything inside a crêpe, and whatever it is will taste better and seem fancier. This filling is a mock curry — more comfort food than authentically Indian.

Makes 6 or 7 crêpes

- Kid-friendly
- Guest-worthy

Tips

You need to mix regular flour with whole wheat or the crêpes will be leaden.

The batter should be thin, about the consistency of cream.

You can make the filling while the batter rests in the fridge, then reheat it as needed.

One key to success is making sure the pan is very hot before adding the batter. Don't be discouraged if the first crêpe doesn't turn out perfectly — it never seems to.

- **Blender**
- **10-inch (25 cm) nonstick crêpe pan**

Crêpes

1 cup	milk (see Tips, page 269)	250 mL
2	large eggs	2
1/4 tsp	salt	1 mL
1/2 cup	all-purpose flour	125 mL
1/2 cup	whole wheat flour	125 mL
2 tbsp	unsalted butter, melted	30 mL
1/4 cup	club soda	60 mL
2 tbsp	vegetable oil (approx.)	30 mL

Filling

1/4 cup	unsalted butter	60 mL
1	small stalk celery, cut in 1/8-inch (3 mm) dice	1
1/4 cup	red bell pepper cut in 1/8-inch (3 mm) dice	60 mL
1	clove garlic, minced	1
1 tbsp	curry powder	15 mL
1/4 tsp	salt (approx.)	1 mL
1/4 tsp	freshly ground black pepper	1 mL
1/4 cup	all-purpose flour	60 mL
2/3 cup	chicken or vegetable stock	150 mL
1 1/3 cups	milk	325 mL
1	can (7 1/2 oz/213 g) salmon, drained, deboned and broken into chunks	1
1/4 cup	chopped parsley leaves, divided	60 mL

1. *Crêpes:* In blender, combine milk, eggs and salt. Add all-purpose and whole wheat flours and blend at high speed for 30 seconds. Scrape down sides. Add butter and blend at high speed for 30 seconds, until smooth.

Tips

If you've ladled in too much batter, quickly pour back the excess.

The first side cooked is the more attractive, so keep this on the exterior when serving.

I like the texture of these crêpes when the batter is prepared with 2% milk. For the filling it's okay to use skim milk if you want to cut calories.

2. Scrape batter into a large storage tub, cover tightly and refrigerate for at least 1 hour or up to 2 days. When you're ready to cook, whisk in soda.

3. Heat crêpe pan for 1 minute over medium heat. Brush with a thin layer of oil. Lift pan off heat and ladle in about $1/3$ cup (75 mL) batter. Tilt and swirl, coaxing the batter to coat the pan thinly but completely. Return pan to burner and cook for about 1 minute, until bottom is golden and top looks dry. Flip and cook for 30 seconds more. Slide or flip crêpe onto a plate and lay a sheet of foil overtop. Repeat with remaining batter, greasing skillet each time before adding batter. Wrap foil over plate.

4. *Filling:* In a saucepan over medium heat, melt butter. Add celery, red pepper and garlic and cook, stirring often, for 4 to 5 minutes, until softened. Stir in curry powder, salt and pepper for 1 minute. Whisk in flour for 1 to 2 minutes, until golden. While whisking constantly, gradually pour in stock, then milk. When mixture comes to a simmer, reduce heat to medium-low. Simmer for about 5 minutes, until thickened. Stir in salmon and 3 tbsp (45 mL) parsley. Add salt to taste, if necessary. Remove from heat and set aside.

5. To assemble, one at a time, place a crêpe on a serving plate. Ladle about $1/3$ cup (75 mL) filling over the center. Create an envelope shape by folding the left third of the crêpe over the filling, folding up the bottom third, then folding down the top third. Close the envelope by folding over the right third. Repeat with remaining crêpes (you may have some filling left over). Sprinkle remaining parsley over crêpes and serve immediately.

Variations

If you prefer, add a bit more liquid to the creamed salmon and serve it over toast or rice.

Substitute an equal quantity of tuna, mackerel, shrimp, crab or lobster for the salmon.

Tuna à la King

In the beginning, there was chicken à la king. Not long after, seafood à la king appeared, featuring anything from tuna to lobster. During wartime, à la kings made with canned seafood became symbols of thrifty dining. Ladle this dish over puff pastry shells with little caps, which are known as vols-au-vent, or mate it with rice, noodles, toast or crêpes.

Makes 4 servings

• Kid-friendly

Variations

Substitute 2 tbsp (30 mL) dry sherry for the wine.

Substitute an equal quantity of salmon, mackerel, shrimp, crab or lobster for the tuna.

1½ cups	chicken stock	375 mL
¼ cup	all-purpose flour	60 mL
¼ tsp	dried thyme	1 mL
¼ tsp	freshly ground white pepper	1 mL
1 tbsp	unsalted butter	15 mL
1 tbsp	vegetable oil	15 mL
2½ cups	chopped button mushrooms (about 8 oz/250 g)	625 mL
1	small onion, diced	1
1	carrot, chopped	1
½ tsp	salt (approx.)	2 mL
¼ cup	dry white wine, optional	60 mL
½ cup	half-and-half (10%) cream	125 mL
1	large egg yolk	1
1	can (6 oz/170 g) tuna in water, drained and broken into large chunks	1
¼ cup	pimientos, drained and chopped	60 mL
1 tbsp	chopped parsley leaves	15 mL
	Sweet paprika	
4	lemon wedges	4

1. In a large measuring cup, whisk together stock, flour, thyme and pepper.

2. In a large saucepan over medium heat, melt butter with oil. Add mushrooms, onion, carrot and salt and cook, stirring, for 10 minutes, until mushrooms release their liquid and carrot softens. Stir in wine, if using, and cook for 1 minute. Gradually stir in stock mixture. When mixture comes to a simmer, reduce heat to low and simmer for 5 minutes, until thickened. Stir in cream.

3. In a small bowl, stir together egg yolk and a small ladleful of the warm cream mixture. Return to pan, stir to blend for a few seconds, then remove from heat. Do not allow it to boil.

4. Gently stir in tuna, pimientos and parsley. Add salt to taste, if necessary.

5. Sprinkle paprika overtop and serve immediately, with lemon wedges alongside to squeeze over.

Sardines with Roast Spuds, Smoked Paprika Oil and Lemon

This simple meal of sardines, greens and potatoes is exceptionally tasty.

Makes 2 to 4 servings

Tips

I recommend using yellow-fleshed potatoes in this dish. They are creamy yet hold their shape.

Sardines break easily. For the best presentation, handle them gently to keep them intact.

Variations

Kick up the spiciness of the dish with smoked hot paprika.

You can use mixed baby greens or baby spinach instead of arugula.

Substitute an equal quantity of tuna, salmon, mackerel, cod, sprats, kippers or octopus for the sardines.

- **Preheat oven to 400°F (200°C)**
- **Rimmed baking sheet**

¼ cup	extra virgin olive oil	60 mL
1 tsp	smoked sweet paprika (see Variations, left)	5 mL
1 tbsp + 1 tsp	finely grated lemon zest, divided	20 mL
½ tsp	salt (approx.)	2 mL
⅛ tsp	freshly ground black pepper	0.5 mL
1 lb	mini potatoes (about 1½ inches/4 cm in diameter), scrubbed and halved (see Tips, left)	500 g
4 cups	baby arugula leaves (about 2 oz/60 g)	1 L
1	can (3.75 oz/106 g) sardines, drained	1
4	lemon wedges	4

1. In a measuring cup, whisk together oil, paprika, 1 tbsp (15 mL) lemon zest, salt and pepper.

2. In a bowl, toss potatoes with 2 tbsp (30 mL) of the oil mixture. Arrange, cut side up, on baking sheet and roast in preheated oven for 40 to 45 minutes, until tender and golden. Transfer to a bowl and toss gently with 1 tbsp (15 mL) of remaining oil mixture. Set aside to cool for 10 to 15 minutes (you don't want to make the arugula limp).

3. Line a small platter with arugula. Place potatoes on top and arrange sardines alongside. Drizzle remaining oil mixture over sardines. Sprinkle salt, to taste, overtop. Scatter remaining 1 tsp (5 mL) lemon zest over potatoes. Place lemon wedges alongside to squeeze liberally over sardines and potatoes. Serve immediately.

Fish & Seafood Substitutions

⚓ = used in recipe
● = suggested substitution

Use this chart to quickly find which fish or seafood is the best substitute for the main ingredients used in each recipe in this book.

Recipe	tuna	salmon	mackerel	cod	sardines	sprats	kippers	anchovies	roe	shrimp	crab	lobster	clams	oysters	mussels	squid	octopus
Avocado and Shrimp in New-School Marie Rose Sauce										⚓	●	●					
Basque-Style Shrimp, Ham and Potato Salad				●						⚓		●					
Blini with Caviar		●							⚓								
Brandade	●	●	●	⚓			●			●		●	●				●
Cajun Pasta Salad	●	●	●	●						⚓	●	●					
California Salad, Starring Salmon	●	⚓															
Caponata	⚓		●					⚓		●							●
Catalan Clams and Ham												●	⚓				
Caviar and Avocado Sushi Rolls	●	●							⚓		●	●					
CBLT										●	⚓	●					
Cheesy Tuna, Broccoli and Rice	⚓	●	●	●						●			●				
Chinese Takeout Egg Rolls										⚓		●					
Chipotle Salmon on Rice	●	⚓															
Citrus Quinoa with Crab and Cress	●	●								●	⚓	●					
Citrusy Crab and Sprouts	●	●								●	⚓	●					
Citrusy Linguine with Smoked Mussels and Baby Spinach						●								●	⚓		
Clam, Bacon and Chive Dip		●								●	●	●	⚓				
Clam, Bacon and Spinach Lasagna		●										●	⚓				
Clam Carbonara	●	●	●							●		●	⚓				
Clam Maque Choux	●	●	●	●			●			●	●	●	⚓				
Clams in Herb Broth with Angel Hair Pasta										●	●	●	⚓			●	●
Classic Salmon Salad	●	⚓	●		●	●				●	●	●					
Coulibiac	●	⚓	●														

	tuna	salmon	mackerel	cod	sardines	sprats	kippers	anchovies	roe	shrimp	crab	lobster	clams	oysters	mussels	squid	octopus
Couscous with Tuna, Feta and Lemon Mint Dressing	⚓	•								•							
Crab, Watercress and Egg Drop Soup										•	⚓	•	•				
Crab and Corn Griddle Cakes		•	•				•			•	⚓	•	•				
Crab and Sesame-Lime Rice	•	•								•	⚓	•					
Crab Cakes											⚓	•					
Crab Étouffé	•	•								•	⚓		•				
Crab Foo Yung with Soy Glaze	•	•	•							•	⚓	•	•				
Crab Louis	•	•								•	⚓	•					
Creamy Crab and Poblano Soup	•	•	•	•			•			•	⚓	•	•				•
Cuban-Style Crab and Plantains with Mojo		•								•	⚓	•					
Curried Scrambled Eggs and Crab	•	•	•				•			•	⚓	•			•		
Curried Shrimp Pilaf		•								⚓	•	•					
Deviled Crab	•	•	•							•	⚓	•					
Deviled Eggs with Tuna	⚓	•						•	•	•				•	•		
Devilish Angels on Horseback														⚓	•		
Diner Tuna Melts	⚓	•	•							•							
East Coast Lobster Rolls										•	•	⚓					
Easy Ham and Clam Jambalaya										•		•	⚓				
Express Chinese Noodle Dinner	•	•								⚓		•					
Express Coconut Tuna and Pea Curry	⚓	•	•							•	•	•					
Farfalle with Cajun Shrimp and Broccoli Pesto		•								⚓	•	•					
Farfalle with Smoky Tuna, Mushrooms and Green Peppercorns	⚓	•				•											
Faux Pho		⚓								•		•	•			•	
Fishloaf	•	⚓															
Fish Tacos	⚓	•															

	tuna	salmon	mackerel	cod	sardines	sprats	kippers	anchovies	roe	shrimp	crab	lobster	clams	oysters	mussels	squid	octopus
Legend: ⚓ = used in recipe, • = suggested substitution																	
Fishy Telescopes	⚓	•	•		•	•				•	•	•					
Frisée with Salmon and Poached Eggs	•	⚓			•	•	•			•		•					
Golden Purses		•								⚓	•	•					
The Grand Aïoli	•	•	•	⚓	•	•	•			•	•	•		•	•		•
Greek Pizza		•								•		•					⚓
Hot Crab Dip	•	•	•	•			•			•	⚓	•	•	•	•		
Italian Tuna, Potato and Green Bean Salad	⚓	•	•	•	•	•											
Jamaican Crab and Okra Curry										•	⚓	•					
Jumbo Shells Stuffed with Salmon, Ricotta and Zucchini	•	⚓	•				•										
Lemon Pepper Shrimp Pasta	•	•								⚓	•	•					
Lemony Salmon and Asparagus Risotto	•	⚓								•		•	•				•
Lip-Smacking Anchovy Butter								⚓	•	•							
Little Italy Tuna Melts	⚓	•	•		•	•				•		•					
Lobster and Shells in Ginger Tomato Sauce	•	•								•	•	⚓					
Lobster in Américaine Sauce	•	•								•	•	⚓					
Lobster Mushroom Bisque		•								•	•	⚓	•	•	•		
Lobster Tikka Masala	•	•	•							•		⚓					
Mack and Cheese with Peas	•	•	⚓				•										
Mackerel and Green Onion Sushi Rolls	•	•	⚓						•	•		•					
Manhattan Clam Chowder										•		•	⚓				
Marinated Tuna and Radicchio Salad	⚓	•	•									•					
Maritime Quiche	•	•	•	•			•			⚓		•	•				
Mediterranean Diet Tuna Salad	⚓	•	•		•	•					•	•					
Mediterranean Roasted Peppers and Tuna	⚓	•	•	•	•	•											
Mediterranean Salmon and Rice Casserole	•	⚓	•							•							

⚓ = used in recipe
• = suggested substitution

	tuna	salmon	mackerel	cod	sardines	sprats	kippers	anchovies	roe	shrimp	crab	lobster	clams	oysters	mussels	squid	octopus
Moroccan-Style Salmon Quinoa	•	⚓								•	•	•					
Mussel Salad with Capers														•	⚓		
New England Clam Chowder	•	•	•	•			•			•	•	•	⚓	•	•	•	•
New Haven Clam Pizzas										•		•	⚓				•
Niçoise Tuna Burgers	⚓							⚓									
Nutty Salmon and Spinach Wraps	•	⚓															
Old-Fashioned Tuna Noodle Casserole	⚓	•	•				•			•			•				
Old-School Spinach Salad with Shrimp and Poppyseed Dressing		•								⚓	•	•					
Orzo with Salmon, Asparagus and Smoked Mozzarella	•	⚓	•	•						•		•					
Oven Orzo with Shrimp and Feta										⚓		•					•
Pan Bagnat	⚓	•			•	•		⚓									
Parmesan Tuna Sandwiches	⚓	•															
Party Antipasto	⚓							•									
Pasta with Spicy Salmon and Rapini	•	⚓	•	•				•		•		•	•				
Pasta with Tuna, Beans, Sage and Olives	⚓	•	•														
Personal Pizzas with Lobster and Roasted Garlic										•	•	⚓	•				
Pinwheel Sandwiches	⚓	⚓															
Portuguese Rice with Clams										•			⚓			•	•
Potato Salad with Smoked Oysters and Roasted Peppers					•	•								⚓	•		
Presto Lobster Newberg	•	•									•	⚓					
Quick Mock Paella										⚓		•	•				•
Retro Tuna Salad Pasta	⚓	•	•		•	•	•			•							
Roasted Vegetable and Salmon Strudel	•	⚓	•	•													
Salade Niçoise	⚓	•	•	•	•	•		⚓		•	•	•					•

Substitutions   275

	tuna	salmon	mackerel	cod	sardines	sprats	kippers	anchovies	roe	shrimp	crab	lobster	clams	oysters	mussels	squid	octopus
⚓ = used in recipe **• = suggested substitution**																	
Salmon, Avocado and Red Onion Club Sandwiches	•	⚓								•		•					
Salmon, Corn and Herb Chowder with Pepper Jack	•	⚓	•	•			•			•	•	•	•	•	•		•
Salmon, Spinach and Sweet Potato Frittata	•	⚓	•				•			•	•	•	•	•	•		
Salmon and Egg Smørrebrød	•	⚓	•			•	•			•		•		•	•		
Salmon and Green Onion Yogurt Dip	•	⚓	•	•			•			•		•		•	•		
Salmon and Leek Pot Pie	•	⚓	•							•		•	•				
Salmon and Olive Puffs	•	⚓	•	•			•			•							
Salmon and Rapini Lasagna	•	⚓	•				•						•				
Salmon and Roasted Garlic Bisque with Cajun Croutons	•	⚓	•	•						•	•	•		•	•		•
Salmon and Sprout Quesadillas	•	⚓								•							
Salmon and White Bean Soup with Oniony Croutons	•	⚓	•							•							
Salmon Cheese Balls	•	⚓			•	•			•	•				•	•		
Salmon Herb Agnolotti		⚓	•							•							
Salmon Pâté		⚓						⚓									
Salmon Picadillo	•	⚓								•							
Salmon Pizza Pinwheels	•	⚓	•														
Salmon Wiggle	•	⚓	•	•			•			•							
Salsa Verde	•							⚓									
Sardines Caprese	•	•	•	•	⚓	•				•							
Sardines on Toast with Drizzle	•	•	•		⚓	•	•				•	•					
Sardines with Roast Spuds, Smoked Paprika Oil and Lemon	•	•	•	•	⚓	•	•										•
Scandinavian Dilled Shrimp on Party Pumpernickel										⚓		•					
Seafood Summer Rolls	•	⚓	•							•	•	•					
Shiitake Frittata with Garlicky Shrimp Sauce		•								⚓	•	•	•				

Recipe	tuna	salmon	mackerel	cod	sardines	sprats	kippers	anchovies	roe	shrimp	crab	lobster	clams	oysters	mussels	squid	octopus
Shortcut Lobster Thermidor											•	⚓					
Shortcut Shrimp and Sausage Gumbo										⚓	•	•	•				
Shortcut Tuna Pot Pie	⚓	•	•							•			•				
Shrimp, Pomegranate and Almond Quinoa	•	•								⚓		•					
Shrimp and Cuke Croissants										⚓	•	•					
Shrimp and Grits with Tomato Gravy										⚓	•	•					
Shrimp and Shiitake Risotto		•								⚓		•					
Shrimp Creole	•	•								⚓	•	•					
Shrimp Fried Rice		•	•							⚓		•	•			•	•
Shrimp Mac and Queso	•	•	•							⚓		•	•				
Shrimp Margherita Pizza								•		⚓		•	•				
Shrimp Pad Thai		•								⚓	•	•					
Sicilian-Style Sardine Pasta			•		⚓	•											
Smoked Salmon and Wild Rice Chowder	•	⚓	•	•				•		•		•					
Smoked Tuna and Avocado on Baby Greens with Lemon Chervil Dressing	⚓	•						•									
Smoky Tuna Dip	⚓	•	•	•				•		•		•		•	•		
Spanish Noodles			•							•		•	⚓				•
Spicy Salmon and Asparagus Sushi Rolls	•	⚓	•							•	•	•					
Spinach Linguine with Salmon and Caviar	•	⚓	•						⚓	•	•	•	•				
Tagliatelle with Tarragon Lobster and Asparagus	•	•	•							•		⚓		•	•		
Tangerine Salmon Salad	•	⚓									•						
Tarragon Lobster Rolls										•	•	⚓					
Thai Coconut Crab Soup		•	•	•						•	⚓	•					
Thai Shrimp Noodle Salad		•								⚓	•	•					
Thai Tuna Salad	⚓	•										•					
Tortellini Toss-Up	⚓	•	•				•										
Triple-Decker Triangle Sandwiches	⚓	⚓	•							•	•	•					
Triple-S Pearl Couscous	•	•	•	•	•	•				⚓		•					•

⚓ = used in recipe
• = suggested substitution

	tuna	salmon	mackerel	cod	sardines	sprats	kippers	anchovies	roe	shrimp	crab	lobster	clams	oysters	mussels	squid	octopus
Tuna, Egg and Fresh Bean Salad	⚓	•	•	•								•					
Tuna, Tomato and Herb Spelt	⚓	•	•		•	•											
Tuna à la King	⚓	•	•							•	•	•					
Tuna and Artichoke Panini	⚓	•	•														
Tuna and Bean Salad on Arugula	⚓	•															
Tuna and Cucumber Sushi Rolls	⚓	•	•						⚓								
Tuna and Olive Rotini	⚓	•			•	•				•							
Tuna and Spinach Risotto	⚓	•	•							•		•					
Tuna Cobb Salad	⚓	•	•		•	•	•			•	•	•					
Tuna Croquettes	⚓	•	•	•			•			•	•	•					
Tuna Fettuccine Alfredo	⚓	•	•							•		•	•				
Tuna McMelts	⚓	•	•							•							
Tuna Muffuletta Sandwiches	⚓	•	•					⚓									
Tuna Salad Cream Cheese	⚓	•	•		•	•	•			•	•	•					
Tuna Salad with a Greek Accent	⚓	•	•		•	•				•	•	•					
Tuna Salad with an Indian Accent	⚓	•	•		•	•				•	•	•					
Tuna Salad with an Italian Accent	⚓	•	•		•	•				•	•	•					
Tuna Taco Salad	⚓	•															
Tuna Tapenade	⚓	•	•		•	•		⚓									
Tuna Tetrazzini	⚓	•	•							•		•	•				•
Tuna with Artichoke Heart Relish	⚓	•	•		•	•											
Tuscan Sandwiches	⚓	•	•		•	•											
Updated Tuna Noodle Casserole	⚓	•	•				•			•		•	•				
Vintage Tuna Mac and Cheese	⚓	•	•														
Vintage Tuna Salad	⚓	•	•		•	•				•	•	•					
Whole Wheat Crêpes with Curried Creamed Salmon		⚓	•							•	•	•					
Whole Wheat Penne with Tuna, Arugula and Roasted Tomatoes	⚓	•	•						•								
The Ziti Caper	⚓	•	•					⚓									

Library and Archives Canada Cataloguing in Publication

Sampson, Susan
    200 best canned fish & seafood recipes : for tuna, salmon, shrimp, crab, clams,
    oysters, lobster & more / Susan Sampson.

Includes index.
ISBN 978-0-7788-0415-4

    1. Cooking (Seafood). 2. Cooking (Fish). 3. Canned seafood. 4. Cookbooks.
    I. Title. II. Title: Two hundred best canned fish & seafood recipes.

TX747.S345 2012   641.6'92   C2012-902818-5

Index